KNOWING
HOW TO KNOW

KNOWING HOW TO KNOW

A Practical Philosophy in the Sufi Tradition

by

IDRIES SHAH

THE OCTAGON PRESS
LONDON

Requests for permission to reprint, reproduce, etc., to:
Permission Department, The Octagon Press Ltd.,
P.O. Box 227, London N6 4EW, England

ISBN 0 863040 72 1

Published 1998

Printed and bound by
Redwood Books, Trowbridge, Wiltshire

CONTENTS

Preface

A book of 200 pages may contain nothing of any value at all.

Another may contain as little as one hint, one fact, which is of supreme importance to readers.

Most books could be better written, and very many of them are padded in order to produce a length which the author, the publishers – or the readers – (or all three) regard as worthwhile.

This book contains material which, if expanded even in the most acceptable way, could easily fill many hundreds of pages. Such expansion, however, would not necessarily be of any use.

If you are influenced by some prestige-content in a fat book, this book is not for you, for you will be disappointed because it is not crammed with words.

If you could, however, have benefited just as much from seeing the same materials printed in pamphlet form, then you would not have thought that you needed to read this book: you would already have the information which it contains, and would not be reading books like this.

If you can take its message and apply it, while benefiting from its handling qualities, bulk and unspoken communication: this book is for you.

SECTION I

Inclusion and Exclusion
— a prologue

We are all interested in spiritual, psychological and social questions, and particularly in our personal problems, but in order to understand how we should learn, what we must know, we must have information.

The first important principle which we must understand is that there are two pre-eminent concepts; one is inclusion and the other is exclusion. Now this is extremely important – what we include in our studies, and what we exclude from our studies.

Although this concept is not instantly familiar in this form to most people, they can usually understand that it is necessary. However they have often made certain mistakes. These mistakes have been made by people who are studying higher things, and also by the culture in general.

The mistakes arise from not understanding or not emphasising correctly what is inclusion and what is exclusion. And although that error is not hard to correct, it has great consequences. Therefore we must clear it away, right at the beginning.

We start, simply, by giving some definitions of this problem.

I will first give you an example of how people ordinarily imagine 'inclusion and exclusion' is carried out. Religionists, (notice that I do not say 'spiritual people') for example, attempt to avoid things which are unpleasant, undesirable, and which are not permitted by their religion. This is exclusion: 'I will exclude myself from the world. I will exclude myself from contact with bad people. I will exclude myself from the study of things which are not religious.'

This is familiar, traditional exclusion. When you are among this kind of religious people, you will find that you are forbidden to study certain things, or to go to certain places, or to carry out certain activities – even to think certain things . . .

That is exclusion. Therefore, for example, if you are a good monotheist, you are expected not to go into an idol temple and ring their bells – you must exclude that form of ritual, and you must include your own form instead. Even in the case of idol-temples, where I have seen statues of the Virgin Mary and Father Christmas included: on making enquiries I have been

6

told that the priests of this temple – while very permissive about images – would not permit, say, the removal of idols . . . So this is exclusion.

This is not a strange concept to any of us, no matter what our culture is; it is standard procedure in all countries to include in this way and exclude in that. Yet people do not think of it in these terms.

If we go back to the origin of the reason for inclusion and exclusion, we find that the problem arises where there was in the past a different definition of an enterprise from the one which we understand today.

In other words, the activity has changed because the definition has changed. We must, therefore, go back to an earlier stage in order to understand how we can best employ exclusion and inclusion in our studies. When we do this, we immediately face a problem.

The problem is that those people who have become accustomed to including and excluding in a mechanical way will imagine that we are against them, or that we are opposing them.

This is not our intention, however.

We are fortunate in some respects to be operating in the present-day world, the actual world. I would like to draw your attention to our good fortune. Thus, when I talk about exclusion and inclusion, I am able to refer you to the modern methods of studying any subject. The difference is that I am trying to introduce into this type of study the very ancient methods which have been lost, the method of specialisation. Specialisation is a modern phenomenon, but it is also a very ancient one. It had for long been lost. We are trying to specialise. As a small example, we can say that if we want to study something we *must* exclude.

If, for instance, we want to study Spanish we must exclude French, and we must include Spanish. If we want to talk in this room, we must exclude the children and the noise and we must 'include' the walls of the room and the language in which we are speaking; these are part of the necessities of the situation.

This is in fact a specialisation. We are narrowing down in order to see more clearly.

There is another method, however – still very well established in the mind of modern man. The method to which I refer is called, in modern terminology, 'conditioning'.

Conditioning is not just specialising; it is becoming trained to certain responses so that one cannot think flexibly. We see the faults and the problems produced by this in political, religious and social life everywhere in the world today.

People become obsessed; an idea gets into their heads and as a result they become less capable, less – not more – able to learn. They are capable only of acting and feeling, emotions and intellect, and they are not capable of learning deeper knowledge.

We can help to restore to people the flexibility of specialisation and changing of focus. This is quite a different method of study from that which is familiar to most people today.

In the modern world we are in a paradoxical situation; because although in theory man knows that he can extend his attention to something and then remove it, he very often does not do so. In many areas he does not look at something and then detach from it, and look at something else.

Once he has found something to interest himself in, he cannot detach himself from it efficiently, and therefore he cannot be objective. Note that, in most if not all languages, we have words like 'objectivity' which leads people to imagine that they have it, or can easily use it. That is equivalent (in reality if not in theory) to saying 'I know the word "gold", so I am rich.'

The consequences of this lack of flexibility surround us everywhere, in every country, in every culture, and this lack of flexibility is a major danger to the existence of humanity. It can be said that man may even destroy himself in consequence. Such is the degree of importance which this matter possesses.

I would like to invite your attention to the consequences of this mentality in a situation such as that which I am trying to develop. What has happened on many occasions is that a lot of people come and they want to study, they want to learn, they want to organise, they want to develop themselves; and they say to me, 'Give me the guidance, give me the material, give me the information, give me this, give me that.'

If I gave them those things, (or such of them as I might be able to) while they were suffering from this disease of obsessing themselves, I would be their worst enemy.

It is for this reason that you will probably have read that some of the stories which I have published make this point; they illustrate this seeming paradox that I can be your enemy if I give you something. This may be strange to our thinking, foreign to our ordinary thinking, but it is very true.

You have seen the operation of this malaise yourselves already in your lives, and therefore it is not necessary for me to emphasise it: but it would be worthwhile thinking about it.

If you do, I think you will agree with me that you have seen the consequences of this yourselves in past years.

Fortunately the malaise is not irreversible. It can be reversed: but only if we have the right conditions and the right people involved in the effort.

But we cannot say that we have the medicine, or the remedy, for everybody in the world, on demand, and we cannot say that we can reverse the tendency in five minutes, and we cannot say that we can do this without perhaps some discomfort.

We must say these things so as to be realistic, and in order to tell the truth.

We are not dealing in promises and imagination; we are operating an enterprise. Although it is not romantic to talk in this way, (and most people demand, as their 'price' for giving attention, some degree of romanticism and imagination) we are interested in the results, and let other people be interested in fantasies. There are plenty of people who are emotionally-minded. We must be serious.

And we must also remember that many people are, effectively, asleep, dreaming romantic dreams. These people will always oppose this approach, dislike it, as they always have; and undoubtedly we *are* spoiling their amusement: or interrupting their dream.

They will not, however, realise that this is their condition, and they will therefore oppose these ideas, as always, on other grounds. This helps the cause of sleep, and therefore it is important for us to remain calm, and to recognise the disease. When a person has a disease, you do not attack him, but neither do you worry about all that he is saying.

If a man is in pain, or is in a fantasy world, you do not love him nor do you hate him, for that. You do not take very great notice or pay unbalanced attention to what a certain kind of sick person is saying or doing; because he is not capable of understanding you, and therefore you are in a false position if you react emotionally or even intellectually to his behaviour. It is very important to remember that. Remain calm, above all.

Therefore you will see that charity and kindness towards other people is not a virtue, it is a necessity – a necessity of the situation. It comes from a true diagnosis of the reality, and not directly from a high spiritual source at all. Charity and kindness is not a high quality, it is a realistic quality, and a necessary one. It stems from duty, sympathy and measure.

I invite your attention to the historical situation in which a teacher is dealing with a primitive people who have no sense of the situation, and no diagnostic capacities.

This teacher must appeal to them to be charitable and to try to be objective; he must initially appeal to them emotionally. He may represent charity as a virtue to them, because they do not understand anything else. But this is a primitive stage before the development of understanding. You do not need to be emotionally charitable towards a diseased person, a sick person, if you are a doctor. If you can see he is ill, you don't need to say, 'it is for the sake of God that I am being kind to him'.

It is for the sake of man that you are being kind to him; it is for the sake of the necessity that you are being kind to him.

If a man is suffering from pain, and he attacks you because he has got this terrible pain, you do not say, 'I will not hit back because I am a religious man.' You say, 'I am a doctor, I know

10

what's wrong with him. My emotions are not involved and I must, from duty, try to help him'. You have here gone one stage beyond the primitive, and this is a very important argument, because most of the people in this world are still being taught as if they were primitive people.

They are being told: be charitable, be understanding, it is divine. They are thus being treated as if they were primitive savages: regressed, even, to an earlier stage than they were before. But they're not so primitive any more: their supposed mentors are in fact treating them with something like contempt.

As a result they are easily confused. Because they are really capable of understanding this sleep, this narcoleptic malaise, they should be told about it on that level. This is the shortcoming of certain forms of allegedly spiritual instruction, which continue to treat people as if they were primitive tribalists living one, two or more thousand years ago.

And it is because the audience does not correspond in its cultural level with those who are teaching it, that very little progress can be made. As an example, I will tell you quite plainly that you will find, in certain forms of supposedly spiritual teachings, the audience are given promises and treated to threats. They are told, 'If you do this, it will be good for you; if you do that it will be bad for you.' And they are alternately frightened and promised wonderful things. Now this is the most primitive way of dealing with human beings, and it can indeed be necessary with a primitive community. It is not necessary for all members of all the communities of today. This is not to say that there is not a place for threat or promise; but only a place, and a specific one at that.

It is for that reason that a very famous woman, Rabia, one of the saints of our tradition, has left us a very beautiful prayer. She said, 'Oh God, if I worship You from fear of Hell, then put me in Hell, and if I worship You from desire for Paradise, exclude me from Paradise.' This is what that prayer means. That she is not doing something to please or displease God, she is doing it for another reason: because she understands something. This is a very important principle, and it brings us to a higher

11

level than the generally familiar, primitive version of religion.

So you will see that if we are dealing with a primitive individual or community, we may well use threat and promise. But where we are dealing with a more advanced community, if we use these methods of fear and hope too strongly, we will actually regress the person to a more primitive condition even if he or she has already passed that stage; we will not only be doing such a person no good, we will be doing damage to a person who is now trained to respond mainly to fear and hope.

This fact has been known, of course, for many thousands of years, and has been taught for as long a period of time. But there have always been large populations of the world which have been at some time ignorant of it.

Fortunately at this time, with the development of sociological and psychological knowledge and experimentation, there is a great deal of material published not by us but by experts all over the world which verifies and proves this point, and there is now no need to rely on our unsupported word for this information.

We are able to direct your attention to the scientific work which has been done in this field. This is a very great advantage which we have, which we would not have had even one hundred years ago, because the research material was not then available.

Therefore we must be thankful and grateful to the scientists who have placed these instruments in our hands, and we should not imagine that there is some conflict between us and the scientific method and scientific work.

We should also note in passing that such has been the power of the scientific revelations in the late twentieth century on this subject that even the traditionalistic religious people must take account of it, must take notice of this, and they must adjust their teaching in response to this scientific knowledge, otherwise their form of training will die out.

Now there was a very famous Sufi called Muhiyuddin Ibn el Arabi in Spain who pointed out in his writings that when you are teaching somebody something, you must first assess the level of that person, and you must have different circles of people in accordance with their capacity to understand.

For saying this, Ibn el Arabi was very seriously criticised, because he was 'being unfair' and people said: 'There is no monopoly of truth. Tell the truth to everybody and they will understand.'

It is only in the last few decades, in the last few years, that Ibn el Arabi's theory has been understood properly. We have been able to verify it because we know that you must speak to everybody in accordance with his understanding, otherwise you may be doing damage.

Now we can return to exclusion and inclusion. You will be aware that in traditional spiritual teaching we are told that we must make sacrifices, and we must hold back from gaining certain things which we want, we must not be over-ambitious. We must be considerate to other people, we must not make a great noise and must avoid pride, and so on. These are some of the virtues which we are expected to cultivate. There is a profound psychological reason for trying to cultivate these abilities.

This is what we must now understand: that these virtues which we are supposed to cultivate have a scientific background, and they are necessary, not for our social happiness, but for our psychological integrity.

When this has not been fully explained, and when it is not understood, there will be serious mistakes in the development of a group of people. It is not rare to find such diseases – in many if not all religious organisations. For example, people behave as though they are very humble externally, yet this is just a mask, this is a *persona*.

It happens when people judge others by their behaviour; 'This man is very simple, he only eats one meal a day: therefore he must be good'. They judge him externally, and that is because we have been taught to judge externally. How does he behave, and not 'what is he really like?' It is this confused kind of mind which imagines that 'miracles' presuppose divine guidance, contact or the rest.

13

To refer again to the woman Sufi Rabia: when people claimed that onions had appeared by a miracle in her kitchen, she said, 'My Lord is not a greengrocer!'

Here is another important example: the idea of sacrifice and service. These are two important necessities for humankind. If they become diseases, if they become obsessions, then they are destructive to humans.

As an example: a week or two ago I was at a meeting where a lecture was given by a very famous religious figure in London, a man who has been teaching and preaching for fifty years.

He was constantly asking his audience to be humble and to repent and to sacrifice and to feel guilty, and the result was that they were all extremely unhappy because they had already sacrificed, they had already felt guilty, they had already served as much as they could, and they didn't know what more to do.

But he was just going on like a recording – saying 'You must suffer, you must sacrifice, you must be humble', as if he were a doctor giving an aspirin to somebody and telling him that he must have 50 aspirins, 100 aspirins, 200 aspirins.

But too many aspirin tablets will kill you in the end! Any psychologist will be able to tell you that the people who are the audience of that religious man, his followers, have been conditioned into feeling unhappiness every time they meet him. Until he tells them that all will be well: is this a religious objective, or is it not?

There is another teacher of this sort, who is doing the reverse. He collects large numbers of people together, and he makes them feel happy by saying pleasant things to them, by telling them that everything is all right, and all they have to do is this, that and the other and they will be happy and successful – and they love him, and they feel very happy.

But unfortunately if you study them you find that they have become extremely inefficient and useless people. All they have is a sensation that they are happy. Now if this is what you seek, then that is the man to follow. But all he is really doing is mental engineering.

He is an engineer, just like the first man of whom I spoke was an engineer.

In both cases these gentlemen are excluding certain things and including certain things. But unfortunately the mixture which each has ended up with is a very unsuitable one, although nobody will blame them. That is one of the serious problems, that once people believe in something or somebody, they will never reproach or blame the person who is manipulating them, because they are unaware that any manipulation is being carried out.

Now you must note at this point that I have attacked what people imagine (quite erroneously) to be the very basis of the so-called spiritual teaching of almost the entire world, and I cannot hope to attack people in this manner without producing a very savage reaction.

But I would like you to remember that what the majority believes is not necessarily the truth.

This brings us to the point that it is not only a question of inclusion and exclusion, but it is: what are we including and what are we excluding? We must be specific as to what things it is necessary to exclude.

At this point we must say that the things which we include and the things which we exclude are offered to you to study and to experiment with, for the purposes of familiarisation. We cannot prove that the things which we include and the things which we exclude are different or superior, we can only say we offer them for study.

It is for this reason that we cannot convert you to a belief in what we are doing. And it is for this reason also that we can never be called a cult of any kind; because by definition we do not expect belief.

Those people who call us a cult are only showing their own ignorance of what a cult is. It is interesting to notice that the people who imagine that we are a cult are the people in the developed countries of the West, who have not yet become aware of the scientific research on this subject carried out by their own specialists. In the East we are not considered to be

15

a cult. There are, of course, both in the East and the West, cults which use our name and imagine that they are Sufic. I exclude these, for they are obvious for what they are to all sensible people.

Our imitators are criticised in the West, and so they should be. We suffer from this disability, that what we are doing is so unfamiliar to this culture, which has not yet reached a knowledge of its own discoveries, that we are at a disadvantage, still.

As a matter of interest, I will illustrate this. I have here a list of more than 20 international authorities in literature, philosophy, science, and so on. All these authorities, some of whom are professors and some of whom are heads of departments in universities, and some of whom are respected individuals of the greatest importance in their own countries – all these people are writing chapters for a book on Sufism.

There are Cabinet Ministers, ambassadors, ministers; some are millionaires, some are commercial people, all of them are what is called, in English, household names. Everybody knows them as people of great achievement, greatly respected and of great calibre and importance. These people are all familiar with, and know a great deal about, the history and development and value of Sufism.

Some of them are Turks, some are Persians, some Pakistanis, some are Indians, some are Arabs from Egypt, of Iraq, from Syria, from Jordan, from the Lebanon, from North Africa and the Sudan, not to mention countries like Afghanistan. One of them is the Chief Justice of India, that is to say, he is the most important judge in India, and another one is a Christian ecclesiastic of the Coptic Church of Egypt; another is a hermit of India. Many of these people are not Moslems. They are not influenced by money or propaganda; they have their own communities, their own achievements, and so on. To each one of these people the Sufi history, philosophy and culture is well known, respected and understood. No such equivalent can be found in the West.

⋆　　⋆　　⋆

There was a peasant working in a field ploughing the ground with his horse, when a general in the army was going along the road beside the field. His horse got a stone in its shoe and became lame. The general, being accustomed to authority, shouted to the peasant:

'Hey, you, come here, and give me that horse', and the peasant came to him and said, 'Why should I give you my horse?'

The general said, 'My horse is lame, with a stone in his hoof'. The peasant replied, 'Who are you, that I should give you my horse? If I give you this horse, then I will be nothing, I will lose all my money, I won't be able to do anything. I'm not going to give you my horse; my horse is my life.' And the general said, 'I am a general, don't you understand?' The peasant said: 'What is a general?'

'A man in the army.'

Said the peasant: 'Ah, now, I don't know what a general is, but I know that when I was in the army, the sergeant was my chief, and if the *sergeant* told me to give him my horse I would give him the horse. But I don't know who or what you are, because I never heard of your kind of people. If you want my horse, you go and get the sergeant, because I know whom to obey. I know that the man above me is the sergeant, but a general – God knows what a general is!'

The obvious 'application' of this story is that a man cannot see anything much higher, he can only see one degree higher and if he is just a peasant, a sergeant is like God to him.

That is perfectly true, but it is the crude moral. The interpretation I want to give you here is one of structure, that the man, the peasant, is working in a certain structure. The story is supposedly about hierarchy, but in fact it is concerned with structure.

The peasant has been in the army, so he has got two structures; one is the horse in the field. If he loses that horse he may die, or become penniless. The other structure is when the general mentions the army, he immediately understands the structure up to sergeant, and that is perfectly right for him, that he should work in that structure.

So it is structure I am talking about, structure and not hierarchy. The man received orders from somebody in the structure, and that was what he understood.

It is not sufficient for us to produce a structure in which to learn, and then to abandon that structure, and allow the people to continue studying in that structure for the rest of their lives. This would simply automatise them. It is for that reason we cannot have a mass movement. For that reason we must have an organic movement.

The difference between a mass movement and an organic movement is that a mass movement is composed of a mass of people, and an organic movement is more like a plant, in which messages are received when they are necessary and according to a certain requirement.

For example, if the plant needs more water it calls for water and water comes up from the roots to the stem and so on.

With a mass movement you don't get that, you just get 'the mass wants to do something'. But a plant is, of course, a very delicate, complicated and varied thing. Not all of the plant needs all of the water at the same time, so it must be properly organised. And that is why we use the term *organic*.

Many people talk about organic organisations, but they do not in fact have such an organisation, they have mass movements, and they call them organic. So you must not only listen to the words, you must look at the phenomenon. We have the phrase: *Al mujazu qantarat al Haqiqa* which means 'The phenomenal is the channel to the Truth'.

That is the phrase which we use for this process.

We have forms in which we work. Now the form in which we work may be a vocational one, some kind of activity of manufacturing something. So we relate a number of people together, with an objective to manufacture something, it might be carpets, it might be tables, it might be artisan work. Providing that the people are carefully enough selected, and provided that the objective is correctly enough chosen, we will develop a remarkable result. This is the sort of operation which in the past

18

has produced very great art and very great achievements in human culture. This is the type of operation in which we are working, the kind of operation of which you constantly hear rumours such as those about the Cathedral builders and about the great artisans of the past who had spiritual objectives as well as vocational ones.

It is this type of operation. However, in the West the information about who these people were and how they operated has been lost. People are anxious to know all about them. What they do not know is that if they did have this information, it would be of no value to them: it would only be museum- or catalogue-information.

The consequence of the attempts to rediscover these methods has been that people in the West have become emotionally aroused by art, because they can see and feel something in this art: and because emotion is so important to them, they have joined the two things together and they have become emotionally obsessed by art.

In doing this, they have lost the idea of method. Slowly, some people are rediscovering some of this, quite independently of us, and we are delighted to find that this is so.

I will give you an example which I used in a television broadcast, and which created a tremendous amount of interest, mainly in the form of letters.

The particular example which I chose and which created so much interest, was this: In the United States of America it was discovered that there is another way of teaching than the way which we have normally been accustomed to.

Other, that is, than the way of indoctrination and of tension, repetition and anxiety: 'do it again, do it again'. And if this method of learning can be applied to human beings as it has been applied to animals, then our whole ideas about education will have to change.

I will summarise the method: It was discovered that if you take cats, and you teach them how to perform simple tasks, it takes a certain time because cats are difficult to teach; they have very little attention-capacity and they are not interested in trying to learn. They are not, therefore, taught very much.

A group of cats were taught certain things, to perform various tasks, and it was recorded how many hours it took to teach these cats.

Then the researchers took one of the 'educated' cats and they put it in a room with 'uneducated' cats, of the same age and of the same group, of the same family, and they discovered that the cats which had not been educated learned from being in the presence of the educated cat and watching it.

They learnt fifty times faster than the other cats. In other words, they learnt by association with the educated cats, only fifty times faster. The interesting thing is that when these experiments were first published in England, the man who wrote the article – the popularisation of this work – ended it with some significant words.

He said that it was possible that we are now learning why, in the Middle Ages, great artists and great thinkers used to have disciples with them all the time who simply adored the master and stayed with him, waited on him. They worked with him, and they learned; and they became masters in their turn, and therefore it may be that we are rediscovering a method of learning which is superior for certain purposes to our present-day methods of education.

Today, particularly in the Western world, it is difficult to apply this method of teaching to humans, and the reason for that is extremely important to observe.

The reason is that if you want to learn from a contemporary man or woman who is at the top of a profession, the only way you will be taught is by a mixture of propaganda and repetition and anxiety.

This will interrupt the learning system; he will not be content for you to learn from him as he goes about his daily work; you will not move into his house and live with him and learn from him, because this is considered to be inefficient. In fact, the truth is that the man who is an expert nowadays is too vain, too full of self-importance, and he insists first, generally speaking, on transferring that to you, his sense of self-importance. This interrupts the learning process.

But the cat which learnt didn't feel anything – not 'I am a great cat because I have learnt' – therefore he could communicate. And so you will not find it easy to learn certain things from a Westerner nowadays because he just feels that his learning gives him some kind of importance.

This in turn is a barrier between you and him. And now you see the wisdom of the people in the past who taught us all, you and me, that we should have humility towards our teacher because this means that you are open to whatever he or she can teach. But unfortunately the tradition perhaps did not insist so strongly upon the humility of the actual teacher, and therefore the learning process has effectively been interrupted. We can, though, reclaim our heritage in this respect.

It will not have escaped your attention that the habit of people to sign their work and to become well-known as artists in their own name is a modern one; that none of the ancient artists put their name on their work. And the names of the people who produced the great objects of art of the past are totally unknown.

On a visit to India I seized the opportunity to talk to one or two spiritual teachers there. When I went to see one of them, a very important one, I was sitting with him when an American gentleman who had made great sacrifices to come there, was announced.

He said to this guru, as he is called, 'Tell me, what is a guru? How can I recognise a guru? Who is the greatest guru in the world?'

That is all he wanted to know. In that respect this American gentleman's questions were very much paralleled by my own post-bag. I get the same sort of questions every day from correspondents who read my books. And this Hindu gentleman, who was the guru, smiled and said to the American gentleman: 'What I am going to say will not please you. I hope you have not come here to be pleased.'

And the American said: 'Oh, no! I want the truth!'

'Very well, the answer is this. If I am walking through the

21

jungle on a path and there is a stone in the path, and I trip and fall on that stone, and if I learn from that stone to look where I am going, that is my guru, because it has taught me something; not somebody who is going to teach me, not somebody who might teach you, but somebody who has taught you something. And if it is a stone, it is a stone. But you no doubt are thinking about human beings, about god-men.

'A guru is something or somebody from whom you have learnt something, not from whom you might or will or whom you respect or whom other people respect. If you can't learn, the teacher, effectively, "does not exist".'

Now we will return to the question of the structure and the learning.

There are real Sufic study-centres in many, if not most, areas of the world. They exist wherever they are needed, and have done so for many centuries.

These are organised deliberately. That is to say, we don't use a Western system. Western and other primitive systems collect together people who are interested in a certain subject. It is then assumed that they are eligible and that they can learn. It is also imagined that someone who wants to do so, or who has been chosen by Heaven knows what process, will be able to teach them. Or even that, given enough effort or orientation, learning will come about.

To us that is an intolerably 'oriental' mentality. We regard this as oriental nonsense because you are impractical in this particular area: in this particular field you are not only impractical, but you imagine that you *must* not be practical, that this is not a practical area, and when I start to talk about practical things, you think that this is not spirituality, this is something else.

We find it difficult to work with such people. Naturally, the representatives of such thinking who come to Asia to study spiritual things are unsuitable to learn or to teach. Call it a paradox. It is a fact.

In other words, they go and look for the people who look like gurus to them. We don't, generally, tell them because they don't listen.

In fact I've tried to tell people but many don't listen. Here is a very important point that you must remember: the people who advertise themselves and the people who have great visibility, people who make a lot of noise and people who are known to be great spiritual teachers, or the like – such people monopolise the communications media, the TV, the radio, the newspapers. They all have active, loud-mouthed disciples, which gives the impression that this is the spirituality of the East, because there are thousands of them going about.

If you go to places in India, for example, you will find thousands of Americans and English people, and Indians. In fact you may even find millions of Indians, because in India you can easily collect a crowd of one million people.

And everybody imagines that this must be a great spiritual teacher because he has got a million people listening to him at one time. But I must beg of you to note two things. One is that quantity is not the same as quality. Visibility is not the same as quality. And although I am saying this here, you must remember that if I say this in public, ten thousand important and respected people in England will shout me down and say that I am a liar and I am wrong and that it isn't true and that I hate them; because they're obsessed, and I am taking away their toys, their amusements.

But I am afraid it is the truth, nevertheless. It revolves just the same, as Galileo's famous saying has it. But we continue to operate nevertheless. Now you will probably understand some of the reasons why we cannot go into competition with these people in the mass communications media or in forming a mass movement.

Now we will revert to this question of working format, of structures. We find it difficult to convince people in the West that generally we can work only with people who have been chosen as suitable for this work, not people who want to do it, even if they want to give up all their money and all their loyalty, and everything.

Suppose some people are not suitable: especially at any given moment. What are we going to do with them? I must remind you here that when we demand the right to choose the student, we are doing exactly the same as you are doing.

In your own educational institutions nobody has a right to study an advanced subject if they are illiterate. You choose a student according to capacities and previous education.

We insist on the same right. But do you see how far you have strayed from the path of your civilisation, your culture and your traditions in permitting the collection of people without any sort of preparation, without any sort of testing as to their capacity, in these extraordinary groups? Now there is a delicate point here. You may believe that in a democratic society everybody should have a chance to get some of what there is to obtain.

I agree. However, another mentality co-exists in Western people. It is, unfortunately, the mass-production mentality, the mentality which regards the human being not as a human being but as a product. This often lies behind modern thinking and you must be careful of it. The consequence of that mind-set: the factory mentality, is to think, 'bring all these people into this room, tell them something, train them, and then push them out there as finished products'.

Our conception of humanity is far higher than that. To me you are individuals, not objects to be processed by me and go through my course, just as if you were all the same, so that you all get exactly the same, and you all come out exactly the same at the other end. This is for manufacturing sausages, this is not for developing humans.

Now, you might say, 'well that is not very efficient, there must be some way of overcoming this problem. How do we deal with a mass of people?' And I have good news for you, because I can tell you we have developed means to overcome this problem. But we have not solved it in your way, and therefore you must look at the way in which we do solve it.

Our solutions are not the same as your theoretical solutions would have been. They are determined by possibilities, not fantasies.

In the first place, we know that when a group of people

24

becomes too large, it must be sub-divided, in order to maintain the organic nature of the group, of the movement of people. This is not a strange conception to you, you can understand it, and you can see its advantages. And in order to deal with, to work with a large number of people at one time, it has been necessary to overcome the evils, the drawbacks, the disadvantages, which exist when you concentrate all the people in a geographical area which is the Western method. Consequently, we have a different communication system.

In talking about this special communication system, we must be careful not to become excited or emotionally involved with it, because this will interrupt it.

It is in two parts. The first part is that we give a task or an assignment or an activity to a group of people, and we ask them to follow that activity until we ask them to stop it.

This activity which we have designated for them contains all the requirements for that group of people up to the point when we want to stop their activity, or change it.

This is the first thing − the work, the elements are contained in the ambience, in the activity: that is the first communication. The atmosphere in which they work is communicating with them through the objects with which they are working.

In other words, the situation in which we put the people contains the elements, or half the elements which they need.

It is just the same as if we sent you on a journey somewhere, and we gave you some food and that food was sufficient for that journey. This is the first communication element.

The second communication element is that when the group is operating correctly in accordance with the requirements and in the proper balance without too much emotion, and without too much intellectuality, there is a direct communication among all the people connected with this work, and that communication is telepathic.

Now the problem is this, that in general most people in study groups do not want to study, they want attention. And they want to go and see some guru, or they want to be told something fantastic, they want to feel something in their stomach, therefore they are not learning at all; they are a sociological phenomenon, and therefore they cannot learn, therefore they want to learn desperately, and therefore nothing will happen.

It is a vicious circle. We are dealing with a sociological phenomenon, in such instances, and not with a spiritual or a learning one at all.

You will have observed in the groups in which you have worked, all kinds of groups, that there are a lot of people who want to attract attention to themselves, or want to make trouble, or want psychotherapy, or want money, or want comfort, or want parents, or something, from the group. Now we say that you can obtain all these things in the ordinary world much better, much more easily and much more satisfactorily, and therefore we always encourage everybody to have proper friends, proper social relationships and proper outlets, all their lives, so that they do not come to depend on us for those things. And the reason for that is that otherwise you will convert your study group into a social organisation and its objectives will be lost, its objectives will become social.

This is what has happened to spiritual groupings all over the world. It always happens. We must try to prevent it. Now there is not an infinite variety of people nor is there an infinite variety of groups. They fall into various categories. The number of types of people and the number of types of group are limited, so this helps us, because if they were infinite, we would not be able to work with them.

Therefore we generally find in a group of people, people who are at different stages, or who really belong to different groups. They should be in another type of group instead of the group in which they are. Now, our concern is that the majority of people in a group should be suitable for that group. Some of them will not be suitable, but it doesn't matter as long as the majority is suitable for that group of people. So what happens in actual fact is, that people form groups, and many of these groups have no hope of developing into anything at all. But the members of the group will not accept that, because it is

26

too uncomfortable for them to accept it, but nevertheless it is the case, it is the condition.

Fortunately, groups which have not got the stability potential, which have not got the potential of stabilising themselves, generally break up relatively soon, relatively early, or we help them to break up if we can.

There are many easy ways of helping these groups to deteriorate, and one uses those methods. For example, when we get letters from these people which reveal that they are seeking emotional excitement; or they ask questions which show us that they are merely looking for a social stabilisation, we send them the kind of direction which will cause the group to dissolve through dissatisfaction.

In an exactly similar manner, when somebody comes to me looking for a guru, I always talk like a materialist who is not interested in humanity and I behave in a very frivolous manner. I tell jokes, and my visitor soon decides that I am not a serious person, and goes away painlessly.

The verdict: 'This man is no good at all. Thank God I didn't get into his hands.' And therefore we are all happy. This is rather an oriental technique, because in the West people do not like to lose their gravity, they do not like to lose their sense of dignity, and therefore they have deprived themselves of this weapon, they have thrown away this tool.

Do you notice how we include and others (through the desire for dignity) exclude an activity?

SECTION II

Real and Imitation Sufi Groups

Like anything else which becomes well known and well thought of, the Sufi study group is constantly imitated. Few of such imitations are intentionally spurious. By far the largest number are based on the idea which also underlies such apparently different activities as sympathetic magic and fashion: 'If I look like it, I can, in some way, BECOME it.' Sometimes this concept takes the unwitting form of 'If I can think about it, I can make it happen'.

We must avoid magical thinking. Religious thinking requires one to become worthy of something; magical thinking tries to cause or to create effects.

I came across an example of how far the human mechanism of rationalisation can go towards the absurd twenty or more years ago, when leaders of a large number of study groups in Europe and America approached me, seeking advice on what – and how – to teach.

I first asked, in surprise, how long these groups had been at work, and how they had managed to keep going without any real content or any idea how to teach.

They had existed, like that, for up to forty years! But on what basis, I wondered, aloud.

'Well, you see, we heard that the source of the Teaching was in the East. We reasoned that, if we formed centres of study here, the real teachers would hear of us and would be attracted. In fact, we were told this by our leaders. It seemed logical at the time.'

'We reasoned'? At first I thought that these remarks were intended as a joke. But when I laughed I only found that it distressed these honest but wholly misguided folk.

The 'will to power' may be unacceptable to most people: but when it is entirely unconscious, that is even more bizarre. They were trying to make things happen . . .

You may not think that the people I mention were dishonest, but what else are we to call them? First, they spoke frankly and openly to me, admitting that they knew next to nothing. Second, they even told their disciples that they were 'waiting for the message from the Eastern teachers'. And the pupils themselves, many of them highly intelligent people, saw nothing strange in the theory.

Yet, to any half-way lucid person, surely, the theory could be paraphrased thus:

'Somewhere in the East, we know not where, there is a body of people who have a special, advanced knowledge of man. These people have cultivated this knowledge for aeons, and they have schools and systems through which it is taught. Engaged, as they are, in pursuing this activity for the good of humanity, they carry on the teaching in the way which is necessary for its fulfilment.'

It had never, I gathered, occurred to any of these good people to think that, given the existence of such people as they constantly spoke of, the Eastern Teachers must surely have the means to project the teaching wherever they like: or, at all events, wherever it was necessary or advisable.

It was a strange experience to see the faces of the eager esotericists when I said: 'Your Eastern teachers must be a rum lot, if they have all that wisdom and are incapable of carrying on their job without you.'

I had visions of a parallel, equally ludicrous, hypothetical situation: of the good people of the Kentish village near which I lived collecting together and agreeing that they would like some advanced knowledge (let us call it microelectronics) and then trying to puzzle their way around in such information they had of it, until such time as some technologist, stimulated by their heroism, should take pity on them . . .

There are still hundreds of groups like the seekers I have told you about: and they have many thousands of members.

That is one form of imitation group. By far the commonest, however, derive their energy from a more familiar, though less clearly articulated, source than a mere lack of common sense.

They are thought to be Sufi groups, but their dynamic, that which holds them together, is something quite different. It is the unperceived contract between people who want to be in a social group and those who want to exercise (most often unconsciously) leadership.

This phenomenon is now well known and documented by workers in the fields of sociology, anthropology and psychology. But it is not yet well understood by the population at large. The reason is not difficult to find. When a number of people combine for a common purpose, it is always taken as axiomatic that they are brought together, and kept united, by the label, the apparent aim of the group.

The reality is the other way about. If the desire to group were not there, nobody would think of forming a group. If the alleged purpose of the group were not there, another would be adopted. It is as simple as that.

One reason why this knowledge, fascinating and important as it is, (and verified by much sociological research in the West) is so slow in percolating down to the ordinary person is this: People cherish their groups. They also have a genuine interest in the avowed aims of the group. Anyone who seems to them to be deriding or in any way threatening the group, even by raising legitimate questions about it, is perceived as hostile.

Psychologically speaking, then, there is a factor in group-behaviour which can have serious consequences for the group and its members, the most conspicuous one being that people find it hard to get away from the group, even when it is not desirable for them to stay in it.

There is an added complication: groups are often very valuable, and carry on excellent and important work. Because of this, there is a subconscious impression that a specific group MUST be good, must be useful. This is fortified by the fellow-feeling which often accompanies group membership: People are deriving satisfactions from being members. Yet such groups are not Sufic ones, whatever their members may imagine. So, if someone comes along and says, 'This group is only a social phenomenon', he will be told, 'You cannot understand how valuable it is to us. We feel something which you do not'. In these circumstances, the group becomes a self-protecting entity.

33

But, of course, it is not a spiritual one, no matter what its members may imagine. And it is imagination at work, no matter what it feels like.

Well, it may be asked (and I have often been asked it), what is wrong with that? One man put it in this way:

'I accept that group behaviour is rooted in instinct. But this, surely, is only the form and not the substance. People need that instinct, or they would never combine at all. We should be glad that the tendency exists. People may form a group to practise, for instance, first aid, and do a lot of good. How would they manage it if they did not have a tendency towards concerted conception, planning and action?'

The statement, though articulate and seemingly reasonable, is in reality based on incoherent thought and lack of information. Far from being connected with higher consciousness, it badly needs an injection of lower (normal) consciousness. You see, I was talking about Sufi learning groups, not about first aid.

There are any amount of non-Sufic efforts which can be carried out by groups originating with, and making use of, the natural human tendency to combine: and this should be encouraged. The incoherence comes in when it is assumed that there is only one kind of group possible, and that this is the best way to attempt anything. Sufic groups are highly specialised entities, and certainly no job for amateurs.

Perhaps you recognise the logic within the incoherence. It is our old friend the logic of the man who says 'I admit that I do this from habit or instinct. But look at what a lot of good I do, and, besides, there is no other way to do it!'

Another form of this kind of fallacious thinking runs: 'If God had wanted us to fly, he would have given us wings.'

Besides, no Sufi will say that there should be a group which is not based on natural human proclivities or which should be completely other than any familiar human group. What he will say, however, is that no Sufi group can usefully exist unless the group mentality operates to the minimum. For this to be possible, for a Sufi group to come into being, those in the group must, as a priority, know about groups, and know how to reduce the compulsive element inherent in the drive towards grouping.

So a true group, in the Sufi sense, is one which has the minimum of 'groupiness' about it. Imitation Sufi groups are in-groups. A good test is to see whether complete strangers (with no esotericist interests at all) feel at ease in the group. If they do not, it is not a Sufic group.

Furthermore, a Sufi group is not a permanency. It may be dissolved, recombined, suspended for months or even years, so that the unwelcome characteristics of a group are avoided.

The next characteristic of a real Sufi group is that its members are chosen and harmonised so as to develop the maximum learning advantage from the group. To do this requires not a touching faith in the Eastern Masters who may be attracted, but a thorough Sufic knowledge of harmonisation.

Sufi study groups are not recruitment groups. They are not collections of people who have all answered a newspaper advertisement, or formed a group after reading a book or hearing a lecture, or because they are related to someone, or have been made interested in the Sufi Way; or people who simply seek a group. Such non-Sufic groups may be recognised, even by complete outsiders, by the personality conflicts which arise within them.

People in a Sufi group are those assigned to a group by someone who knows what this really means. And that means by a Sufi. And a Sufi is someone who has completed the learning, who is the end-product, not a learner in any sense. Seekers are not Sufis.

Any other form of group whose members imagine that they are following Sufi study will have as little chance of acquiring anything of Sufic knowledge as any collection of people (like my villagers trying to understand technology) who lack the basic requirement of fundamental guidance.

In this sense, it will now be obvious, a Sufic group is a specialised one; something very different from a random assemblage of people, something distinct from people simply sharing a similar outlook or having similar objectives.

35

For this reason alone, no group can be called Sufi which is not organised by a Sufi. It should be noted here that Sufis are not claiming that the Sufi group is in some way superior to any other kind of group. But it is simply quite different. You can learn to be a Sufi (if a member of a group) only in a Sufi group; which is not the same as saying that any Sufi wants to try to turn people into Sufis. But a Sufi is obliged to make clear the difference between Sufically purposeful groups and others, however attractive or apparently determined these others may be.

There is another common (though often unwitting) rationalisation found among would-be 'seekers'. Having been informed that a Sufi group should be one directed by a Sufi, they promptly backtrack and rename themselves 'preparatory groups', or some such label. The name may change, but the reality does not. You may be full of goodwill, want to inform people about Sufi matters, know little but think that you can do little harm by giving talks, having meetings, and so on. But this activity is full of pitfalls, which are far more numerous and objectionable than the advantages. Wisdom does not come out of ignorance; and the matter does not even end there. Out of ignorance and self-deception may come a great deal of harm. The least that can happen is that imitation groups will proliferate, because there is nothing which can be done to prevent this.

The test for those who are really interested to learn what can be learnt from the Sufi way is easy. It is exactly the same as the test which common sense applies to the learning of anything: Does the would-be learner want to learn what there is to be learnt, in the manner, in the company, and with the materials, timing and methods, which are necessary to the time, place, situation of the pupil and the learning? Or does the learner want to proceed in ways which he or she feels are the right ones?

'Increase your necessity' is a Sufi phrase, speaking, you should observe, not of a desire, but of a necessity. Most people extend the wrong side of themselves to Sufi teaching. They may be seeking: but they are seeking what the Sufis are not able to give.

There is another bizarre element which can creep into study

groups, a sort of poison, which does not originate in the Sufi attitude or teaching, but in the 'contaminant of the World'. This is when someone gets hold of the idea that the Sufi ideas have to be promoted, and forms a group while not yet fitted for the task. Such a person is easy to identify, by the use of common sense. Unfortunately, one of the first things that such a person does is to oppose common sense.

Such people will take, for instance, our books, which are publicly distributed, and set people to study them. The next step is to oppose rational interpretations of their contents by saying (or implying) that 'there is a different, hidden, special, meaning in this material'. Or it might be put thus: 'What is written here is not intended to be understood as it stands.' Or even 'this is a test.' They tend to like the idea of 'a test'. But Sufi tests are never carried out in a way which is ever discerned by the pupil: and never at all in a 'preparatory group'.

Anyone who teaches but says that he or she does not understand; or who says that things in our published materials have a special and different meaning from the overt one is – at best – very self-deluded.

Another common statement or implication from such an unsuitable individual is 'We do not understand, but understanding will come if we persist'.

This kind of person is particularly difficult to deal with; because he or she is suffering from a concealed desire to dominate. This is concealed both from the individual in question and also from the group, under layers of 'greed' and self-deception. Only the restoration of real humility can change that. That, in turn, requires repentance of the desire to dominate. This is usually too much to ask from those who have developed a taste for it.

People say 'this person is so dedicated, is taking nothing from the group, how can he or she be deluded, or want power?' This question ignores the fact that there are other things to be taken from situations than, say, money or overt power. Generally one can recognise such a self-deceived, if – to some – plausible, person because he (or she) gives the impression of acting under

37

the instructions of someone else, the Teacher, living or dead. There is a familiar pattern in the life of this kind of person. More often than not, he or she has tremendous personal and social difficulties, constantly having problems which are attributed to some kind of 'test' or 'cross to bear'. All that is happening is that this individual is ascribing a different cause to events, and the pattern continues, sometimes for many years.

Luckily, such a situation can sometimes be retrieved. But such a retrieval partly depends upon the group-leader recognising his or her need to learn before one can lead. There is a gap in such a person's knowledge. Until that gap is filled, there will be no progress.

And the onus is not only on the 'group-leader' to reform. In one sense, the members of the group are also 'guilty'. Their desire to be involved in something important, special or promising, their allowing a sense of dependency to become too strong, causes the suspension of the common sense which the Sufis need before progress can be made.

I have come across many people who have said, 'But I have only persisted with this group because I really want to learn, and can find no other opportunity'. That sounds all right to the person who is saying it. But how does he or she explain the fact that there are thousands, perhaps millions, of people who are just as interested and who do not stay tied to such unsuitable company?

This phenomenon is not confined to supposedly Sufic groups: indeed, it is rarer among them than among all kinds of esotericist groupings. And, as any sociologist will tell you, this kind of social group will continue to be formed, almost everywhere: simply because it makes use of the dependency wish and wonder-seeking characteristics which are present in everybody. The Sufi tries to reduce these characteristics. The esotericist feeds off them. He or she seeks wonders, 'promptings', meanings and messages. This attitude is highly undesirable.

Apart from certain natural proclivities, what are the factors which produce such problems among people who are often otherwise quite sensible?

There is, interestingly enough, only a single reason. We have found it to be a constant wherever we have come across the peculiarities which I have been describing. The reason is, quite simply, that the people involved have failed to stick to a single curriculum.

They have collected all kinds of esoteric, religious and similar fragments from all kinds of sources, and tried to link them; or, at all events, to include them in their thinking. In other words, they have attempted to do the reverse of what any lucid teaching system requires.

Sufi study does not differ from any other purposeful and acceptable teaching in any area. It requires the student to follow a series of carefully selected and graded steps, without incorporating imagination, assumptions, materials from elsewhere, or concepts originating with other times, places and people. In a word, it is a complete system whenever projected.

This approach does not appeal to those who, while imagining that they want to learn or to progress, in reality merely want to spin on their own axes. They have, effectively, removed themselves from any real teaching or learning.

An Assumption Underlying All Human Cultures

All human cultures, no matter how diverse they may appear to superficialists, are ultimately based upon exactly the same premise. This is that *greed is wrong,* and that *renunciation, as the opposite of greed,* must be right. The cultures continue, in their automatic reasoning (as one can see not from their arguments but by their actions – a far better method of assessment) that if *total greed is totally objectionable, total renunciation must be totally praiseworthy.*

39

In basing themselves upon such an idea, the cultures are, of course, acting in a manner exactly similar to the useless way of thinking of the infant or the savage, who thinks: *one aspirin cures a headache, 1,000 aspirins will give me illumination.*

The truth lies in the middle. It is not contested that greed is destructive, something which can easily be illustrated even by such apparently bizarre logical extensions as saying: 'If one person's greed reached its total maximum, there would be no food left for anyone else to eat, and then he would be alone. Greed might in that way become abolished, since consumption would not be at anyone's expense, but humanity would die out.'

Smaller groupings of people, however, have almost always existed who have realised that the barbarian methods of thought are not only inefficient but insufficient, and create more problems than they solve.

It is these groupings which have communicated the much more sophisticated patterns of thought which all current cultures can easily be seen to lack.

All members of current cultures, in exercising their capacity to understand this patchy development of their thinking patterns, must realise that they should never be expected to abandon customary methods of thought. If they were to do so, they would become incomprehensible to their fellows, and this would seriously disturb the possibility of their being able to continue to live amicably and successfully among them. But this does not exclude the possibility that the 'refined barbarian' can add to the dimensions of his understanding, even if he cannot make these dimensions understood to his fellows within the impoverished thought-structures wherein they demand to be informed.

But before he tries to add to his breadth of knowledge and his objectivity, the individual must ask himself whether he really does desire to do so. I say this because it is entirely obvious that most people, no matter what they imagine, do not in fact want to learn more. If they did, they would have been able to observe at least some of the absurdities and the shortcomings of their present patterns of thinking. There is no real evidence that this has occurred in the past few thousand years on any significant scale.

Nobody who tries to increase this knowledge in the human milieu can remain unaware that, among those who believe that they are trying to increase their knowledge, perceptions and awareness, only a very small number are actually trying to do so. The rest are using the same words, but they are in fact demanding certain satisfactions from the enterprise: social, personal and community diversion being among the most obvious.

Acceptance

A characteristic of almost all human societies is the general belief, hallowed by institutions and uncritically accepted, that something must be:

- Convenient;
- Plausible;
- Believed;
- Allowed by precedent;
- Accepted as true;
- Capable of 'proof' within confines laid down by self-appointed authorities or their successors;
- Admitted by some established body of experts:

otherwise it is not allowed to be 'true'.

The fact is, of course, as we can immediately see once we pause to analyse it:

> An idea, scheme, or almost anything else, really needs no other qualification than that it *is* true.

Rule: Truth is not dependent upon whether any given individual, machine, or body of people regard it as true or otherwise.

41

Attention

Man seeks attention because he needs it.

It is part of human nutrition.

The obtaining and employment of attention follows a nutrition pattern.

Too little attention causes symptoms of deprivation.

More than a certain amount 'fills up' man, in that he cannot perceive other things.

Man is at a stage where he craves attention and does not realise it. It is not the object which he desires, but the attention derived from the object.

He is like a child, savage or animal that has a need which disables him because he has not organised it.

Human beings who had not developed regular eating habits would be similarly inefficient, breaking off all kinds of activities to have food.

Those people who give and take the necessary quality, quantity and variety of attention are incomparably more effective and free than those whose lives are dominated by attention-craving, but who have no clear picture of the situation.

Notice

People who claim that they are not getting the notice which they deserve would not behave as they do if this were true.

Equally confused are those who claim that they do not want attention and who do. When they are given what they say they want, they often reject it, because what they wanted all the time was − attention. But it should not be called attention, since they like to feel that it is something 'more important'.

A Real Community

Ours is a real community. Ordinary communities come into being, grow, develop, die and regenerate, in certain very similar patterns.

People think that these communities are different from one another because of their outward shapes.

But they have characteristics which utilise human tendencies like self-esteem, greed, the desire to receive approval (or, failing that, attention of any sort) and so on.

Unable or unwilling to resist a community's demands for these and other satisfactions, almost all the leaders of human groups have, knowingly or otherwise, made use of them.

The inevitable result has been that almost all human groupings – whatever their overt aims – structurally resemble one another. They are, or rapidly become, manifestations of the same characteristics. They only masquerade as being 'in search of knowledge', or as 'uplifting the people', or as 'spreading information', even as 'increasing wealth or productivity'.

This is because they are only able to appear to do such things so long as the individuals and mass of the community are gaining or being promised some lower satisfaction.

This fact has been observed, only too well, by sociologists and psychologists. It is so marked that these experts have gone so far as to believe that no human community can come about, progress or survive unless it panders to the lower human proclivities.

If this were so, there would be no hope for the human race.

While it is understandable that at a lower level human egoism may be harnessed to social action ('do something "good"and you will feel good') the higher philosophy must take effect at some point. If it does not, if a higher community does not develop, nothing can happen beyond the social common denominator.

The Sufi enterprise concentrates upon developing a knowledge in the human being that the satisfactions of his accustomed 'self' may be legitimate in smaller things. He cannot use them as a springboard to higher understanding.

Our community remains faithful to the higher development of man only to the extent to which its individual and group studies can recognise the possibility of the existence of a higher aim than disguised personal satisfactions.

Are Men Machines?

People do not like being called machines. And yet most people are not even machines in lacking faculties for evaluating the qualitative nature of experience. Instead of being able to perceive the spectrum of influences in a single experience, they feel it transcendental *if it moves them.* Unlike a machine, too, the human being has no switching gear to turn experience on and off. And man has no means of engendering experience except by the most hazardous trial-and-error ones such as throwing himself into random situations or ingesting drugs.

One of the purposes of a real esoteric training is first to acquire lower control, control such as a machine might have, before higher controls can be attained.

Assessment and Service

Visualise a child, a primitive man or an uninstructed one watching a skilled worker performing a series of actions.

This observer, if he lacks information (and perhaps also experience) comes to certain conclusions about what he is witnessing.

Among the conclusions might be the opinion that the actions were random, were a game, were a mechanical ritual, were a dramatic enactment, and so on.

The observer might imitate the actions. This imitation, for subjective or even physical reasons, might cause him pleasure. If this were the consequence, he might well conclude that he had discovered the reason for the actions themselves.

The imitation, on the other hand, might for one of many reasons fatigue him or might 'produce no result'. Such an experience would almost inevitably cause him to entertain and even convince himself of the truth of suppositions concerning the actions which might well be quite at variance with fact.

The imitation, again, might obsess him until he felt constrained to perform those actions repeatedly. He might very well form an opinion based upon this experience. Such an opinion, yet again, might well be totally at variance with the facts.

And there are of course numerous other possibilities of experience and interpretation, all stemming from the simple situation with which we started.

Now note that there are many circumstances in life when any one of us, and any collection of us, might behave virtually exactly as would a child, a primitive man or an uninstructed individual. This is especially likely when people are faced with ideas, behaviour, actions or other phenomena based upon knowledge (and even on information) which they lack.

People make mistakes which are seen to be ludicrous when they encounter circumstances arising from bases of which they lack knowledge, or of which their instruction is defective, insufficient, too generalised or otherwise inapplicable.

This kind of situation is almost exactly duplicated in the relationship between the student (or would-be student) of higher human knowledge, and a teacher of it.

As you will readily understand from the foregoing, the onus is very much upon the teacher to make sure that the student has a sufficient background of information, knowledge and experience so that he can benefit from the teaching itself.

The teaching, too, must be presented in a volume, quality

and manner which will correspond with the pupil's needs, abilities and previous thinking, as well as with the teaching's own minimum requirements for its effective expression.

Without all these conditions, real teaching is not possible.

It is the teacher, not the student, who assesses the condition of the student and prescribes his studies. Without adequate supervision over the curriculum and the student's exposure to study-materials, progress is inadequate.

It is by no means uncommon, too, for two students to undergo very similar studies with the result that one of them emerges mechanically conditioned, and the other correctly developed.

The second student in such an instance would graduate to even higher studies, while the first one would either become a happy but limited devotee or else would have to be 'deconditioned' so that he could really learn.

Striking examples of these differences are to be seen in human-contact situations where the matter of service to an individual, a goal or a doctrine is involved. This is what we call the 'Stage of Service'. All human beings have to learn how to serve in such a way as to benefit and to be benefited concurrently. Superficial organisations provide only a travesty of this process, of priceless value as a warning but useless as an example.

Academics Anonymous

This is the name which could be given to a group of disaffected scholars, formed from those who cannot stand the narrow-mindedness of the very structures which sustain them. I get more and more letters from such people. Some are distinguished men in their own fields. They, however, cannot say or publish ideas which have not been 'proved' by the criteria of the mass. This saddens them. Sometimes they liken themselves to Galileos and other martyrs, and it is possible that some of them are, or might become such. They plead, touchingly, for someone to publish their papers under pen-names and to guarantee their anonymity. It is only fair to remark, however, that if they were suffering as much as they say, one would expect them to bear the consequences and become real Galileos. If many of the letters from conventional 'specialists' read like papers written by one-eyed mummies, some of these others write like suppliants in the advice columns of women's weekly papers:

> 'If I say what I think, my colleagues will put it about that I am insane. But I do not know how long I can go on like this, knowing that the academic method of thought and so-called 'proof' is bogus and rests upon deception in mind and gross deceit in the handling of materials . . .'

Are You Above or Beyond This?

Anyone who has worked for a time with candidates for specialised 'higher' studies will have had borne upon him again and again that:

> The people who are most likely to imply, to say or think that they are 'above' or 'beyond' certain ideas, statements, undertakings of a psychological or spiritual nature are the ones most likely to be those who are in need of them.

This is, of course, only because one way of preventing oneself from being exposed to something for which one fears a lack of capacity is to say 'I am not to be included in that'.

Those who know more about such things know that the people who are really above, or beyond, the elements mentioned above intimate their stage in a very different manner from the imitators. They do not think, imply, say such things.

47

All Knowledge is Everywhere

It is as true as anything else which can be spoken to say that all knowledge is really available everywhere.

In practical terms, however, it is only the presence of a teacher which makes it flow in the students.

The human element is absolutely essential.

Teachers are not, as you might hope, people who make you feel peace and harmony. They may give you love, knowledge, the capacity for action which are of such an advanced order that these concepts as formerly known to one now seem imitations.

Adopted Methods

If you adopt the methods or institutions which have been developed by people with one set of ideas, these methods or institutions will eventually take over. The result will be that your ideas or objectives will be overcome by the ideas which were originally present in the instrument which you tried to adapt.

This principle may be seen throughout human history.

A religion, for instance, which adopts the structures and procedures of another will end by resembling the previous one far more than itself. If it has prevailed over another religion in the same area, it will develop the same old-age symptoms or weaknesses as the original one. All that the second religion will have contributed is a certain amount of energy, which will soon be spent.

This is why monotheistic religions adopting aspects of paganism are eventually overcome by paganism.

Economic and political systems suffer the same fate.

So do nations and communities organised on other bases, if they are grafted upon convenient but, as always, still-active, roots.

Special ideas, new developments, if they are to flourish, need absolutely characteristic institutions and methods.

Structures originally built for one kind of thinking, or by people who think in a certain way, will always produce – like plants – the same kind of fruit. 'Everything returns to its origin.'

Apparatus

'Photosensitive sensors mounted in the upper part of a semi-rotating central turret, capable of lateral and vertical and some rotary movement to permit this and other equipment to bear on specific sources of stimulus. The turret contains chemical and electronic evaluation systems. The efficiency of the analytic sections varies considerably from one sample to another. The entire object has a relatively poor thermal resistance.

'Two prominent gas intakes contain a system for the identification of certain solid substances. A further twin evaluation system mounted on either side monitors vibrations. The entire object processes three thousand gallons of gas in twenty-four hours.

'A centrally-situated reactor system – at the lower part of the turret – serves as a primary fuel intake.'

Scientific description of a human head.

Books and Reading

Have you noticed something about books and book titles?

If I mention, in speech or writing, a book, even as a location footnote, people rush to get hold of a copy. If I recommend a book (which is rare) they rush to get a copy. If someone mentions a book that I have mentioned, people rush to get a copy. If I ask someone to get me a book, others rush to get a copy.

All these people are doing the same thing (rushing to get a book) as a result of several different intentions. In the one case, the book is mentioned just for identification; in another, because reading it will benefit some people and not others; in yet another, because I myself propose to supply notes or translation of that book because the existing version is unsuitable or incorrect.

Behind all this book-reading activity, lamentably, lie two unacceptable factors. These are:

1. Some sort of greed, some sort of primitive feeling that there is something in 'the book', grips people because their covetousness is stronger than their reason.

2. The students assume that a book is being recommended, even when there is no reason for this, and in selectively subjective blindness to the fact that I have actually said, time and again, that books belong to the community for which they are written, not in interior value to anyone who tries to possess their meaning.

You can do yourself harm by seizing all the books I mention and trying to understand them; especially when you choose to ignore other things I say: in particular that many books, supposedly in our field, are misleading.

Parts of these books may be suitable for our community and our time. These are made specifically available for study. Is this not enough?

Many special books on traditional studies are really like encyclopaedias: some parts are relevant to some stages. What would happen to you if you memorised the whole *Encyclopaedia Britannica* when all you needed was to read the entry on perfumes? You would end up with nothing at all except an uncomfortable obsession with reading or with the *Encyclopaedia*.

Small wonder that after reading some of the books cited in

short passages or matters of detail by me, people come or write
and so many of them say:

> 'I didn't understand.' or,
> 'I don't accept.' or,
> 'I want to discuss this,' or,
> 'This is marvellous,' or,
> 'Give me more books,' or,
> 'I have had enough of books, I want action.'

At best, these people are wasting time.

I am not engaged in an academic, literary or editorial
endeavour. I am fulfilling the function of providing you with
what you need when and where you need it. Neither you nor
I can abdicate responsibility by acting like semi-literates or
adolescents, looking for answers in books. Thousands of years
ago the sophisticated use of literature, whereby it was adapted
to guarding in a special way real knowledge, was accomplished.
Its unlocking has to be no less sophisticated.

Learn this contention. If your excuse is that you did not know
it before, remember that you have now been told it.

If I want books to be studied, I will tell you. If I wanted you
to scramble for books, I know how to say, 'scramble for books.'
I don't need to hint by listing books as references which are
in reality intended to be obtained and read.

We need to read, to write, to hear written material, to be read
to. We also need to meet, to have meetings, to carry out studies
in a wide variety of ways if we are to avoid panaceas and the
gimmickry of 'finding' truth in some simple thing, be it an
exercise or a book.

The difference between the useless and the useful lies not in
what it has but in how it uses it.

Your studies must be composed of the right proportion of
a number of elements. Books are both essential at the present
stage and also only a part. Only stupidity or greed or infantilism
underlies any action which basically says: 'By this simple method
I will arrive.' Rather than pretend, you might as well adopt the
theory of conditioning, and simply say: 'By this token, totem,

51

book, exercise, I will train myself to feel as if I am on the way to something.' That, at least, would be more honest.

Boredom, Study and Entertainment

Some people enrol for a course of study, and the course starts to bore them. The next stage is either to give up the study, because they do not want to be bored; or else to say, 'This cannot be any good, because it bores me.'

What they mean, of course, is 'I did not come only to study, I came to be entertained. I did not realise that it is possible to get entertainment from one source and studies from another.'

As soon as the real problem (that the person needs a source of entertainment) is seen, it can be solved.

The studies 'cease to be boring' if the person is not in need of entertainment at the time when he is attending classes.

The whole problem has been very much confused by the theory that 'all instruction ought to be enjoyable'.

Such theories are without any more foundation than the following:

> 'Some studies can be made entertaining. We find that those people who are entertained by their studies make progress. Therefore we imagine that all studies can, or must, be made entertaining.'

In fact, of course, it is a happy thing if a study can be made entertaining. But not all of them can. When they cannot, the need is for the entertainment to be found somewhere else in the person's life, so that this part of his requirement is fulfilled. He can then undertake studies without being bored by them. Unless he is conditioned to being bored, which is a separate problem.

52

'I have never learned anything unless I really liked it' does not (contrary to general imaginings) mean: 'Nobody can learn anything unless he really likes (i.e. derives recreational benefit from) it.'

On the contrary, when people are frustrated in their search for entertainment, they will seek it everywhere, trying even to turn serious and non-entertainment study into diversion. When they do this, they often prevent any real study in that subject taking place at all.

This is very evident in certain scholastic circles, where academics and students 'niggle' on minor points and opinions, gaining some small emotional satisfactions, because they are deprived of these through their poor social adjustment.

Basic Considerations

A remarkably small number of suppositions about higher, inner, deeper, knowledge of man (and about the people engaged in transmitting it) underlie the errors into which most would-be students, disciples, followers and seekers are inevitably led.

The result of accepting these suppositions is always the same: the production of obsessed ('conditioned') people – sometimes called 'believers' – and the production of a restless state in people when things do not seem to measure up to their expectations.

A close study of these pitfalls is essential to anyone who wants real knowledge, let alone real fulfilment, tranquillity, real attainment.

CONSIDERATION 1

Inner knowledge cannot always be approached as an answer to one's psychological problems. It may be approached in this way by certain people, or by people at different stages in their lives. But it is not to be thus treated for all of the people all of the time. To think that it can, creates more problems than it solves.

CONSIDERATION 2

To believe that one can get everything from books is as good – and as bad – as believing that one can get nothing from books. Here again, the individual must abide by the instructions of his teacher, as to what books to read, when to read them, when not to read, how to read.

CONSIDERATION 3

Reliance upon a prestige-figure, a great teacher, a body of literature, practices or an appeal to tradition alone is a chimera. People must learn how to extract the nutrition from all of these things, and from many others. They cannot 'go it alone' in this search.

CONSIDERATION 4

The confusing of emotionality or sentimentality with spirituality is one of the major basic mistakes of would-be mystics, of false occultists and of dishonest religionists alike. Emotion is a powerful consideration in human life. It must be understood. Understanding it can only be accomplished under competent direction.

CONSIDERATION 5

Competent direction is defined as direction by a competent

teacher. Such a person, rare in the extreme, is not one who has called forth an emotional reaction because something which he says is acceptable to the hearer at the specific time when he hears it. Neither is he someone who relies (overtly or otherwise) upon strange or authoritative dogma. He is a teacher.

CONSIDERATION 6

Looking for mystical or other higher aims as represented in individuals and societies with an outward mystical tinge is perhaps an obvious attempt. But there are – and always have been – innumerable individuals and organisations carrying on this teaching in such a manner and characterised by such externals that no superficialist would dream that they were engaged upon this high task.

CONSIDERATION 7

When a real teacher prescribes a course of study, or enjoins individuals or groupings in action or inaction, or anything at all, this is the current form of the Teaching: and none other.

CONSIDERATION 8

The belief that one is a teacher, or a seeker, or anything else, does not make one into that thing. People can – and do – believe anything and everything. Their beliefs are less important than their real state. The individual is generally unaware of that inner state. It takes a teacher to assess it and to prescribe for it.

CONSIDERATION 9

Just as the outward form of teachings changes with times,

peoples and cultures, so does the outward form of one and the same teaching appear to change. People who cannot adopt a 'new' phase of a traditional teaching have shown themselves incapable of the necessary adaptation, and probably nothing can be done for them.

CONSIDERATION 10

'Ancient' systems do not work in modern times. They may train people to believe certain things: they do not improve those people. No true system is ancient. The knowledge upon which it is based is ancient. The trappings, formulae, externals must alter, sometimes frequently, if its operational efficacy is to be preserved.

CONSIDERATION 11

Patience and impatience alike are pitfalls. This is because the exercise of patience and impatience are preparations for something else. People who are one hundred per cent patient are as ill-equipped for learning as people who have no patience at all.

CONSIDERATION 12

People who cannot tell the difference between a real feeling and one which has been trained into them are not capable of learning on their own. Their course of study must be prescribed for them until they can discriminate. Only after that can they begin a real 'search'.

CONSIDERATION 13

People who mistake good fellowship, relaxation of tensions, or a mere sense of well-being for progress on a road to higher things have to back-track and learn certain earlier lessons. Otherwise they are merely candidates for encapsulated 'wisdom' and superficial systems.

CONSIDERATION 14

People who think that spiritual, esoteric, higher movements spring suddenly into being have to learn that nothing could be further from the truth. Immensely intricate planning and preparation must precede any real teaching.

CONSIDERATION 15

Learners cannot expect to stipulate which parts of a teaching specially appeals to them, on which they will concentrate. They have to learn the whole background of certain things before the inner content can have effect upon them in an effective sense.

CONSIDERATION 16

When a teacher has announced that a true contact exists between him and an individual or group, it never becomes severed, even if the participants are not conscious of it. What makes them impatient or fearful is the superficiality of their emotion, not the reality of contact.

CONSIDERATION 17

An individual or group may continue in contact with a teacher for long periods of time, working effectively without being conscious of it until he can bring them what they need. If, on the other hand, they cannot sustain any separation or apparent break in contact, he cannot help them, because his task is never to entertain them and work on a crude basis of assurance or reassurance, or 'conditioning'. Such people are hypocrites. They need games, not studies.

CONSIDERATION 18

When a teacher gives an individual or a grouping something to study, observe, to carry out, they should do so, even when it does not appear logical or necessary to them. This is because it is seldom that the patient knows his ailment, whereas the physician does.

CONSIDERATION 19

The 'tests' and studies which will yield the greatest results are those which are least familiar to the students. This is because if people are given tasks with which they are familiar (through reading, report or practice) something in them will 'cheat' in their performance.

CONSIDERATION 20

People who are put in charge of others, whether individuals or groups, in the current formulation of the teaching, must regard themselves always as mere channels. If they take any personal advantage or exercise any unnecessary pressure, they themselves will suffer in proportion.

CONSIDERATION 21

People must now learn something which was formerly only taught in secret: that there are many varieties of spiritual, social, religious grouping. They are all time-centred. Most of them are anachronistic. In all of them except for real inner teachings there are serious contaminants stemming from their sojourn in the terrestrial sphere which makes them hazardous to everyone to a degree at least equivalent to their value.

CONSIDERATION 22

People should familiarise themselves thoroughly with the materials or tasks given to them, instead of making them a source of criticism, self-aggrandisement or bickering.

CONSIDERATION 23

Any form of greed – even for knowledge – effectively prevents real learning in a degree directly proportional to the degree of greed present in the individual, group or organisation.

CONSIDERATION 24

Pride, in an individual or a group, is a form of greed.

CONSIDERATION 25

When you look at a child, you notice that it has three kinds of qualities: those which help its progress, such as eating instinctively; those which could harm its future, such as eating poisonous things; and those which are neutral. In respect to higher teaching and learning, the adult human being is the same. He can acquire valuable nutrients in knowledge. He can acquire dangerous ones, while thinking they are good for him. He can take in irrelevant ones, thinking nothing or thinking that they are significant. Like the parent, the Teacher knows which are which.

CONSIDERATION 26

Almost all people interested in metaphysics have at some time been studied for responsiveness to teaching by those who can teach them. Frequently, such would-be students are unaware that such a study has been made. They continue to seek higher knowledge through attempts to contact crude forms of what they imagine to be real teaching.

CONSIDERATION 27

Organisations and other groupings set up for true higher study have, as it were, a life of their own. They are 'concentration-points'. It is vital that they continue to operate, and not be neglected nor turned into centres for 'making golden calves'. This is because they are entities through which, in due time, higher communications are made.

CONSIDERATION 28

Chronological repetition, meetings and studies, activities and exercises, which are carried out by means of a fixed schedule are almost always a sign of a deteriorated tradition. A real School varies its operations and movement in accordance with a special pattern. This pattern is non-repetitious.

CONSIDERATION 29

Man (and woman) has an infinite capacity for self-development. Equally, he has an infinite capacity for self-destruction. A human being may be clinically alive and yet, despite all appearances, spiritually dead.

CONSIDERATION 30

Experiences of an unusual kind are often given to people in order to test as to whether they will react correctly to them. Most people fail in this test. The commonest example is with people who are made to feel something of true reality, and who immediately imagine that they should teach it.

CONSIDERATION 31

Perceptions of another kind of being, when not accompanied by correct preparation, can be more harmful than a lifetime without any such perception. This is because unprepared people misinterpret their experiences and cash in on them at a low level. An example is people who become superstitious because they have sensed something at work which they are too lazy to try to understand. Another example is when people imagine that some true but minor 'sign' gives them an importance or a divine contact or character. Such people are already almost lost, 'even if their repute rises to the heavens'.

CONSIDERATION 32

The original motive of religious preaching is not social uplift, moral indoctrination and so on, but specific techniques of preparation of individuals and communities to enable them to endure and follow higher development. Most religious systems known to us, however, are today stabilised upon superficialities and emotionality and have lost all contact with the higher levels of meaning within their exhortation: they have the meat but have lost the recipe.

CONSIDERATION 33

Inevitable pitfalls in human learning are two: 'conversion syndrome' when people believe anything said by an individual or institution; and obsessional opposition, when they believe nothing. These are the two factors, though they may be combined in one person in varying proportions. The task of real higher teaching is to contact people and inform them quite aside from the question of faith or unfaith. Both the latter factors are aspects of brain-engineering, and have no place in real teaching.

SECTION III

Background, Techniques and Theory of Esoteric Systems

1. Misleading information is included in order to divert unsuitable people. This is a 'filter'. It includes behaviour on the part of the esotericists designed to annoy or otherwise deflect the unsuitable.
2. The outward appearance of an esoteric organisation, and even its avowed principles, are unlikely to be significant. Those who adopt them as central to belief remain exotericists.
3. Many study materials have two or more meanings/dimensions. The revelation of these meanings can be done only by a special, not a familiar, technique.
4. The commanding principle is that a certain number and quality of individuals must be related together in some form of association. It is this, and not indoctrination, persuasion or even human service (for you cannot serve until you can serve), which is the basic intention.
5. All institutions commonly known to man will alter, becoming social groupings, unless special knowledge keeps them free of this or regenerates them.
6. There is a distinction between the emotional, the intellectual, the social, the therapeutic demands of man. Genuine systems are those which still have vitality: do not mistake one for another of these.
7. Literature, ritual, exercises and other ingredients of study or observance as generally known very often represent deteriorations of what were originally specifically functioning enlightenment factors.
8. Man is imprisoned by time and space. There are two methods of releasing him: (a) processes which negate these factors; (b) using timing and 'place' to act as and when their rhythm is conducive to making 'break-throughs' in human consciousness.

9. The human tendency is to attach oneself to people and objects. The esotericist's object is to help people find a 'self' which can attach itself to something more refined.

10. Esoteric cults and formulations become superseded by time and other factors, becoming fossils which are nevertheless still believed in as functional by unenlightened followers.

11. It is not possible effectively to mix two or more formulations for development. Man choosing from such systems what he thinks may suit him is mixing recipes and could produce a poison for himself.

12. A group of people engaged upon esoteric work may to outward appearances have quite a different function.

13. Many religious and other organisations retain traces of conscious higher work. In fact, it is possible to recognise the cultural and other conditions of the original group from what remain of the religious theories and practices.

14. In a true higher organisation functioning correctly the concepts of love, devotion, effort, discipline and self-training, as well as moral principles, must be in balance. Deterioration of function takes place when an organisation stabilises itself on one principle or a narrow range of theory or technique.

15. Ignorance of human thinking processes has for many centuries caused otherwise admirable systems to be at some point shaped by the relatively ignorant into mechanisms for implanting and maintaining obsessions; or of maintaining information in the belief that it is knowledge, or of encouraging behaviour which is of sociological, charitable, psychological or recreational value in the belief that it is fulfilling some other function.

16. Superficial tendencies of human thought have been adopted and encouraged, when they are often obstacles to understanding. Examples are the profiting by the human proclivities to prefer things which are new, old, remote, said with authority, mysterious, emotion-arousing, and so on.

17. The apparent clash between the principles of certain

systems is only due to the fact that different 'rules' have held good for specific communities at different times and places. The remedy, in fact, has been prescribed for the disease. Those who have the disease should accept the remedy. Conversely, if they have not got the disease, the remedy may be bad for them. Or they may need another remedy.

Conceit

To people of lower development, superior ideas often seem to be couched in almost unacceptably 'superior' language. This feeling, however, stems only from subjective reactions.

If you tell a backward man, ignorant of medicine, that you can cure an infection by means of a tube of cream, he may well think that you are a liar, and giving yourself airs.

He may, equally inaccurately, think that you are a god.

Both attitudes conform to his stage of understanding, not to the reality of the situation.

This is one reason why it is valuable to establish the differences between wishful thinking and useful thought.

Charity

The other day, travelling in an underground train in London, I was sitting in the midst of six young people who were talking about someone they wanted to help, but bemoaning the problems involved in their enterprise.

After various interchanges on this subject, one of them said:

'After all, being charitable is one thing – but having to go to trouble about it is another!'

I thought that someone might disagree. But no: they all agreed upon this summing-up.

Consideration

If you give people more than a certain amount of consideration, they come to develop a taste for this consideration. As a consequence, they regard you as the source of the attention which they may have formerly obtained elsewhere.

The drawback of this condition is that, in the expectation, enjoyment and memory of consideration, people get nothing else out of the relationship.

This does not prevent them, however, from swearing that the basis and function of the relationship is almost anything else than ritualised mutual enjoyment.

This is particularly so in cultures where the theory that enjoyment is somehow wrong has taken root to any degree.

Constant Exhortation

Those people whose performance is subject to deterioration only remedied by emotional and intellectual exhortation are unsuitable candidates for our Teaching.

In fact, though these methods are widely believed to be the only ones which will work with the human population, the fact is that these are methods which will work only with those who are subnormal. By subnormal, I mean that they are not products of the culture to which they belong. This − contemporary − human culture is one which claims that man should be able to operate, to study, to keep going, and so on, without propaganda, conditioning, emotional arousal and so on.

Few people are wholly emotional, responding to command, excitement, constant exhortation alone. But this kind of treatment is like a drug: the more you are exposed to it the less you can do without it, and the more you can be pointed out as being prone to it. So we have a situation equal to people saying: 'Look! He does nothing unless he has had a shot of heroin. That is, of course, the human condition.'

You are at this moment being reminded that that is not the human condition. Bad as it is, the human condition is better than that. Those who say otherwise are either abysmally ignorant or else trying to use the primitive to make people more primitive than they need be.

Until this has been learned, few other things of any significance can be learned. Therefore learn this, and do not indulge a desire to be idle and forget by scurrying about imagining that you are learning other things. The other things would only be of equal, not greater, quality than the things you know already. And that is not a sufficient basis for higher learning, no matter what some sentimentalists who are more vociferous than us, have to say about it.

Criticism

You ask me why I criticise only one side, when I could be pointing out the strengths and weaknesses of both.

By doing so, you ignore the fact that nobody nowadays needs to write a book criticising, say, the plague virus.

Equally, when antibiotics are so well known, you merely record their efficacy or otherwise: You do not have to rhapsodise about them when this has already been done.

One must know the difference between constructive description and sheer wallowing in words.

In order to know this, one must have a basis of knowledge as to how words are used, and what is didactic and what is not.

Otherwise, you will merely be at the mercy of the conditioning power of words and personalities.

Corrective

The superficial behaviour and irrelevant linking of social behaviour with 'higher things' can be righted.

The method available to everyone is to become thoroughly familiar with and to digest the materials – such as these – which are designed not just to enunciate and warn, but also to help educate.

Clarity and Perplexity

It is an interesting and dangerous facet of contemporary thinking that people will do anything if they imagine that they understand issues, and that the matter is clear to them. This gives plenty of opportunity to others to create the impression that issues are clear. Over-simplifications are provided, and believed on all sides. The result is confusion.

If, on the other hand, there is initial confusion, and even perplexity, this can lead to clarity as soon as the people have understood that there is a problem to solve, a clarity to be achieved. If they only accept other people's clarity – which is pretended clarity more often than not – they are astray.

Cause and Effect

Every person must learn to ask himself:

> 'Am I attributing this or that thing, this appearance or that effect, to some cause or origin which may not be its cause?'

All cultures teach their people to do this in certain subjects and in a few areas. But the net result of this has been for people to do it in as *few*, not as many, instances as possible.

Cult-Makers

Man is a cult-making creature. That is to say, he formalises what could be constructive procedures and uses them for recreational purposes.

This is done in the same way that beavers build dams whether they need a dam or not. Superficialists, ignoring this, applaud beavers unreservedly.

In the human being this recreational tendency is bad, because instead of taking what diversion he needs and also working constructively towards self-fulfilment on a higher level, he may think that when he is playing he is fulfilling a 'higher' function.

Caution

Many people, quite rightly, approach metaphysicians with caution.

Yet the very same people may be seen to abandon all caution when they try to deal with their own selves. They then frequently, daily, allow wholly unreliable criteria, dogmas and caprices to dominate their selection of associates and even what they are pleased to call their studies.

Unknowingly, they are candidates for a form of slavery more insidious, if less instantly perceptible, than that of the wayward geniuses of many esoteric bodies.

People use words to justify their adherence to cults and fixations. Similarly, their opponents use words to justify their basic hostilities to such cults. Both parties, apparently opposed, are in reality the same phenomenon: people with obsessions.

Experienced observers can see this. Such experience has to be made available to the obsessed as well. And it has to be a certain kind of experience, otherwise the mere intellectual knowledge that he is fixated upon something will avail the victim nothing at all.

Discovery

People want to 'discover themselves'. This seemingly innocent phrase depends for any possible meanings upon invisible but nonetheless essential propositions inherent in the statement:

1. That there is such a thing as man.
2. That any and everyone is a man.
3. That man can be discovered, or some men can be discovered.
4. That there is a self to discover in all or some men, and women.
5. That this 'wanting' is the manner in which one can discover himself, or that it leads to it.

Direct Transmission

Exercises and studies help to develop finer organs of perception. This is the first part of study.

The second part is to be in circumstances in which that which is to be perceived is more richly present. This second part of study confuses many people because it is based upon environment, time, place and certain people. It has a framework which they cannot grasp. Small wonder, since the design is based upon a fine perception which they do not yet possess.

The third part is equally important. It consists of the direct transmission and reception, from one body to another, of communications which are too fine to be perceived by the ordinary methods. When you try to render such a transmission in words, it comes out as nonsense. If you try to draw or paint it, much will be missing. If you put it into sounds, you will capture some of it faithfully, but not enough. The pattern made by rendering some in sound, some in mime, some in words, and so on is incomplete and used in the 'exercises' part of study. In religious behaviour these elements are worked into pious and other observances.

Direct transmission may be called a telepathic communication from an individual or a group, acting as an amplifier for a certain original Truth, capable of transmitting to a less-developed individual or group.

This is one of the functions of a teaching individual or teaching-group. Such people and groups are ultimately dependent upon the existence of a correctly aligned and harmonised 'receiving group' for their operation to be successful.

In addition to 'projecting' upon such groups, they can, however, affect people and groups who have a certain harmony but may be unaware of the source of their 'inspiration'.

Didactic

I have just been asked why my talk and writing is so 'didactic'.

I am glad to have this question because I have been waiting for it for a long time. I needed it so that I could combine it with another question, also waiting for an answer. This other question is: 'Why are you not didactic in what you give out?'

The answer to 'Why are you didactic?' is 'Because I have been asked why I am not didactic.'

The answer to 'Why are you not didactic?' is 'Because I have been asked why I am didactic'.

Until the questioners can make up their minds which I am, I have to answer like this. If they care to fight it out, I shall be delighted to answer the winner with one clear answer to one clear question.

Until then I can only point out that the questions do not yet apply to me: they merely describe the state of mind of the questioners.

Dilution and Concentration

Those who have their being in the domain of dilution can hardly imagine the characteristics, requirements and nature of the area of concentration.

What is an area of significance to a conventional student working on a low level is an area of dilution to one who can experience more.

For this reason, in genuine esoteric activity, students of higher knowledge are transferred from one study-group to another, sent on journeys, retained in one place longer than others, given studies which correspond with their growing evolutionary capacity to benefit from areas of greater concentration.

In an area of concentration there is no visible distinction of rank or privilege.

Depths and Range of Traditional Materials

Most people who try to understand traditional teaching materials have not the faintest notion that some of it was intended for local use, some constitutes answers to specific questions, some is inapplicable or unrepresentative for other reasons; some was intended to mean the reverse of what it may seem to mean.

No single analysis-system can make this material yield its secrets. Attempts at consistent interpretation of it can and do produce a defective system and incorrect conclusions.

You might be surprised how often teachers write or say things which appear absurd in order to convey the rebuke that 'a silly question deserves a silly answer'.

Gravely literalist students produce grotesque interpretations of such material.

This is why one could say: 'Save metaphysics from the metaphysicians'.

A great deal of literature which is most valuable carries its own negating device. If you read too much of it, or do not suppress certain parts in study, it will have no lasting effect.

Effect of Opinion, when Ingrained, even on Scientists

Dr. B. C. Murray, a geologist and Professor of planetary science at the California Institute of Technology studying the American Mars-observing spacecraft Mariner 9, has this to say about how subjective scientists are:

> 'Mars somehow has extended and endured beyond the realm of science to so grab hold of man's emotions and thoughts that it has actually distorted scientific opinion . . . the reason that this has happened is that man has been guilty of wishful thinking collectively . . . the people who have really fallen on this have been the scientists themselves, who have misunderstood the significance of their observations . . . the observations are going to have to beat us over the head and tell us the answer in spite of ourselves.'

Now all this, said at a symposium in November of 1971, is very far from the image of man, of scientist or scholar, which is generally projected by such people. In fact it might well be said that the self-image of man in his own mind is one of the factors inhibiting his observation and understanding of things which conflict with, or are felt to be extraneous to, his interest.

76

Elements being used in our Courses

In our present study courses, we use:

1. Materials drawn from earlier teachings, which have not been corrupted, and which still have validity in the culture whose members we are addressing. Some of this material is available in print. An example is the Eleven Rules.*

2. Materials from past teachings, which are not fully preserved in literature, but of which indications remain. We expand and explain these, and sometimes illustrate them from literature and oral tradition. Examples are mnemonic references in the Sufi and other classics.

3. Materials which belong to the teaching, but which have to be expressed in a form suitable to the audience being addressed, the time and the place. Some of these appear strange, unusual, even contradictory. They are selectively drawn from the huge stock which is itself based upon a knowledge of the design of truth on another level.

Many people try to compare these materials, and as a result become confused. This confusion may lead to conversion syndrome and a sort of fanatical support for us that makes it difficult to teach such people. Others develop from their confusion an opposition to all or part of the material, which, again, makes it difficult for us to teach them.

Ordinary study, of the academic or traditionalistic type, will not know which materials from the recorded literary endowment to use, and which do not now apply. The result is slavish imitation, traditionalism and gaps in effectiveness due to the absence of the third class of materials, leading to an opportunity for automatism to creep in.

On the other hand, during the period of the reintroduction of a study such as this into a culture, the confusion and lack

---

* See: *The Perfumed Scorpion* by Idries Shah (Octagon Press Ltd., London), page 85.

of hard facts about materials which by their very nature are not hard facts, causes gossip, rumour, imagination and so on.

Every real teaching is besieged by a haze of supposition and imagination, report and counter-report. This is in itself a disability, because people on the outside tend to form opinions based upon this unrepresentative material. The result is that, when the operation is complete, there may well be more people believing in the incorrect version of the activity than there are survivors of the real form. The latter, by the usual process of weight of numbers, may even be declared heretics, because of the belief in the importance of consensus of opinion.

There is no easy answer to this problem, except education. By education I mean that people may be told that however much one would like to give them a single simple set of beliefs or activities to concentrate upon, the only result of these would be conditioning.

In the final analysis, true teachings can only work with people who are prepared to learn whatever there is to be learned, not people who want to use us for entertainment and 'game' purposes, however unconscious they may be of what they are doing.

It is in order to carry out this educational project that real teaching institutions first of all have to broaden the basis of the students' attitudes to higher knowledge. There is an analogy here with the ordinary educational systems. In the latter, specialisation and higher studies often have to be preceded by general studies which form the basis for the future studies. Many an undergraduate has wondered why he has to study botany or bacteriology before he can learn how to heal people as a physician. He is in fact receiving factual information, learning a skill and also exercising his brain in a manner which will enable him to cope with more complex things.

Real study centres of higher knowledge really are institutes of higher studies which, up to a point, have to lay the foundation of their studies as they go along.

The habit of questioning the curriculum, however indicative of an enquiring mind, may often be very much out of control.

If one does not know what questions to ask, there is less value in asking questions than one might imagine from the knowledge that questions may be asked.

The very idea that one can learn what one wants to learn, when one wants to, in the right manner, is appealing and therefore not recognised as insidious because it destroys the capacity to learn.

Exercising Power

Almost all human organisations are power organisations.

Since the receipt and exercising of power is imagined to be connected with forceful behaviour, people cannot any longer identify a power organisation. Consequently they do not understand what they are doing and what is happening to them.

As an example, force and influence are contained in the 'emotional blackmail' situation to exactly the same extent as in one where anger or forthrightness are manifested.

When people in authority have the reputation of being kind and soft-hearted, others assume (quite wrongly) that the pressure exerted by such people is not pressure at all. If someone says: 'You must do this because I would be so disappointed if you did not', he is saying exactly the same as 'Do this because I demand that you do it'.

To say that this fact has been observed already is of no importance whatever, because something which has been said or observed and not acted upon is as good as non-existent as a lesson.

People try to exercise power upon those 'below' them. But people upon whom power is supposed to be being exercised are, in fact, by frustrating the effect of that power, themselves exercising power.

Power situations can only exist where there is a contract, arrived at voluntarily or otherwise, in which people will do things or else things can be made difficult for them. 'Do this or I will make you uncomfortable' is the formula for both types of power: the power exerted by people above on those below, and the power exerted from the people below upon those above.

Where there is no such contract – where one party can do without the other one – NO POWER SITUATION CAN EXIST. Neither can it be deemed to exist. But, faced with a situation in which there is no power ingredient, people CONTINUE TO BEHAVE AS IF THEY CAN COERCE OR BE COERCED.

In doing this they give themselves away. To any observer who is aware of the power phenomenon, they clearly show that they belong to the power system and want to operate it.

They generally become furiously angry when this is pointed out to them.

Effort, Stretching and Straining

When people have a hard task to do – one which stretches them – they become less concerned with trivial matters. If you have not registered this yet, observe it in yourself and in others, and you will see that it is true.

When there is an emergency, for example, something which takes up a great deal of attention, triviality is reduced.

In order to enable people to be less trivial, and to tackle things which really help them develop, they should undertake tasks which provide the right kind and degree of stretching.

People who have achieved great things, genuinely effective accomplishments, will be found to have done so through this method: stretching.

When it goes wrong, people apply stress, not stretching. Stress is damaging and does not produce constructive results.

Mistaking stretching for straining: labour for exercise, is what causes a great deal of trouble.

When triviality disappears, even temporarily, people are able to work at a higher level. This is true of all kinds of human endeavour: it is to be seen in attainment of all kinds and also even in the social milieu: people who are less trivial are more respected.

Holding a high or important position is one of the main sources of triviality. This is something which most people do not understand, merely because they have not analysed it.

But when a person has power and does not undertake its responsibilities himself, instead expecting others to obey his orders, he always becomes trivial.

There is nobody more trivial than a person in authority who spends his time telling others what to do and who does not do things himself.

This is because, although in appearance this man or woman is powerful or 'above this and that', he is really below it and is not taking any real part in the exercise of a function. Merely to give orders is not a constructive function. But, since it is imagined that the person who gives orders is in some way more important, people do not register the evident fact that such people fall into two types: those who are really stretching themselves and those who are simply 'little caesars'.

The corrective – and it is an instant one – for becoming trivial, ineffective and disliked through exercising meddlesome authority is for the individual himself to undertake some part of executive action. He should also alternate, sometimes doing some of the work instead of organising it and expecting others always to do it.

The common development of trivial people at the top – when it is frequently said, 'The great are small-minded' is due to this system being in operation without its corrective.

Man has erred in imagining that responsibility and lack of triviality go together. It can be the reverse, and unless the tendency is analytically watched, it generally *will* be the reverse.

Because of this, it should occasion no surprise when people of 'importance' are petty. In any culture in which recognition of the foregoing laws is not embodied in the human training and executive system, we are *bound* to find triviality in the higher echelons.

In past cultures, attempts have been made to redress this tendency by building into human training a dislike for pettiness. This has not been sufficiently successful, partly because the pettiness tends not to be recognised by the person who indulges in it. The disease has to be tackled at its roots: at the point where the individual has to stretch himself.

Although it is not particularly difficult for a person to imagine that he is stretching himself when he is doing nothing or else straining himself, it is not impossible to succeed with this exercise.

In all societies, instruments and institutions, traditions and so on exist to establish and maintain the norms of that society.

In a culture which lacks these safeguards, it is generally necessary for an individual or a body of people who are themselves stretched or no longer in need of such exercise, to preside over the 'prescription' of such an exercise in others.

In some traditional cultures, such an individual is known as a 'teacher' or 'guide'.

If this individual is himself unworthy, which tends to occur in all cultures, he will induce strain instead of exercise. But it is not difficult to identify such people.

Environmental Maladjustment

Whenever you feel that you know more, or have been through more experiences than other people, this is indicative of the fact that you know less, or have been through less, than would be useful to you at the time when you have the feeling.

This is because the real perception of experience and the true realisation of knowledge, are registered and become useful to you in a completely different manner from the one just cited.

The succession is:

1. You think that you know more than others – you do not.
2. You think that you are feeling the need for different experiences – you are not.
3. You realise that you need to know more of what is being offered.
4. You realise that what you have called 'different experiences' are only partial contents of experiences which you have not yet absorbed.

Exercises

There are two ways in which exercises which develop the capacities of man may be used.

The first, and commoner one, is as a sort of magic wand. People imagine, truly for a change, that exercises are a key to higher understanding. But if they are applied upon people who are not correctly attuned for their reception, they will either not operate at all, or else produce a complete illusion of well-being, which is misinterpreted as 'enlightenment'.

Many well-meaning people try to operate exercises in this way. The result is not higher development at all, but recreation.

The other way in which exercises are employed is their original, correct manner. Like anything else of any value at all, they can be used only when conditions are right, when the individual is ready, not just imagining that he is ready, to profit from them.

To collect people and submit them to exercises just because they want exercises is ludicrous, and it has a predictable result. It tends, it is true, to make the good better: but it also makes the bad worse.

'Bad' in this context means people who flatter themselves that they are ready for something when they are not. It also includes those who are so stupid as to imagine that just because they have learned exercises, this gives them the right and capacity to apply them on others.

Eight Points on Initiatory Literature

Few experiences are so ludicrous as when one sees people gravely intoning literature without knowing which passages to use and which to exclude.

1. Many vital books contain parts which, like a safety-catch, actually prevent the meaning from functioning if they fall into incapable hands.

    When, therefore, people seek the 'key' to special literature, they do not realise that the door is locked and the key is in it. The key operates by removing it, not by any other method.

2. Classical initiatory literature, again, contains material for various kinds of people, useful at different times. To devour all the literature without knowing this, and without being able to select or prescribe essential passages, is next to useless. Depending upon the chance choices made, such omnivorous study may actually be harmful.

3. Selecting similar passages from different books or different schools is hazardous and at best a waste of effort. Anthologists and other superficial students,

whatever motives they may think they have, engage in this activity because they really prefer the similarities of associative materials.

4. Some passages in higher literature are enciphered. This is done for a variety of reasons, the main one *not* being as a challenge to individual students to try to penetrate their secrets.

5. Specialists in higher literature perfected, aeons ago, all the methods of using words so that their books would fulfil several functions (instructional, informational, cultural) on different levels. Remember that you cannot perceive the various levels until you are ready, and no simple 'key' will be of any use. This is particularly important for protective purposes. You may have been born and brought up in a single room, as it were. If you are let out while lacking the means to survive in the outside world, you will probably perish.

6. Literature which is seemingly esoteric is often not such at all, but is designed for another purpose. This purpose may well not be one which you can further. You therefore need expert guidance in this matter.

7. Much literature which has no apparently esoteric significance or intent, on the other hand, belongs to the higher domain. If you cannot recognise it, you are in need of guidance.

8. Much higher literature is of no developmental value if studied by itself and depends for its effect upon certain experimental conditions and experiences through sources other than the ears or eyes. If you do not know this, you are in need of guidance.

Energy and Enthusiasm

Enthusiasm to convert or to spread one's beliefs is self-sustaining. That is to say, it feeds off the action and reaction connected with it. No enthusiast is a hero or a saint: he is a producer and consumer of the agitation which is involved in the enthusiasm situation.

It has often been noticed that enthusiasm wilts if left for a time unnoticed. Yet people continue to fall into the trap of enthusiasts, who force them to multiply the nutrition which they themselves seek.

To the enthusiast, no matter what he might imagine, it is not acceptance nor rejection which he pursues: it is the production of an agitation situation. Whether this appears as 'yea', 'nay' or confusion – he still gets his sustenance from it.

Once we learn this, we can detach from being other people's food.

Emotion

How sad that people dignify their activities too much.

They use fine words to describe processes which, if only looked at in the face, would enable them to acquire some humility.

People often have to 'burn off' surplus evaporating volatile substances.

But this is still regarded as significant, because self-esteem is so powerful that man has to conceal his absurdity and even his normal needs by using bombast.

People do not like to be described as machines. It is true that only a man – not a machine or even an ape – could go so far as to describe the processes of physics and chemistry, even electronics, in lyrical, pejorative and hallowed terms.

Emotion and Primitive State

In all human communities, at all times, there is one process which indicates the increasing progress of the individual and the group.

This activity is the development of one's understanding of things in terms of quality and refinement.

In some primitive communities, for instance, the same word is used for 'blue' and 'green' – because the culture has no practical use for these colours separately. The younger a child, the smaller the range of its differentiation between, say, various shapes, sizes and weights.

Really primitive man roams about seeking berries and roots to eat. Because he has not yet organised and made more efficient his food-gathering programme, most of his time is taken up with the search for food. As soon as he learns that he can locate a food-supply and live there; or can grow food; that he need not eat compulsively; that he needs just enough to survive on, – when he discovers these things, he is comparatively free. His life has effectively been lengthened. Instead of spending sixty-nine years gathering food and the equivalent of one year in all other activities, he spends, say, six years collecting food and has available an extra *sixty-three* years for other activities.

'Modern' man is in the same condition where emotion is concerned. He has not yet learned that he has certain emotional needs, has a minimum emotion-intake need. If this is fulfilled, it leaves him free to do other things. In the case of emotion, he has 'an extra sixty-three years' of emotion which he can employ in enlarging and enriching his perceptions. Improving his perceptions enables him to obtain the knowledge which alone makes it possible for him to solve the mysteries of himself and his situation.

But the learning about the usefulness of organising food-gathering was relatively easy, even for really primitive men, since there is a whole, largely visible apparatus, regularly operating, for the rise of hunger, the consumption, processing and elimination of food.

'Modern' man, however, both possesses a greater capacity which enables him to solve the emotion problem, and also retains the primitives' 'making a ritual art of what he imagines to be a necessity.' He has sanctified and glamorised emotion, so it is a modern taboo. Emotion is said to be beautiful, to be the source of inspiration and higher feelings, and so on.

Artists, aesthetes, idealists and people with an interest in manipulating others are unconscious allies in the mutual delusion that this 'holy talisman' must not be broken, that the 'sacred cow' must not be slaughtered.

The only answer to them is the one which the sensible man will give the savage: 'If your talisman can lose its power by being broken, it is not much of a talisman; if your faith is ruined when your cow is made into steaks, it doesn't say much for you. It proves, however, that you are not a man or a woman, but a poor, benighted primitive pretending to be one.'

Egregious

A small group of distinguished philosophers – well-known men of thought, they call themselves – meet regularly to commune and 'assess' living thinkers. These meetings are called by them 'the Sessions', and are regarded as most private and important. They take place in an ancient London club.

At their invitation I went to have tea with them one afternoon. The conversation carried on exclusively in generalities, until the most eminent figure present (a man with a world reputation as one of the greatest thinkers of our time) cleared his throat and looked in my direction.

Since everyone else stiffened, became silent and leant forward in their seats, it was not difficult for me to divine that this was an important moment.

'Tell me,' said the wise one, 'which book most stimulates you when you want to start being intellectually productive?'

I said: 'For such a purpose I would choose a military text, possibly the account of some campaign in which the author has taken part.'

'We cannot be mocked as easily as that,' he said. I haven't been asked back, so the gaffe must have been a particularly bad one. In that circle, it is customary to entertain each person being evaluated at least three times before pronouncing judgement upon him.

Eternalism as a Vice

People often shuffle restlessly when you talk about spiritual techniques being of value for a limited time, merely for attaining specific objectives.

But this reaction is only due to the infantile desire for 'something permanent' which is so vague that they have in that part of themselves failed to distinguish between what needs to be permanent and what not only does not need to be but must in fact not be permanent: unless it is to become a barrier when it is no longer needed.

It is, of course, this primitive desire for 'permanency' – in the wrong sense – which is played upon by people who peddle eternalist panaceas.

But one can get used to other ideas than infantile ones. A technique or a working hypothesis dies when it becomes thought of as a rule or a law. A permanent apple which could not be consumed would not be much use for nutrition, no matter how pleasant as a plaything.

Every Feeling is Qualitative

If you feel love, joy, excitement, interest, focused attention, confusion, disinterest, as the result of sitting down on a pin or hearing a bird sing – these and other feelings *all* contain some negative functions, some self-indulgent ones, and some constructive ones.

This information is the result of higher knowledge, panoramic vision, call it what you will.

You will never reach a higher aim by means of increasing the volume of feelings without any training for perception of the spectrum within feelings.

Only by the last manner of working will you isolate 'worship', 'understanding', 'love', from dross.

Fame and Altruism

Too much thought is given to the real or imagined good and bad effects of fame upon the individual who becomes famous.

There are, in addition, dangers which threaten those who support and those who oppose the famous.

For every single person corrupted by his own repute, thousands are harmed by siding for or against such an individual.

People who court fame, and those who do not try to avoid it, may be to that extent accessories in this process.

The anonymous work of the great men of our tradition is generated by knowledge of these facts.

Real love, real knowledge, real action, depend upon a real basis. This basis is easily undermined by human fame.

The more prominent a real man becomes, the greater his undiscovered contribution to the welfare of man.

The same is true of the fame of doctrine, dogma and institution.

Remember: 'Not the man, not the means, but the work.'

Other kinds of thinking do work, but on a lower level.

The work can only be practised in a true work-situation. These exist only in genuine schools. To imagine that one is 'working' or 'preparing to work' is self-deception.

Fools' Wisdom

The wisdom of the fool is to imagine that he understands something just because he thinks it has been understood.

Fools' wisdom is something from which not only fools suffer.

The delinquency of the authority figure is when he tells people that they are understanding something when they are not.

The confusion of the result of this is that people imagine that they can understand anything because they can understand some things, and that if they are not idiots, they are in every way better than idiots.

Four States of Being

There are four states of human mentation which merit careful attention. In each one of them man can learn, study, develop.

Each state has its own requirements and limitations. Unless these are known, comprehensive study cannot take place.

Unless a man has experienced them all, and each one in a

certain measure, he cannot develop. His perception of true as well as comparative reality is incomplete.

It is almost impossible for this balance of study to occur spontaneously.

Most people pass through each of these four stages every day of their lives, though they are aware of only some of them, or any of them only at times. They can control none of them to any effective extent.

The states or conditions are:

1. State of ordinary wakefulness.
2. State of ordinary sleep.
3. State engendered or reproduced by habit or training, including hypnotic and hypnoidal states.
4. The Fourth State or condition, in which direct and 'extra-sensory' perceptions are possible.

Special studies and exercises exist for the recognition, stabilising, employment and understanding of particular states. Most people know only how to produce ordinary wakefulness from the normal sleep condition. Some know how to produce hypnotic states. But that is the limit of ordinary knowledge, apart from recent research in conditioning.

Fear

If you have fear, you have no need to think of punishment. Fear itself is punishment enough.

Similarly with hope. Intense hope leads easily to fear that the hope may not be realised. To feel that one possesses something may at any moment lead to fear of deprivation.

Feeling that one possesses nothing is a producer of fear.

If you fear, or desire, beyond a certain point, you have lost your way, perhaps completely.

Fill the Pitcher

People who imagine that they are wise enjoin upon others to 'fill the pitcher of their minds before trying to pour anything out.'

This advice holds good, however, only when it follows, in correct succession, the preliminary step:

'A pitcher can only be filled if it has been emptied of those things which prevent more entering. Sometimes even partly-filled pitchers contain elements which, meeting something desirable entering, vitiate it.'

Greed is always Greed

Recognising that the desire for gain is deeply rooted in man as it is in other organisms, all human systems have legislated in a manner which does not abolish greed, but inhibits and diverts it.

Let us not be misled by the words by which this is done. If you are told that: 'Greed is bad, but a desire to do good is good,' you are in fact being told not this, but: 'Wanting the kind of things which we do not want you to want is greed. But greed for what we call 'good' things is permitted, even encouraged.'

Man is now in a condition to understand this point; indeed, with the contemporary breakdown of moral and ethical systems he is being pushed to the point where he will have to recognise it.

It could be of some comfort to him to realise that, if he studies the heritage of the past in human ideas he will be able to find this development foreshadowed in the doings, sayings, writings, theories and teachings of the wise.

Sometimes the greed situation is so clear and so grotesque that anyone can see it. The people who have forsworn material gains and hence think that they have overcome or abolished greed are often a pain in the neck to even larger numbers because of their insensate appetite for 'good'. Very little of this is their own fault. They have been taught, and learnt well, that life is to be lived within a system. That system is based on the imagining that certain things are good and certain others bad.

Well illustrated in psychosomatic illness, the desire for something for oneself is standard in all other human transactions. Greed for adulation makes leaders: greed for attention makes followers. There are always plenty of people who will deny this; but this is only because something tells them that it may be their turn to be analysed next, so they had better pretend that so-and-so is altruistic.

We can only overcome this problem by constant study and practice.

Greed

I am, from time to time, surrounded by people who say: 'I do not like theory', and 'I am tired of attending meetings', and suchlike remarks.

They may dislike theory because it has not been given to them in the right manner or in the correct proportions. But if they react to this ineptitude by deciding that 'Theory is no good' – then neither I nor anyone else can teach them anything while they are in that state of mind.

Again, they may be tired of attending meetings, but if this is because the meetings which they have attended in the past are unproductive, this does not mean that 'Meetings are bad'. If they have developed this kind of attitude, there is probably nothing that I can teach them while they are in this state of mind.

At best, the future of such people is to become attracted towards something which will promise 'No theory', or 'No meetings'.

This, and no supernatural force, is the reason why so many people recently embracing with joy crazes which promise technique without effort and experience without thought, have developed emotional reactions which they have triumphantly identified as transcendental.

If you deprive a person of water, he will drink any available liquid. For the first few seconds even petrol will seem like the water of paradise to such a person. It is only later that he will start to disintegrate.

I am afraid that I cannot use any other word than to say that such people are victims of their own greed. To confuse need with greed involves self-deception as well as deception by others. The only corrective is to be prepared to face one's own self-deception, even if it has existed for thirty years under the name of 'interest in higher knowledge'.

If you cannot do that, you will have thrown everything away.

Guilt, Reward, Punishment

The process of making people feel guilt associated with one thing and pleasure with another may be an essential part of human training, starting from childhood.

If you know more than this, however, you realise what an intolerable evil it is to continue to relate everyone's every reaction only to the reward-punishment process after the time when people are able to understand additional concepts.

Regard, for instance, not only the three possibilities: 'is it good, bad or indifferent?', but 'is it complete, is it relevant, is it superseded? . . . '

Guarding the Wood Supplies

Crying horror and becoming an agitator is characteristic of some people in every human community.

Can't you just see them lining the White Cliffs and saying, of the Romans:

'We must defend our culture. If they once get ashore, they will stop the woad supplies.'

Because it is sometimes necessary to try to stop the entry of a new idea or outside individual, some people can always be made to oppose anything.

Why do they not investigate what they might be better off opposing and which things they should, in their own interests, not oppose — rather welcome?

Because prejudgement has made them believe that they cannot — or need not — judge, so they shout instead.

Group Politics

1. Every human group strives towards premature stabilisation. This is entirely a herd-characteristic, though the participants inevitably interpret it, through concealed vanity, as something of far greater significance. You may tell them that they are wrong, but their capacity to perceive this (or even to entertain it as a theoretical postulate) is observably limited. The result is always the reactions which we have been finding in established groups.

2. We are not engaged in premature unification of groups, because this is superficial and being done by others who are in fact carrying on a mere social activity. Our aim has

always been to encourage people to find their lesser satisfactions in lesser organisations. The 'work' is something far more subtle.

3. A Sufi organisation does not exist merely in order to supplement the mutual-comfort activities of a million other groups. To believe that you are doing anything else than demanding attention or the assuagement of the demands of emotion when you are 'chewing the fat' (even in technical jargon) is an evidence of carelessness and the non-absorption of materials already given you.

4. There is no purpose in simply stressing 'that there are levels in materials which are not perceived'. This is true, but you are given the materials because they operate in 'layers'. If you are looking for advanced layers before you familiarise yourself with the materials, you need a course in basic thinking: and this we cannot give you. You are not ready for anything advanced, and you have to equip yourself by becoming a bit more logical. This is difficult and takes time only if you are cheating.

5. One of the most important characteristics of the randomly-collected group is its comparative ignorance of fundamental facts of human behaviour. This ignorance is usually due to the fact that the individuals are still craving the sort of emotional and mental stimuli of which they have already had enough. They need a rest from this, so that they can digest it. They should note that it needs no advanced diagnostician to see that too many people generally use the group for personal amusement in a thinly disguised manner. This is an unwitting act of hostility, in selfishness, towards more sincere members of the group.

6. The use of pejorative phrases to one another and in referring to their experiences is indicative of the fact that, while still in this state of mind, such individuals will learn nothing. The quality of thought is far lower than its potential. In other words, people are often found to be unworthy of themselves. Their remedy is to

familiarise themselves with the material which they have been offered. If they had done so, they would not have had the problems which they now believe themselves to have. Further, they need to familiarise themselves more with the material which they are being given. Some of them are imagining that they should be doing or thinking or understanding things when they have not used the basic materials, which are still being unrolled in front of them.

7. If you want to use your group for entertainment, then do so, but do not trouble yourselves to listen to or look at our materials, which are intended to inform and instruct. If you lack information, or if you will not take it in, there is nothing that we − or anyone else − can do for you. There are others who can be served and we will have to serve them.

8. At the same time, note that there are still others who behave exactly like this group. Their behaviour is common and unremarkable.

'Gharadh'

In some ways it is easier to communicate Sufi ideas in one language than in another. In English and other Western languages, certain terms and words help in making clear certain subjects. The literature shows that these subjects have had to be laboured at what seems to Westerners an inordinate length in Eastern writings. Equally, of course, the other way around. Of the latter, as an example, you have difficulty in conveying, very often, the concept that the other person is opposed to something because of bias. Bias, like prejudice, is a pejorative term which nobody will readily allow to be attached to him.

But in Arabic and Persian, *'Mugharradh'* (often translated as 'biased') is from *Gharadh*, meaning to have an aim, objective. *Mugharradh*, therefore, can mean that the person has an aim which prevents him from accepting the veracity of something. It does not have to mean that there is anything objectionable in this. You may have something in your hand which prevents you picking something else up. This is only 'bad', if some harm is stemming from holding the first thing or not taking up the second thing. To get to a similar stage of lucidity of the situation – when we do reach it at all – we have to go through elaborate explanations to the man worrying about the derogatory associations of 'bias' which can be quite exhausting . . .

Golden Age

How interesting that people think about a 'Golden Age' and hope for the coming or the return, of one.

I have noticed that they never give any consideration to these concepts:

1. How would they know a Golden Age if they entered into one?
2. Could they survive in a Golden Age?
3. Have they been in a Golden Age, without recognising it?

SECTION IV

Humility and Superiority

You cannot have superiority until you have had humility.

However unpopular, sentimentally speaking, it may be to say that you can become better if you first follow than if you first try to lead – it is functionally true.

Most people who want to learn may not even realise that they have first to submit. Having learned this, they may not know how to submit.

Submitting, in our sense, is acting in a manner other than one which is motivated by unrecognised assumptions of superiority.

When people come and say what amounts to: 'Answer my question', or 'Give me attention', or 'Raise my emotional pitch', or 'Entertain me', they are assuming, generally without realising it, that they at that moment deserve attention, or that their emotions should in fact be raised, or that they rate entertaining.

Their demand should be 'Give me what I need, what will profit me, will profit others, and will profit something higher'. That is a manifestation of humility, when rightly conceived.

This structural character of human thought and action is much more important than the words in which it is couched.

For instance, when a man says:

'Lead me, guide me, let me submit, learn . . .' he is probably in a state in which he is incapable of following, of learning, of receiving guidance. This is because what he is really saying is generally: 'Give me attention'. This has become sadly confused because people assume that: 'Let me lead you' is a different thing from 'You lead me'. But they are, dynamically speaking, exactly the same when, as is usual, both feelings stem only from a desire for attention – both mean: *give me your attention*.

It is necessary to recognise what lies behind words, in order to get to the stage where real leading and following, real teaching and study, can take place.

Until that point is reached, the interchange between people is diversionary, playing games, not useful in any higher sense.

Now this is no new reflection. Many centuries ago wise men realised that man seeks comfort, tries to avoid what he fears will give him pain, wants attention, desires to be entertained – and gives all these things quite different names, thinking unconsciously that doing so will in some magical way banish the process and replace it by a process which is of greater 'moral' worth.

These wise men, in small circles and to select numbers of students, passed on this knowledge. Their method and their opportunities were not such as to permit of public dissemination of these facts. So they built into certain cultural and traditional factors the part of the lesson which could be accepted by the people at large, as a sort of 'Moses basket'. The people, like the Nile, carried the basket. The people of understanding, like the Egyptian princess, could find and care for the content.

In our tradition the undertakings, procedures and methods of organisation and study, provide the means for man to break out of his habit of pursuing inane goals while imagining that they are supreme ones. This, in fact, is the one and only value of a tradition.

For this reason it is of the greatest importance to us all to enter into, maintain and operate the procedures and processes, to keep related together, to stress the unity of the community and the tradition: for it is in this way that we can make use of the hidden deposit of knowledge which is our only true terrestrial heritage and endowment.

Hence the 'work', the organisation, the circles of students, the enterprises, the observances. Hence, too, the relative unimportance of the intellectual study of written materials.

How to Study

When given materials or ideas to study, you have to learn to give all of them equal attention.

Realise that you have in the past been consuming selectively: That is, welcoming what you think you want and ignoring or malforming what you think you do not need.

Such a procedure, in any form of learning, can lead to nothing.

Prejudice, opinion, attitude, are of value in learning only when they enable a person to study effectively. They have, however, been mistakenly elevated into virtues by themselves.

The result is that a person tends to learn only what he has been trained (by himself and others) to learn. This leaves gaps when he is faced by deep knowledge. Unimportant in ordinary matters, these gaps are pitfalls in a more advanced stage.

Man thinks that he needs knowledge. He may, in fact, need techniques: knowing how to learn. This can sound less dramatic, less exciting, less beguiling than vague promises – so people do not bother with it.

Human Knowledge

It is interesting to note how implicitly it is nowadays believed that all man's formal knowledge has been painstakingly collected, by trial-and-error, over the millennia.

The reason people believe this is that they cannot credit any other possible manner of gathering information than:

1. Trial-and-error;
2. Observation and application;
3. Verbal transmission.

Because people believe that there could only have been these methods of collecting facts, they have failed to notice thus far that, had this been true, the human race would have destroyed itself.

True, someone trying caraway seeds on infants might have

discovered that an infusion of them quietened them. This he could transmit. But how could he, and those to whom he transmitted the information, forbear from trying all kinds of other preparations on children, destroying them faster than they could be replaced?

Just imagine the relatively small numbers of people in existence, the poor communications and wastage of transmitted information, the large number of possible trial-and-error experiments – and ask yourself how the human race survived this supposed period . . .

Then look at the persistent traditions among all people relating to the acquisition of knowledge and information from 'supernatural' or other sources . . .

How to 'Broaden Your Outlook' by Narrowing it

Under present circumstances, this trick is performed simply by being a human being.

Man, whatever his culture, constantly prepares for his own dissolution by narrowing his outlook. The method employed is to imagine that one is broadening it. Conviction does not take long to develop, and is continuously culturally transmitted.

Self-congratulatory and self-reproaching societies alike betray this characteristic. They obscure its diagnosis by simple devices such as the pretence that the real issue is the difference between their two forms of approach. This becomes common ground and one may now 'vanish' the necessary thought that it is the problems, not the solutions, which have to be observed first.

Look closely at human collective credos and enterprises and you will be able to see that they are based upon wonderfully few and crude basic assumptions. Man avoids perceiving this by claiming that what really are assumptions are truths, and that what is only emotionality is really something sublime.

This self-deception would only be of use if man were indeed such a paltry and hopeless creature as he pretends he thinks himself not to be.

Institutions, behaviour and dogmas may proclaim human values, significance and dignity, even a high human destiny. In fundamental theory, structure and above all in action, they belie any deep belief in these magnificent concepts.

Instead of acting in accordance with a belief in man, most individuals and societies long ago adopted today's meagre substitutes for belief: indoctrination, conditioning, the implanting of systematic obsessions. This is known, however, as the acquisition and maintaining of 'faith'. Man can, by this change in terminology, induce 'faith' and believe that he has primary or secondary evidence of its existence. Thinking that he has got something, or that he could get it if he wanted it enough, enables man to avoid a search for it. So man 'has faith'.

If encountered among machines, such a tendency to confuse would cause the apparatus manifesting it to be consigned to the repair-shop.

Man's repair-shops occupy themselves with attempts at repairs which are constantly being shown to be ineffective. Even when this is conceded, the automatic assumption following is that the repair-shop needs more knowledge. In fact it needs new repairmen.

There is a poetically beautiful but otherwise horrific situation here. People most concerned about the repairs are generally those least able to carry them out. Those who might make adequate mechanics are generally the ones least interested in the problem.

But we do need repairmen.

Honour

Honour is a preparation, not an objective.

If you teach that crawling is everything, and do not continue to the point when a child can walk upright, what have you achieved?

If you distract people from learning to crawl by talking only about walking, what have you achieved?

If, by teaching and practising crawling alone, you rear a generation which will never be able to do more than crawl until the day they die, what have you done?

If you yourself have only been taught that crawling is the highest attainment, and you don't know about walking, are you a fit instructor?

If you think that it is better to teach people to crawl than to leave them lying on the ground, remember that he who can teach walking can also teach crawling: but he who can teach only crawling may make people incapable of learning the next lesson.

Honour, behaviour, discipline, truthfulness, sincerity: these are preparations, not ultimate objectives.

Higher Ranges of Study

When a new development in learning comes about in a society, and one which can be understood at an ordinary level, this development becomes a part of the educational system. Thus we can see such tools as algebra, chemistry and even literacy taking their place in communities, where their usefulness can easily be demonstrated.

When, however, we come to a higher form of learning, we

must remember that in respect to it, our societies are like a series of tribes at a primitive stage. Only a relatively small number of people in each tribe will be able to assimilate and pass on the new knowledge in useful form.

Do not forget that before even such a simple thing as mathematics became generally accessible, numbers were regarded by most people as magical. Some of those who did understand them preserved the knowledge as a monopoly, for personal or group property and power or superstitious reasons. Primitive and more advanced mathematics continued in use, side by side, for a long time until the development of society demanded the adoption of the superior kind of calculation.

Too many people take for granted that it is just a matter of 'educating' others into the needs of a new knowledge. When they use this word 'education' they really mean 'indoctrination'. This will not do.

Too many people imagine that, because they have for years been on the trail of an advanced knowledge of man, all their friends should be included in the activity as well. This is excellent social spirit. It is an inadequate basis for study.

Take the case of some people accustomed to playing with figures as magical or entertainment objects. A chance is given to them all to use figures for other purposes: calculation. The predictable response will be that some will want to acquire the 'new' knowledge, and others will want to continue to divert themselves.

Let us call them 'type A' and 'type B'. Now, type A and type B, because they have developed (*in addition to* common objectives) mutual psychological dependence, will resist anything which affects this dependence.

If some are to become mathematicians and others to become advanced recreationists (or can learn in some completely different way), it is inevitable that the A and B group will resist, as long as possible, facing this re-grouping if they are preponderantly a social group with mutual transference. Such a resistance will prove that the group has gone so far socially that it is no longer a learning-group.

Since this situation is not visible to the members of the group, only the evidence of actual events and reactions within the group will be able to make it visible: unless the members of the group know enough about human social evolution to discern this tendency among themselves. In such a case they must have sufficient quasi-objectivity not to rationalise the behaviour away. This rationalising is most easily done, and indeed is done in all primitive societies, by regarding any 'new' factor as a threat.

If the 'new' factor expects any loyalty from members of the group, this will be viewed as an attempt to dominate or control. If any material contribution is expected, this will be interpreted as disguised commercialism. If any object, readings or other materials are offered, these will be regarded as dangerous or even as 'useless'.

This behaviour is as predictable as any laboratory experiment in chemistry or physics. This behaviour belongs to the shallow part of human mentation. Like any other useful preliminary study, it should be verified and registered and left behind as soon as possible, so that progress in a higher sense can be made.

But those who cannot learn this lesson, however dear they are to one another as social contacts, cannot continue as students without false pretences or ignorance on the part of the instructor. Such a person's social pastoral function is out of balance with his educational mission.

Human Duty

To help others, to try to be kind and to avoid cruelty, to heal the sick and to protect the weak: these are among the elementary social, not spiritual, duties incumbent upon man as a social animal.

Those who have confused social uplift and psychological

ministrations with 'higher' endeavour, end up by being in a state of bewilderment or forced into sophistry when they find that they no longer have the monopoly of social service.

The fault is at least partly theirs; they should not so readily have taken the easy way of equating something 'other' with something merely civilised.

Hypocrisy

To be a hypocrite is perhaps the worst thing there is. But I can think of something more destructive than that: it is to imagine that one is not false in 'good resolutions'. Neither imagine that you are false, nor lash yourself, for both are forms of self-indulgence.

Have the courage to recognise that, no matter how many people are impressed by the seeming humility and self-reproach of pious people, the real effort is in knowing about oneself, so that one can do something about it. Once you yield to the comparatively easy way of assuming personal guilt, you are guilty of amusing yourself, revelling in your worthlessness.

If you do that, people may admire you, they may point you out as a good example, traditional texts may support your thoughts and actions, society may believe that it benefits from your existence – but you will yourself be lost.

The real men of knowledge can be said to exist for the purpose of indicating to really earnest seekers, that a man is really self-deceived when he feels that he is being righteous – they do not exist to paper over the cracks by agreeing that a certain train of thought or series of actions or both are invariable indications of genuine belief and practice.

Human Thought passing through the Whole Organism

Human thoughts in certain ranges pass directly, without vocalisation, from individuals and groups into the whole human race.

The effect may be all the more effective for its being frequently unperceived by the ordinary perceptions.

If, as an example, many people think in a certain manner destructively, each one of us, and even every other human being, may sustain a debilitating psychic blow.

There are human capacities which, if practised, can operate constructively or destructively, without the slightest contact with the 'higher' mental functions with which they are so often confused.

It is this range of thought which is employed in such systems as those which produce the more dramatic results. Their shortcoming, sometimes assuming the dimension of tragedy, is to mistake the technique for results – for the truth; the manifestation, or the means – for the origin or the end.

Higher Nutritions

The physical organism needs nutrition in a certain quantity, quality and periodicity. The same is true of 'higher nutrition'. To combine various inner studies according to one's whims can be disastrous, just as in the case of a person who is an alcoholic; or one who has indiscriminate feeding habits and is without taste-buds.

Honour of the Wise

The foolish or unimportant often find themselves acclaimed by those who are neither wise nor foolish. Acclaim in itself creates an impression of importance. Such importance, however, endures only in a manner which is objectively unimportant.

Great confusion exists because few people point out that there are different 'densities' of importance. Such densities cannot be measured by everyone – just as you must have a conception and experience of weight before you can estimate how weighty a thing is.

You get to know real significance by feeling, in a similar manner, the relative 'lightness' of something which by ordinary feeling may seem important, and then being able to reject it.

So the wise may honour fools because of the usefulness of 'bulk' in them at any given time. The fools generally imagine that they are being credited with wisdom.

Harmful Ideas

The capacity for development is within you.

The refuge of destructive selfishness is to convince oneself that one has recognised or knows what to do next.

When a person has in fact acquired this recognition-capacity, he feels and behaves in a manner different from the greedy and deluded who merely *imagine* that they have arrived at this point.

Single-Formula Systems

We might call 'the Eureka-system' any which offers you one ritual for everyone, one belief, one authority-figure, one major technique. Such systems are not Ways at all. They are better described as poor jokes, told by the ignorant (perhaps in 'good faith') to the greedy. I talk with directness about this, simply because in speaking about it, as with more obvious infestations, the ordinary social niceties have to be suspended for the sake of an overall good.

Students

A teaching attracts an artificial selection of students (those interested in the way in which the teaching is projected) unless its sponsors are careful to prevent this.

No 'teaching' with a single dogma or unified message can avoid processing its adherents.

Stupidity

Stupidity is not a word which it is easy to define.

It would be worthwhile observing that, while some stupidity is unavoidable, lots of people deliberately make themselves stupid, and thus prevent themselves from understanding things that would be of value to them.

People who appear to be intelligent are often quite obtuse in the methods which they use in assessing something. Because of their repute or ebullient manner, however, they are not regarded as stupid. This is one reason why stupidities of thought are so easily propagated: they are passed on by those whom the public takes as being all-round intelligent people.

Social Concern

Concern over the present and future of young people and others who experiment with methods, ideas and even substances, is part of the whole attitude of 'concern' which most people feel for others.

This concern is dramatised in cases of taking certain drugs, in cases where the underprivileged are highlighted, in times and places where such things as starvation are put into focus by an experience, an organisation or the operation of an attitude.

We cannot really separate one form of this 'concern' from another.

I am the father of three children, I have a wife and other relatives, I am a human being and I have the customary measure of concern about these and other people.

The reason for concern about others is that we all feel that we should do our duty, as others have done theirs, to help, nourish, protect and sustain other human beings. Those upon whom our attention is for some reason most strongly focused generally become those for whom we feel this sentiment in its strongest, most urgent, form.

When there is an absence of objective knowledge as to the causes and the cures of certain difficulties, the concern becomes well-nigh insupportable. We have been taught to love and to cherish others, but we find that this does not seem to work.

This produces a conflict. People in this conflict start to believe all kinds of things: that they have failed, that there must be a solution, that perhaps the former moral structure was unsuitable, and so on.

They turn to others for advice: to psychologists, priests and other authority-figures.

But the real cause of the trouble is that man, in general, has spent so much of his energy and attention trying to help others, or to persuade others to help each other, that he has not had time to study how to find out what help he can give, to whom, when and where. He has so put out of his mind the long-term possibility of attaining an objective knowledge of what is happening to humanity, that many people will not believe that such a view is even possible.

Man's problems cannot be solved by first-aid, trying to tackle them so long after they have taken effect. The root-cause has to be found. When the root-cause of a disease is found and tackled, the symptoms disappear. Man, by attending to the symptoms, solves nothing.

This may seem very harsh, but only when it is being listened to by a mind which is conditioned to symptomatic, topical, treatment. Man does not even suspect, generally speaking, that even the local symptoms which he is trying to ameliorate, and which he mistakenly regards as fundamentals, can be alleviated by getting to the root.

Man, in general, is so conditioned that he wants to bring back a certain *status quo*, even after it has vanished. Even when he does not want this, he seeks a 'new morality': but the one which he is demanding will never occur. What comes into being when an established morality breaks down is something which would not have been acceptable to the earlier generation or community. This is one reason why the earlier community dies. The 'Phoenix which rises from the ashes of itself' does not look like, or even feel like, the original phoenix.

To explain this is unpopular, because people prefer that which they know. They do not know that that which they know is not really themselves, or that which is permanent.

116

The tensions and anxieties man faces in a changing world are assuaged only by self-deception — or by having an objective knowledge of 'what is going on and why'. The tragedy about this is that those who know what is going on and how to teach it to others soon discover that the others, while overtly asking for this knowledge, are in fact only asking for a superior form of tinkering with the existing order.

When a person has this knowledge, which is not bought as cheaply as people would imagine, he is able to be 'in the world but not of it'. His special and sentimental contribution is as great as that of the do-gooders. It is, in fact greater, because none of it is wasted. At the same time he is able to operate on a higher level to help the emergence of the new 'phoenix'.

We are living in an unprecedented age, because, for the first time since the tiny human race was concentrated in a few localities only, when cave-ins of cavern roofs would have destroyed it, we are all faced with the possibility of physical destruction. This possibility has been brought about by the older, not the younger, generation. The older generation has unmasked itself to the younger, and can no longer carry on the masquerade of 'knowing better'.

The new morality and society which will emerge, if it gets a chance, will be equally incomprehensible and unacceptable to the older generation and to the people who are today the younger generation. Today's drug-ingesters and forward-looking individuals will, before a very great period of time, if society lasts, appear grotesquely empirical, random and ineffectual: just as the old system appears to them to be stratified, stultifying and hypocritical.

The only bridge between these three worlds: the old, the present and the new, will be through the overall knowledge which explains and illustrates how such conditions come into being: whose 'fault' it is, and what is necessary and what unnecessary.

The world has at last outlived hypocrisy and mechanical systems which had captured the label of spirituality and in its name had conditioned people into patterns which all alike believed were of higher meaning. The higher content was there: but almost nobody was there to work with it.

Those who over-identify with emotional problems, and those who ignore them are both extreme cases: there is no future for them. Man must first of all learn what 'Rendering unto Caesar and to God' means; what 'Trust in God but tie your camel' means – in their applications as exercises to the transformation of the individual and the community.

Opting out from society is a form of personal greed. It carries its own penalty. Over-commitment with certain causes is a form of personal greed. It carries with it its own punishment. Trying to do good beyond a certain point is a form of greed, and it carries its own consequences. If people would only study this they would see many things which have gone wrong in history and why this has happened. If you love other people, for instance, because it is you who really want to be loved, you are not loving at all, and people (especially the object of that 'love') will hate you, at least in part, and will turn against you, perhaps by turning against your dearest beliefs or practices. There is something in man which can detect real love. We rub it out, or muffle it, by substitute-love.

Man's delinquency is often masked by the most socially-acceptable behaviour. There are two forms of conscience: real conscience and conditioned conscience. The latter is necessary, but it is not absolute. The purpose of the latter is to sustain us while we have a chance to find the former. Few people learn this.

You must improve yourself on a higher level if you are to be able to help people, and not just weep over them: 'Do not think that your magic ring will work if you are not yourself Solomon.'

This is the higher philosophy and the higher morality. Like all subtle things, it can be crushed in individual cases by a cruder thing. The cruder thing is to say: 'I believe that such-and-such is good, and your talk about anything else is disguised evil.'

There is so very little difference in kind between the various contending ideologies: what is 'good' to one is 'evil' to the other: 'A cat and a dog were once fighting to decide which of them was a rat.'

118

The only escape is through more knowledge: People talk about 'service, effort, love, knowledge'. But with knowledge you know what love is, and what it is not. With knowledge you can serve, you can make efforts. Knowledge may not be superior to love, but it is the essential prerequisite. If you do not understand, you cannot love. You can only imagine that you love.

If you cannot help others, you will not be able to do so in any permanent or really effective manner just by asking advice from another person. But you can equip yourself to help others. Another person can help you in this task.

None of us can stop trying to help. But we can stop thinking that there must be a panacea somewhere and that we may be the ones to apply it. This is primitive thinking. Unless we can realise that we have to learn what there is to know, not what we imagine we should learn, the knowledge will not be forthcoming.

Summary of Orientation Points

In order for a study to be launched and its performance maintained, it is necessary that facts which inhibit or prevent the development of the study be thoroughly known. All over the world, at all times, people have been carrying out studies in philosophy, metaphysics, religion, without realising that the materials which they study, the way in which they study them, and the factors which influence individuals and groups must be understood in a certain manner. Here are some brief remarks on this subject:

1. People behave in certain ways due to their cultural, national and psychological background. This behaviour colours their whole being. Not knowing this, they attribute naturally-arising reactions to the 'teaching.' See *Silent Language*, Edward Hall.

2. People organise themselves into groups without realising that group organisation can be fatal to learning. Certain types of group exist only for the group, although the members do not know it. Groups can actually become 'religious' even though no religion is being studied. Study *Human Groups*, W.J.H. Sprott, for popularised material on this.

3. Random or systematised study of certain ideas is next to useless. It is one thing to have an open mind; it is another to think that one can choose the materials which one should study when one is not aware of the special circumstances of study needed and the special personnel of a group needed for special studies. See Shah: *The Study of Sufism in the West*★.

4. Many 'teachings' and ideas come to their students strongly influenced by local cultural modes of expression. Unless this is known, and steps are taken to combat this, the result tends to be indoctrination with superficial and worse characteristics of the vehicle of the teaching. See: *Afghanistan*, by Peter King.

5. People take 'ideas' which were intended to be 'prescribed' for specific situations and groups to enable them to learn. These they imagine are 'laws' or perennial truths. The result is a mechanical system which is next to useless. See: *The Teachers of Gurdjieff* by Rafael Lefort.

6. People study a man and his work through doctrines and personality conceptions which do not apply to that man or that work. They get lost in this enterprise. See: *Rumi the Persian*, Reza Arasteh.

★Part I: *The Way of the Sufi* by Idries Shah (Octagon Press Ltd., London).

Solving Problems

When a problem arises, or is believed to have arisen, the human being's first reaction is not always to solve it – although he will pretend that it is.

This pretence is only the beginning of a whole exercise.

The first reaction is to 'worry' it, like an animal with a piece of food or other attention-object. It is being used, at this stage, as a game or food, to get some juice or reaction out of it. The man is 'getting paid as he goes along'.

Even if the problem is a dispute between two parties, each of them will expect some enjoyment from the very fact of participation. Without this, the solving of the matter will not suffice them.

The man who solves problems 'too quickly', or even the one who ignores them, is signalling by this very fact that he is independent of the enjoyment-content in the problem-game. It is because of this, much more than because of his having solved the problem, that people respect him. They are in some awe of him because he has shown that he can do something that they cannot: dispense with the indulgence of wrestling with a problem.

Seeking and Finding

A Persian proverb says:

> 'Ultimately the Seeker becomes transformed into a Finder.'

A Sufi, taking part of another couplet from Saadi, ended this with:

> 'Even if he is reared among the sons of Adam.'

He interprets it thus:

You will find what you are seeking if you keep looking. There is only one small requirement which the needs of literary elegance have removed from the phrase: You must know what you are looking for, know where it is, and know how to find it.

Showing

The man who has nothing to show, and the one who cannot show what he has, appear equally true or false to the ordinary observer. Human cultures should teach man about himself, not only about other men. The situation at present is why cheats and genuine men of wisdom can both exist.

Specialists

The grinning simpleton has nothing on the people who call themselves 'specialists'. Such people use the word, and – because of the alchemy of associative thought – leave you to infer that they, the specialists, must because of their concentration upon it, know their subject.

Whether it has always been so is doubtful: But currently matters are at such a pass that you may confidently predict (if you have absorbed your experiences) that 'specialist' is another word for 'ignoramus'.

Strange World

In our world real short cuts are numerous, but not easily seen. They lead through jungles where hostile savages abound and provisions are scarce. The fruits which look nutritious are poisonous, and the survival rations appear unpalatable.

The view from the start of the short cut is almost exactly like the prospect from the other side.

These are short cuts with a vengeance. The attractive-looking ones are not short cuts at all.

Single-Minded

The truly single-minded man needs all his concentration capacity. He must work on appearing less than single-minded.

Lesser men, for all their imagined support for single-mindedness, fear it. They will only support what appears to be single-mindedness, or an approximation of it.

The opposition to the really single-minded is carried out in a thousand unconscious, minor but effective ways.

Hence the seeming paradox in which, for defence and protection, for continued efficiency, the truly resolute must frequently appear less than wholly efficient, even vacillatory.

Real capacity, therefore, may be much less common in public knowledge than it is in real fact. There is an ancient proverb: 'In a village where everyone has only one leg, the biped will hop about more lamely than anyone else, if he knows what is good for him.'

This proverb represents the codification of important observation, and is therefore both a record of knowledge and instructional material of the greatest importance.

Sane and Mad

It is agreed that kindness to lunatics is good. Our society does not fail in this important duty. But there is still a certain cultural imbalance, rooted in the pessimist civilisation, which is worth looking at.

When madmen make enormous claims for themselves, they are treated well. But when sane people do so, they are ignored or derided. They may be put through a form of gauntlet-running.

With people at the present stage of development, too much ignoring, too much derision, too much baiting, can produce aggression and irrationality. So the pessimist society, which has said, 'This man cannot really be worth much' actually produces, by the aforementioned techniques, a morbid condition in the attacked individual. This, of course, is taken as proof that the pessimists were right all the time, the man is mad.

As a madman, he does not have to be listened to. The pessimists, who are also humanitarians, having knocked him out, can be kind to him. After all, we are kind to lunatics, aren't we?

Service and Self-Satisfaction

Consideration for others is regarded as the highest good by many thinkers and non-thinkers alike.

But such consideration, if based on personal indulgence, is in fact a vice.

There is a real form of human service, far above the variety which is rooted in self-satisfaction.

Sufism

I have said and written so much about Sufism and the Sufis that some people imagine that I am trying to influence them to join a cult or a religious grouping.

It is, in fact, not possible for me to mount such a campaign, as I will now explain to you.

Hearing and reading what I have had to say about the Sufis has caused the religious-minded to flow towards the theologised versions of Sufism in the East. It has also, with equal force, caused the curious and greedy to flock around the guru-ist cults of the West.

This leaves those who are uninformed, those who want to learn more of what Sufism is, and those who are unconcerned.

This operation has been highly successful, but it has had no higher function for the majority than any other instrument which sorts things – or people – out.

To an Enquirer

You think that I am being foolhardy when I say: 'You will never be able to profit from what I am communicating.'

Here is the explanation: I am, on the contrary, being extremely careful: I am making sure that you will not become a 'follower' of mine, for I can see that you are a person who can lose himself in discipleship. Such a development, far from being a profit to anyone, would mean a loss of a human being – because obsession, by whatever name, is a disaster.

But my initial 'violence' in its effect upon you will never be erased. So you will not now be so prone to indoctrination.

Our relationship, yours and mine, may not be that of teacher and disciple. But neither will it be that of supplier and consumer.

How refreshing!

Time, Place and Materials

Literature and observances are dependent for their effect upon the manner, occasion and circumstances of their study, if they are to be successful as carriers of a truly higher mode of perception.

To violate this rule is to waste time, reduce the chances of understanding, stabilise oneself upon what may appear profound but which is in reality shallow.

We can go a great distance towards profiting from these concepts by making them a familiar part of our information. This does not even have to be done at the expense of more conventional ways of thinking.

Transformation Process

The knowledge of real virtue has been almost lost when well-meaning ignoramuses have felt themselves constrained to practise and further a diluted teaching, often in order to deal with excessively large numbers of people. In so doing they have frequently betrayed the law that:

A few transformed people can transform millions; millions of untransformed people can do – or be – next to nothing.

Such a statement may be unpopular. This does not challenge its authenticity.

Threes and Ones

If someone said to you:

> 'Two plus two equals four, I know that. But why
> should, and how can, three plus one also equal four?'

You could answer — if it were a child — 'It is true, and I will show you.' Then you would demonstrate it, because you would be in a position to gain and to hold his attention, and he would already have been conditioned to accept your assumptions. One of the assumptions is that he must be quiet while you tell him. Another is that he will be prepared to allow you to talk of threes and ones, or mark it down on the ground with a row of beans.

But if you are dealing with an adult, he will not give you a chance. He says, in effect:

'Yes, show me, but show me in "twos"' — in his terms. And: 'Show me without those irrelevant and probably sinister beans . . .'

That is why you can teach a child by a succession of demonstrations along one line of reasoning and illustration, and why you can hardly even get an adult onto the line of reasoning at all.

If that adult were a child, behaving in respect to ordinary understanding as grownups do to higher learning, you would unhesitatingly declare him delinquent or unteachable. He would have to have a course of preliminary corrective teaching . . .

To be Remembered

People in history who were bad are remembered much more than people who tried to make others bad. The same is not the case with goodness. You will notice, if you care to verify this, that it is not the people who were only good who are remembered, but the people who told others to be good, whether they themselves were so or not.

Truth and Belief

Hard-pressed after I had tackled him rather strongly about his beliefs, a man once shouted at me:

'I *know* it's not true, but I *believe* it!'

Before you laugh, consider the more famous phrase:

'I believe it because it is impossible'.

Belief does not have to have anything to do with truth. A thing may be true and believed because of indoctrination, or it may be true and believed by virtue of its truth.

You may find this difficult to understand. It is only so because it is not a customary thought. If you had spent as much time in looking for real and conditioned belief as you have in assuming that there is only one kind of belief and that belief itself is something desirable or important in the crude variety produced by indoctrination or following catharsis, you would find no difficulty at all in understanding what I am saying.

In this respect the only difference between you and me is that I have taken the trouble to spend the time on this which you have spent otherwise.

Transformation of One's Worldly Life

Remarkably many people work back-to-front in their imaginings about higher knowledge. Some assume, for instance, that it is a psychology, or a psychotherapy alone.

It does, indeed, transform the outer life, but this happens only as an incidental of the real seeking.

Any other operation works as mere 'processing', training, not development.

Three Disabling Consequences of Generalisation

Man's tendency to be a generalising animal – to deduce a law or even a rule applicable to one situation from a totally different situation – is one of his greatest problems as well as being of considerable advantage to him. We all know about the advantages. Neglect of the problem has placed whole cultures in the weak psychological situation of today. Let us look at the first major disabling consequence of generalisation in esoteric studies.

FIRST MAJOR DISABLING CONSEQUENCE

People hear it said that experience is superior to formal study, and they therefore leap to the conclusion that they should be given instant illumination or personal attention and not have to read anything or listen to a lecture. This terrible simplification is like saying: 'It is better to wash oneself, because it makes one clean, than to learn hand and eye co-ordination, because that is suitable only for children'. But what happens if one cannot co-ordinate and yet wants to learn washing? Nothing at all. The sad truth is that most people have read too much and got indigestion. What they are likely to need as much or more than personal attention is the right kind of reading or lecture, at the right time. This is why you have been invited to hear these lectures, or to read them.

Generalisation produces simplification. People love to simplify, just as much as they want to complicate. We all know a lot about complication: let us now look at simplification.

SECOND DISABLING CONSEQUENCE:
OF SIMPLIFICATION

The drawback of finding out that one can simplify is that one may simplify something which then becomes worthless because of the simplification. This is the situation with esoteric studies. Because people have become accustomed to studying esoteric things through words and symbols, rituals and books, regalia and customs, images and authority-figures which by some sort of simplification process have been assigned to the 'esoteric realm', they are unable to imagine (let alone recognise) the esoteric process in existence and action outside of these attenuated fields. As a consequence of this they have actually deprived themselves of the opportunity to learn from those things which they regard as irrelevant. Because of this, much that stares them in the face seems secret and elusive, much that they could immediately understand seems esoteric and uncertain. Any real teaching of higher understanding today must unlock those things which do not seem by association of ideas, to belong to the higher realm. These lectures and other materials now being offered do not, therefore, limit themselves to the familiar terminology nor to the poverty-stricken fields which represent today's ineffective 'higher world', as understood by what are in reality externalists who imagine that they are metaphysicians.

THIRD DISABLING CONSEQUENCE:
OF GREED

Human greed and impatience, which has largely been brought under control in social areas where it has been extensively made unprofitable, still operates at full blast in esotericist fields. As a consequence, the very thing desired by the would-be illuminate is out of his grasp and will remain so until he learns what steps he must take first.

The very first step is to realise that there is no genuine esoteric study in which he will get simple answers to simple questions, and where he will be able easily to attain what he wants. He will have to expose himself to what appear to be the most diverse and improbable materials and experiences before he has the basic preparation upon which alone he can build. If he frequents circles which purport to give him something higher through a logical system, he will have fallen into the hands of scoundrels or superficialists. His greed will disable him. He can decide whether he is to be disabled or not.

If the student is capable of giving his attention to the course of study now being given, he will have a chance of developing through it. If, however, he uses it as a means of amusing himself, of filling time, of social intercourse, of feeling that he is engaged in something significant, of passing it on to others, or any other similar superficial aim, which includes intellectual or emotional indulgence, the material will yield him nothing at all, no matter what he may imagine that it provides him.

It is for him to make the resolve, and he is fully capable of following such a course. He might as well, however, not start at all as give up part of the way or as mix it with other systems or quotations or teachings. It is within his capabilities to exercise this much discipline, and nobody else can ever do it for him, no matter what anyone may, deludedly or otherwise, promise him.

*   *   *

In the above statement, you will note that the word 'man' is used to import 'man or woman'; as we often use the word 'chicken' to refer to 'the young of any bird'. This kind of conventional generalisation is ordinarily adequate to the situation.

If, however, we note the associations attached to another word also found above, 'esoteric', we realise that this term is ordinarily generalised to mean 'any hidden knowledge, anything inner, secret, mysterious, taught to a select few'. Its technical meaning, however, for those who are familiar with such lore, is 'that knowledge, ordinarily concealed from men in one way or

131

another, which leads to the ultimate understanding of man by man.'

And, of course, once someone knows it, it is no longer 'esoteric' in quite the same way to him – or to her.

Thought

Man is accustomed to considering intellect as a consistent thing. Thinking varies in intensity, he will say, but not in quality. In actual fact, there is an infinite gradation of the quality and perceptiveness of intellect itself. The scholastic may be indulging in hypertrophy of intellect, like a man who exercises his biceps just because they are there and because he therefore considers that they should be exercised to their limit: having discovered that he can develop them by exercises. Thought is a much more effective and sublime thing than this. The Sufi is one who has become aware of the harmony and possibility of thought, like the athlete who realises the harmony and completeness of the body, not the man who has discovered some possibilities of the biceps and is obsessed by them. To the Sufi, the scholar is as ungainly as the man with developed biceps, made as massive as possible by exercise, would appear to the ordinary gaze.

There comes a Time

There always comes a time when instruction-materials originally employed to direct the attention of certain people towards a certain aim are adopted as 'gospel', or else simplified out of all usefulness and shallowly interpreted.

An example of the latter is the current idea of the meaning of Diogenes' looking with a lamp in broad daylight for an honest man.

People think that he did this to indicate how rare were honest men. In fact, this procedure is a perfectly obvious example of directing attention to the whole question: not only to the rarity of honest men, but to the whole question as to how they might be found.

Thought and Property

Thought and belief are a property interest.

Because belief does not look like, say, a piece of land or a possession, people of all kinds are unable to realise what is going on within them.

All human systems exchange the two kinds of property: material and thought.

The people who have no property are more readily indoctrinated: that is to say, more ready to accept thought, which behaves like a substance.

The people who have so much property that they are bored with it will take up forms of thought. This is because, while endowed with property, they are in a state of surfeit. They seek and accept a different form of property – that of thought.

When a person says: 'My belief is my dearest *possession*' he is unwittingly describing his situation with scientific accuracy.

When an academic refers to 'his field', he is speaking of his alternative to physical possession of property.

This is why the human being can be indoctrinated: he is not just the helpless receptor of ideas or implanted obsessions, he is a partner in the transaction. Someone is saying to him: 'I have something; I am offering it to you.'

As with cross-tolerance in ingested substances, there is cross-tolerance in thought. The human being will not normally be able to distinguish between thought which is nutritious and that which is manipulative to him.

But some thought builds him up, while some will only enslave him.

Anyone can study this for himself in everyday life, once he is prepared to look at what really is going on, not just at the labels we give to it.

Terminology

In communication by words, if you use archaic terminology, your audience's mentation is instantly regressed to an inapplicable stage.

If people crave the use of certain formulae, this is symptomatic of their condition, not necessarily indicative of any need whatever.

In certain cases it is better not to speak about 'Everlasting Life'. This has acquired a misleading image. More advantage would be gained by referring to the 'Project for the Infinite Increase in Human Durability'.

And even that could be abbreviated to PIIHD.

The Worst Ailment

There is one ailment which really is the worst of all.

It is the one which makes you think that not you, but others, are the sufferers and you are free from it.

In mild forms, it concedes that you may suffer from it a little, but that it is others who have it in a far worse form.

The Meaning of Life

The 'meaning of life' is only to be found if our studies include things which people generally call 'meaningless', and consequently do not study, rendering their efforts incomplete.

Incomplete effort leads to incomplete results.

The purposes of a teaching-entity include ensuring that every relevant and essential form of study is covered.

'The Right to Know'

People talk about the *right to know* this or that. This implies that something which people might or should know is being withheld from them, or that they are not allowed to find it out for themselves.

The Sufic activity is perhaps the most powerful supporter of the RIGHT TO KNOW. Not only have you a right to know about yourself, but you have a right to know what it is that is stopping you from knowing. As an instance, bias and ingrained beliefs about all kinds of things prevent people from knowing, because they imagine that there is nothing to know, or what they might know is not a good thing to know. The right to know must also include the right to know that there is something to know.

Politically-minded people harp on the right to know what, for instance, their government is doing. This may be all very well. But what about the abolition of the concept that there is anything at all to know? In the case of certain enslavers of the human mind, there are those who literally say: 'A right to know about man's potential: about, say, mysticism? Why, THERE IS NOTHING TO KNOW . . .' They have prevented even the idea that there is a right to know by denying that there IS anything to be known. Thus, centuries before the Orwellian concept of a people denied a right to know, there was the discovery that cleverer and more effective than denying any right to know is the claim that there IS nothing to know . . .

The Higher Learning

When you realise the manner in which the Higher Learning protects itself it is small wonder that so very few people attain to it.

When you see how dishonest is ordinary human expectation, you realise how the Higher Knowledge can be said to lie in directions contrary to expectation.

If you really know humanity, you can know the Higher Knowledge.

The Sufis and Worldly Success

The Sufis hold that they can achieve worldly success because there is a relationship between this world and the other one: though this does not mean that they are attached to mundane matters – very much to the contrary. The reality, therefore, is not so much what they have, but whether what they have is a shackle for them.

The analogy of the 'two worlds' is given by the Master Hisamuddin among many others. He points to the effect which moving has on your shadow.

Take this world, he suggested, as the shadow, and the next one as the sun, for the purposes of the analogy.

Now note that if you move towards your shadow (the world) it recedes, and if pursued cannot be caught.

If, however, you move towards the sun (the other world) your shadow will follow you.

The Use of Initiatory Texts

Certain great writings in a variety of different languages are rightly regarded as great textbooks of higher thought and mysticism.

People therefore read them, intending to obtain by concentration and application something of their higher content.

But each one of these books contains, in addition to its developmental ingredients, materials which effectively prevent people from misusing them.

In order to obtain the inner meaning of the materials, it is necessary to deal with the book in certain special manners.

You must know, first of all, which passages to read and which not to read. If you read the wrong one, or if you read the whole of the book, you will be absorbing the antidote, the security-device, as well as the materials contained. The result will be that the book will not act in the manner which it could.

The book may obsess you, or condition you, or give you emotional reactions, or interest you for reasons of intellectual dilettantism. These phenomena you may misinterpret as special to that book. What you do not know is that almost any book, if you thought that it contained great teachings or secrets, would have the same effect. You are still working with the mechanical part of the mind.

It is for this reason that people in our tradition make special selections from certain literature, in order to offer the student the materials which will suit him, and reduce the effect of the buffer-materials placed there to protect real meaning.

It is the same with ritual, and with exercises. Many exercises, prayers and other routines have been specified in great or little detail, but they all have specific use. If you violate, even through ignorance, this need to remove the skin, as it were, you will be biting the bitter peel of the orange. Certainly, something is happening, but it is that the bitter oil is being felt, not the pure juice.

On less advanced planes, literary selections are made by, say, teachers of literature, in order to provide useful texts for students. On a higher level, similar considerations apply. The more enlightened man in the esoteric sense will be able to provide appropriate nutrition for his own students.

Ordinary 'spiritual' people are really disguised emotionalists. They choose the materials which have moved them sentimentally, and they are always found to be unwittingly training their followers to similar subjective experiences by offering them anthologies of stimulating material. Real inner materials are not in this range of crudity of perception.

These are some of the hazards of random study.

SECTION V

The Nature of Sufic Study

Sufi teaching is effected through imposed experience, and training to benefit from experience. People are subjected to written materials designed to 'strike' them in such a way as to allow the mind to work in a new or different manner. Sufi circles, their members carrying on all manner of (often seemingly mundane or irrelevant) tasks, are settings for seeking the imposition and tasting of experience. The words, the actions – even the inaction – of teachers are a further form of impact teaching. The content of Sufi literature and contact also enable the student to obtain impacts suitable to his state from what are to others simply some of the ordinary events of the conventional world. He can see them differently and profit from them more extensively, while still retaining his ability to cope with events in the ordinary world on its customary, more limited, levels.

Because the foregoing is not properly understood, there are three, not one, reactions to Sufi-offered experience in evidence:

1. The individual becomes a wisecracker. Instead of profiting from the Sufi impact, he learns how to 'deal with it', answering back, as it were, to frustrate the impact.
2. He becomes hopelessly indoctrinated, obsessional, a 'believer' in Sufism who is nothing other than a sensationalist.
3. He (or she) *is* able to observe and to feel the special function of the Sufi impact, on himself, on his fellows, in literature and in other areas. He can detect, and profit from, this activity in many different ways, without being imprisoned by method or associations.

The Nature of the Study Circle

As soon as you join a study circle, you come into a certain special relationship with its members, with its teacher, and with the whole of the studies.

That is why it is important to maintain a special sort of relationship between the members, and a special sort of attunement in the student.

The study materials themselves, the membership of the group, the activity as a whole of the school, the proceedings which are carried out – these are the means whereby the special harmony and receptivity, as well as the inter-relation between the students and the study, take place.

Most people are familiar only with the sort of inter-relation which is brought forth by sentiment or indoctrination, sad though it may be.

Remember, too, that the advantages which you gain from the study circle and its materials vary from time to time. That is to say, we cannot, and should not imagine we can, extract all the nutrition from any piece of study material at one time.

What we have to do is to familiarise ourselves with certain information, techniques and so on, so that our attention is not focussed upon them when the time comes to use them. Then, as and when we can do so, we extract the use of the materials on successive occasions.

In addition to this process, several others are taking place at one and the same time. One is the relationship, invisible and sometimes unperceived, with all others on the same Path. Another by-product of the studies is the change in our outward lives which takes place almost without our noticing it.

The study circle is the kernel of the community. It is from this essential grouping that all kinds of social, religious, psychological and philosophical schools have been formed. But the formation of such an institution sacrifices the organic nature of the inter-relation between real, living people, correctly grouped, and a real, living teaching, all operating as one whole.

Remember, the real inter-relation is so far advanced compared with the artificial one as to be almost unrecognisable when set side by side with it.

The Anopheles Mosquito Situation

In order to explain the difficulties and necessities of a teaching situation, there are few better methods than transposing such a situation into a context which answers well enough as an illustration, and which deals with factors equivalent to those actually involved; these factors to be ones which are already familiar to your audience. This is what I am now about to do. I am bringing the efficient and time-honoured methods of teaching by means of fable into the usage and format of the second half of what we now call the twentieth century.

The assertion which we first make is that the people with whom we are dealing in trying to deliver our message are spiritually underdeveloped. There is no shame in this, and the matter is not open for discussion. All teaching begins with an assertion, such as 'I am here to teach you, and you have to give me the minimum amount of attention.' It then goes on to a second kind of assertion (such as the one above) which is equivalent to saying: 'You do not know the method by which I will teach you, say, French; you may not know how little you know. I am not going to discuss this point, but will teach such people as will go along with me on this.'

There are some of you who are beguiled by 'method', and who will listen to a man if he offers, or seems to offer, a 'method' other than you have been accustomed to. I ignore these, because in this context a change is not as good as a rest. Some of you like theory, some practice. I am here to give you what theory you need and what practice you need, as and when you need it. As this is not a recruiting, advertising nor psychotherapeutic organisation, I will not attempt to ascertain what your symptoms are and offer remedies. I am here to teach, not to make you feel good or bad or satisfied with what I am doing, or the reverse.

Now we will get straight on to our anopheles mosquito. You will now have to place yourself in my position, by means of a trick of illustration, which we call parable. You are a medical or hygiene worker. You arrive at a place where the people have almost no knowledge of such things. Let us call it a primitive community which nevertheless has considerable achievements in other fields. They are better than you, for instance, at survival in the jungle, have a fine sense of justice and valuable institutions of many kinds. But, because they have no real idea of hygiene as applied to themselves in their current situation, they are dying in large numbers, their infant mortality is high. Let us say that because of this wastage of human potential this community is unable to expand to take advantage of its possible cultural, economic and other potentials. You have the expertise to address this.

The people say to you: 'You are a miracle-worker. We know, because we have seen you make fire without rubbing sticks together.' This to you is irrelevant, to them important. You cannot pursue this line of thought, because they are still reluctant to believe that your matches are man-made. So you merely say: 'I may seem something to you. But what I really am is what is important.'

Now the people say to you: 'How can you help us?'

You say: 'I am here to make it possible for you to have a better material life, I know the method. I am also here to save life, and I can do other things, which you can learn from me.'

Some say: 'Teach us, NOW!!!' You say: 'I have to teach you the rudiments, because my skills depend upon a basis.' This does not please them. They want to have a better material life NOW, or some evidence of its coming in a form which is *perceptible to them.*

Some say: 'He is lying!'

144

Some say: 'We will do anything you say. Here are a brace of chickens, just like we give to the ju-ju man. Make us live forever!' You cannot accept this basis either.

Some say: 'What should we do?'

When you say: 'The first thing to do is to take oil and spray it on a stagnant pool, because this will inhibit the growth of the larvae of the anopheles mosquito, which in turn will not then be able to infect you with malaria. As a consequence, many people who are lying about unproductively will be able to work, there will be no death from complications, and the pool of water will also eventually be reclaimed for useful purposes': What do they say?

Some say: 'You are talking on such a high level that we cannot make any sense out of it. How can a mosquito more or less make any difference to death, or water? They don't drink much. They don't prick much! The ju-ju man has told us of the dangers of breaking taboos. Perhaps you are saying that mosquitos are taboo in some way?'

You say: 'Give me a chance and I will show you.' They say: 'How long?' They want to be shown NOW. You say: 'Very well, we will get microscopes, DDT, books on Lister and Ross . . .' They think you are raving mad. At the best impossibly irrelevant.

You say: 'How do you want me to tell you?' They say: 'Keep on talking.' Or, 'Tell us in the way we are accustomed to hearing it.' You say: 'Only primitive ideas can be expressed in medicine-man talk.' They say: 'Teach us the new language, then.' You say: 'Very well, this is just what I have been trying to do, but you don't try to keep the concepts in mind.' They say: 'Yes, people have told us we are hopeless before. We do indeed feel hopeless when faced by you. Is this not a good sign?' You say: 'There are degrees of hopelessness, and there are periods for feeling it and relationships of it' and they say: 'This is a strange new doctrine; it may not even be true. That is, it may be something different from what we have heard in the past.'

145

The Sociological Problem

There is no problem with the communication of the Teaching to new or old students which can be tackled, or even said to exist, until the sociological problem has been settled.

The sociological problems are connected with the point of view, set of thought, attitudes of the people towards any cult, creed, set of ideas, community, familiar or unfamiliar approach.

This series of problems was until recently in this culture considered to be psychological, but their roots lie deeper and the problems are more easily seen and can be tackled with relative ease within the sociological context.

The acceptance, rejection, uncertainty on the part of individuals and/or groups towards the projection of the Teaching all stem from attitudes already shaped by the native community of the individual or group. Prejudice against or for any approach 'from outside' or even 'from inside' exists as a symptom of adjustment or maladjustment with the social norms of the individual or group.

Hence, for example:

- If an individual or group is accustomed to deriving its social solace and advantages from an authoritarian system, such an individual or group will seek similar stimuli from the 'new' approach.
- If the individual has been trained, through his social environment, to regard things which he does not understand as sinister, he will bring this attitude to bear upon anything which he does not understand, and this will include, not be confined to, any manifestation of the Teaching.
- Only hopelessly ignorant individuals and institutions adopt the view that 'conditioning' people (giving them a new social outlook) is a part of teaching. It is a part of processing.
- Only social groupings masquerading as 'higher' ones (including those belonging to religions) imagine that the

induction of an emotional breakdown followed by acceptance of certain beliefs is 'conversion'. It is reprogramming.

Therefore any approach to individuals and/or groups, whatever their complexion, must take into account these social factors. It must, in addition, be able to present itself in such a manner as to communicate the fact that it is not concerned with the shallower factors which are truly social. It must illustrate, as clearly and as often as necessary, that what most people take to be 'spiritual' or 'higher' experiences are induced by methodologies which interfere with the customary social, chemical or electrical milieu of the individual.

If such information is unknown to the would-be student, he will have to assimilate it from current available sources of information. To 'teach' what can be learned elsewhere is a waste of time and effort.

The social problem being interposed between the student and the Teaching means inevitably that, in the absence of efficient information about the matter, the student will continue to study and attempt to employ higher developmental materials as a means to further his social adjustment.

Such usage is a travesty of what can be done, and causes the instructors of the teaching to become reduced to social integration engineers: a task which can equally well be performed by people with conventional knowledge in current cultures.

Such importance, however, does the social adjustment factor assume in the brain of the student, and so confused with 'higher' things is this factor in his thinking, that it is a very real problem and a test for him to allow himself to see that this situation exists.

Self-deception will cause him to oppose, deny or by-pass such a realisation. But it is a central fact of the Teaching that the Teaching itself is lost when it becomes a mere means of helping social adjustment. This is doubly true where there are adequate methods and facilities for social adjustment available already in the wider community, the 'host culture'.

It is well established that good social integration into the wider

147

community produces a better student of the Teaching. A person whose entire life 'is the Teaching' will be found to be a less capable student.

It is for this reason that the Teaching is addressed primarily to those who have acquired this social balance. When the Teaching takes any responsibility for existing groups which regard themselves as working with the Tradition, the first necessity is to determine whether the group and/or its individual members have an adequate wider social integration.

Diagnostically, it is easy to tell those whose 'dedication to the Teaching' is obsessional and implanted, and those who 'belong to the Teaching'. The former can think of little else, and are not able to cope with the ordinary world. The latter, being motivated by capacity and not conviction, are able to operate in all societies.

A vital, preliminary and basic requirement is to establish, with all necessary emphasis, the mistake in diagnosis whereby obsessionals are regarded by some institutions as praiseworthy and valuable individuals. They are, in fact, able only to give. Because of this, they are of the greatest value to an institution which is trying to make its own existence the object of its efforts. But the purpose of an institution developed by this Teaching is as an instrument, limited in scope and objectives: a tool which takes the minimum of energy, dedication and sacrifice from the individual and the group, and gives to them the maximum of instruction and potentiality.

Most human societies contain several, often well-loved social organisms which operate the self-perpetuating rhythm. Since these are generally organisations which command respect, and because their simple method (implanting and reinforcing enthusiasm) is the one with which the general run of people at all levels are familiar, it is necessary to make sure that the message as to the truth about institution and organism be made clearly known. People learn such basic things as this relatively slowly. To have recorded the argument is no proof of one's really understanding it.

It is in making the understanding permanent that the Teaching's courses and activities are of such great value.

The Age of the Fish

Exposure to teaching can improve man.

If it has made him worse, it is the absence of knowledge on the part of the teacher, who has exposed him to study materials before correcting the inner tendencies of the man. In this case, effectively, there has been no teaching and no learning.

If the man has been studying on his own, there has been no studying and no teaching.

Hope of improvement is not a substitute for capacity to improve.

Some who have studied and worked may learn more than those who have not. But all depends upon the time. It is as if you were to say: 'I have this fish, which means that my nutritional needs are provided for' without realising that the fish will be bad and poisonous in three days.

Remember, an eater must be a digester. To devour without a stomach is pleasant, may feel rewarding. Does it provide anything more?

The Faculty of Speech

The capacity to speak, considered so valuable in forming and maintaining communication between people, has been captured and dominated by another factor. It is now employed just as much to obscure facts, to influence judgment, and even to talk around matters so that they can be made to seem not to exist at all.

Were it not for the existence of other faculties, (even though these are not shared by everyone), man would have created a complete insanity, even out of his own world.

The Influence of a Teaching

The influence of a teaching is very little greater than the capacity of its pupils. When the pupils are mainly of low quality, teaching momentum is lost, and the pupils dominate what is taught. The teacher has to select, therefore, who can best benefit, for the sake of all.

The Emperor's Clothes

We all know the story of the Emperor's clothes: how, because he was foolish he imagined that he was wearing gorgeous robes, and how people imagined he was because they had been told that anyone who could not see them was an unworthy person. And we all know that it was a small child which broke the spell by crying: 'But the Emperor has no clothes on at all!'

So we all assume that there is a hope that someone will always be there to point out the absence of clothes . . .

But what happens when we find a situation in which it is the crowd which has no clothes on, and even the child thinks, as children often do, that it really is wearing its 'pretend' clothes?

The Unknown

In the face of something not understood by him, man will always tend to react with rejection and hostility – or else with uncritical acceptance.

The fact that he may do either of these things confuses many people. The result is that when a new situation arises, people range themselves into 'for', 'against', and the rest.

What should be realised is that the 'fors' and the 'againsts' are not in fact opposed. They are merely two varieties of organism reacting to the same stimulus in what is essentially the same way: with energy. Compared with what they imagine about the situation, their 'for' or 'against' stance may be unimportant.

The More You Think

The more you think about your teacher, the less you may learn.

The more you think you should not think about teachers, the less you may learn.

The more you think about yourself, or books, or against books, or for or against teaching materials and exercises, and the spreading of a teaching, the less you may learn.

The only way to learn is to keep these and other factors in constant balance.

This can only be achieved by practice under direction.

Some people at some times do not like practice.

Some people at some times do not like direction. This would be excellent if these attitudes were based on any real insight. Unfortunately, they are based on self-amusement. Wanting this and not wanting that are manifestations of lower aspiration, and as such not genuine enough to bear the weight of study.

The Eighth Day

Circumstances have overtaken man. His old languages are not sufficient to describe what is happening, and what is about to happen. To think in terms of a millennium or such tame concepts as 'the eleventh hour' is ridiculous.

Better that he should realise that he is in an era which might be more accurately described as the 'eighth day of the week'.

The Village

To escape from being made into something mechanical, you have to see the customs and the rightness of the village, the systems and the coherence of the world outside it, and the logic and the processes of the greater world.

The Greed of Generosity

Don't you see how people use your greed?

They only have to say: 'Do not be greedy' for you to develop a greed for generosity.

Do you imagine that a greed for generosity is not a greed, with all its destructive aspects?

When are you going to register that anyone who develops greed in the belief that he is stimulating generosity is more likely to be ignorant than evil, and that ignorance is what greed feeds off?

152

You have all the data with which to register this: because its perception does not come into some metaphysical domain. It should have become common knowledge and useful information ages ago, like how to tell the time on a clock.

The Hidden Current in Man

All living organisms are connected by a normally invisible force.

All communities have this force in them, and they themselves become organisms.

All the human communities may be viewed and treated as one organism.

In this sense there is no difference between those who are clinically alive, those who are 'dead', those who are here, those who are there.

There is another, vital, range of relationships.

Instinctively trying to find, or to 'prove' this, man still does some very stupid things.

The increasing of sensitivity of the individual and the total organism's perceptions can transform the individuals and the organism alike – constructively, destructively or by mutation.

The Value of Opinion

Opinion is simultaneously one of the best and the worst things we have. If your opinion is right, all is well. If it is wrong, you may be lost.

The weakness of the opinion-structure lies in the assumption that there is always someone or something available who will help one to change or modify opinion.

Because people are not conscious of the flimsy or transitory basis of most opinion, they over-value it.

Most opinion is used as a substitute for knowledge. If opinion is over-strong, being cruder than knowledge, it blocks the action of knowledge.

The Values of Alchemy

A value to us of the alchemical formulation is to note the emphasis placed on the right materials, the right treatments, and the right conditions. These might be called the essence of alchemy, whether of the chemical or 'spiritual' variety.

In the latter form, of course, alchemy preserved the teaching of specialisation in people, places and processes which had been banished by institutional religion at the point where the latter decided that it would 'popularise' itself.

The price which such simplified religion has had to pay, of course, is that since it has not managed to supply the fulfilment sought by its practitioners, it has had to retreat further and further into sophistries or dogmatics, trying to preserve its position.

'Time, place and people' is, as a consequence, coming back into its own: but regarded as a theory for heretics.

The Cycle of Human Thought

There is a cycle in human thought. Note this characteristic in it:

People are at first hostile to what they imagine is 'new', even when it is only the current application of the most ancient. Next they adjust to a state of support for the 'new', which now becomes the 'received, attested' doctrine or practice.

By now it has coalesced. Its most energetic supporters are, at this stage, the people who want 'no change'. They are the overtly important people. In fact, though prominent, they are functionally unimportant. Others carry on the evolutionary task.

The stage becomes set at this point for a recrudescence of the teaching. Those who are to be its most implacable enemies are the enthusiasts who would, in earlier stages, have been martyrs for the 'new form'.

The only variants in this pattern are in the time-scale. Some enterprises in thought decay or atrophy faster than others.

No terrestrial organisation or individual can resist the decline-cycle of thought. This is why those who know set up institutions only designed for a limited effective life.

The Use of Direct Language

I talk in direct language partly because it serves the purpose of communication. Also because traditional terminology coined for higher studies has been usurped by shallow thinkers, and its communication value thereby reduced. More advanced phraseology has become loaded with paltry associations.

The main opposition to direct language is to be found today among those who have interests which might be imperilled by its use. Their version, of course, is 'this is crudity, not spirituality, not higher'.

Make your choice.

The Rewards of Virtue

Virtue is rewarded in a closed system, a social system, where certain thoughts and actions are treated as good, and others as bad.

Everyday experience can teach anyone that this kind of classification holds good only in the short run and in the narrow field. Even within short runs and in some areas of life, as the proverb has it, 'circumstances alter cases'.

To attempt to assume that any virtue-vice system has more than a very limited potential, however useful it is within those limitations, leads inevitably to a stunting of understanding, accompanied by dishonesty of thought. We all know how crooked are the thinkers who believe that all life can be simplified to certain dogmas. In order to conceal the fact that the reverse is true, or in order to be able to maintain superficial plausibility for their argument, they are forced first into impossible sophistries. Secondarily, they seek to live in or operate closed societies.

But the qualifications which the attempted practice of virtues bestow are a very different matter. In the course of developing a 'virtue', a person always has to acquire discipline, restraint, patience, truthfulness. These are all efficiency capacities which have inestimably higher value than the virtues which were in fact frameworks to enable these exercises to take place.

If, for instance, a person tries to tell the truth, this is regarded as a virtue. If he is so truthful as to say that he cannot be sure what truth is, he is exercising a capacity. But closed systems which purport to concentrate upon truth will not allow the process to develop. Their answer is not to say: 'Good, you are now really trying to be truthful.' Instead they say: 'If you knew truth you would know that *our* dogma is true;' or else: 'You do not yet know truth. Practise such-and-such cathartic thoughts or actions until you believe in us or become a disbeliever.'

The Third System

There are three convenient stages of human growth: infancy, adolescence and adulthood, which provide us with an adequate comparison standard for three stages of community development.

In the first, visible crudity and destructivity is evident. This is childhood, equivalent to the conquest of territory in the community's life.

The second is characterised by intense emotion, mental activity and insistence upon objectives. Its equivalent is the 'derivative baronial' phase. Instead of conquering national territories, its spread is in domination of the brain (propaganda and publicity) and in energy concentration – commercial and industrial empires.

Communities of all social, political and economic labels operate these systems.

The third type, which is the final phase, and the most effective and constructive, is an organisation which can contribute in so many fields that it cannot be singled out as an enemy, or even as a friend, for its members come from every section of every community. By providing positive and demonstrable gains in such diverse fields as literature, commerce, art, science, psychology and human thought and social relations, it penetrates throughout the interstices of the existing relatively crude systems.

In order to do this, such an entity must be directed by people who understand it as well as the baron understands war, or the tycoon understands business. There are not many such men and women, but they already exist.

This development has been foreshadowed by the attempts of nations, companies and systems to offer their members a wide variety of advantages. But they have all failed because they cannot control their people (control is the wrong method, but they depend upon it) and because they have not been able to supply the creative quota of varied developments

157

which alone could make their organism viable in the new system.

So they have to be content with the new peasantry. Remember: a peasantry is not a community of impoverished people ruled by rich ones. A peasantry is a community, national or international, which is 'owned': which has its beliefs engineered by propaganda, and its material activities and its diversions provided for it to someone's gain.

Recognise yourself?

The Defeatist Culture

Overlapping all the differences of various current human cultures is the invisible 'defeatist culture', with common denominators among all peoples.

A child learns from its parents and those adults who surround it. It learns not only the positive injunctions of problem-solving which its elders think they are teaching it. In addition it is learning to emulate the parents; and it emulates their defeatism. This includes their rationalisations of why they do not attempt certain tasks, why they are 'too tired', or such-and-such an effort is not 'worthwhile'.

This is true in the individual as it is in society. Nobody on record had run a four-minute mile before someone did it. After that, because the unspoken taboo had been beaten, it became more and more common. A similar process takes place in children learning, perhaps sometimes without words, not to make a certain effort, an effort of will or of experiment.

The innocent Sudanese warrior who told me that his compatriots who broke the British Square at Omdurman did so 'because they did not know it was impossible', could have been talking about the lack of unspoken conditioning in their upbringing.

158

The human culture, in spite of prizing in some of its manifestations positive action and belief in the human being, incarnates and passes on defeatism and negativity as a sort of contact-disease. The 'pool of infection' as it would be called if there were a bacterium at the bottom of it, is coterminous with mankind itself.

It is largely because this has not been realised on a wide enough scale that nothing is done about it. In apparently progressive cultures it is believed that any traumatic disabilities occasioned by the behaviour of the parents can be 'engineered' out of the children by psychotherapists. But the practitioners themselves are not tested for the presence of cultural negatives. Furthermore, when the child is returned to his environment there is no established way to make sure that he will not be reinfected.

Unusual Experiences

While there are many people who have partial or imagined 'higher experiences', and who as a result imagine that they are receiving mystical communications, there is another problem, too.

There are quite a number of highly rational people who, on experiencing genuine special forms of thought, tell nobody at all, for fear of being laughed at, or because they do not want to become cranks, or even, as some had put it to me, because they fear that they may be insane.

At present the only quasi-respectable manner in which such people may try to follow up these experiences is through what is currently called 'ESP'. But their faculties are not capable of verification by ESP-related doctrines.

159

What Cannot be Answered

I have circulated a lot of letters which I have written, because it has been felt that they are of interest, and we have received a very large number of appreciations as a result.

It may now be of interest to see a letter typical of the kind which I *cannot* answer. This is an extremely common type of letter; dozens of them, every week, contain one or more of the phrases which distinguish this one:

> 'I want to integrate myself with the real world; to develop my potential, to find that which is missing in my life. To see and feel things more objectively, I will have to detach myself from the background which has been imposed upon me by my country, my parents, my culture. I feel that we have all left the Natural Order, and we must re-enter it . . . I seek a spiritualising of the material, and an improving of the restrictive life in which I find myself . . .'

This incoherence, when you come to meet the people who write like this, always masks an over-development of the virtues which Sufi activity seeks to reduce, and a near-absence of those things which Sufi action seeks to develop . . .

This is the realm of real study and real development. In the meantime, in the current coin of garbledom, write or talk like my correspondent above, and you will please and impress him, or her; even when you are only feeding back to him his own incoherencies, lightly paraphrased.

If you don't believe this, you are welcome to try, for not only will nobody try to prevent you, but you will make many more friends – if you can stand them. If you *can* stand them, you should have been talking like this all along.

When 'This is not the Time' does not have to mean 'I am Busy'

One can illustrate extremely important facts by the use of apparently trite examples. So banal are such incidents, moreover, that they often escape completely unnoticed by observers.

Here is one:

A young man came to see me and said: 'I want to talk to you about learning from you.'

I said: 'This is not the time.'

He said: 'You are busy, are you?'

I said: 'This is not the time.'

He said: 'You haven't got time, then?'

I said: 'I did not say that I hadn't got the time.'

He said: 'Why don't you say that you're busy, and we can leave it at that?'

This shows that he was in a condition of mind in which he could only accept that I was busy, and had no time for him. He was capable of listening to the words 'This is not the time', but (like most people) his mind was 'programmed' to accept only the interpretation of what I had said that he himself was providing.

This gave him an opportunity of thinking to himself, or saying to others: 'He would have talked to me, but he did not have the time.'

So he went away without any gain at all. If he had bothered to think over the phrase: 'This is not the time,' he would at least have been able to say to himself: 'He claims that this was not the time. This may mean that there might be another, more suitable time. Such a time is not necessarily connected with whether a person is busy or not.'

He might have learned. Or he might have found the time contention too unacceptable, or absurd. But, as he was, he could not get past the answer 'too busy' which he had brought with him.

Walking

People say: 'Do not try to run before you can walk.'

They do not say: 'Do not try to walk before you can crawl', simply because such advice would have to be given to a child which, at that age, would not be able to understand words.

But when we are dealing with literate adults, who understand the words, and we have to say the equivalent of 'Do not try to walk before you can crawl', all we get is a loss of interest or else – worse – a depressed audience.

Why should it be regarded as an attack, or an outburst, if one speaks descriptively? Probably because the listener is not hearing the meaning, nor yet the tone of voice. He is hearing the words echoing through some hostility within himself.

I have never learned anything through being what is generally imagined to be acquiescent. Only by being what I can only call 'transparent'.

World of their Own

It is often said, and almost as often seen, that those who imagine that they are scholars 'live in a world of their own'.

How little it is noticed, though, that this world of their own is not the world of whoever or whatever they are supposed to be studying.

Note this and you will not be surprised at the otherwise amazing imaginings of the armchair scholar.

Words and Violence

First, man had no words. Then he learned to use words instead of physical violence.

Now he uses words to lead him into violence. He has to unlearn the misuse of words. He has to learn the use of the physical and of words. This is the creature which is called man.

Will Travel

There is a pseudo-advertisement in American folklore: 'Have gun, will travel'.

A more general, unspoken, motto of the human race is:

'Have pessimism, laziness, superficiality: *will* use them'.

And if you have these things, be sure of another fact: just as surely as other people will use your possessions if they can, they will use you through your proclivities, because they certainly can.

Why People follow lesser Aims

Basically, people are interested in history because something in them wants to know about their own origins, present state and possible destiny. People are interested in the lives of others because something within them is asking for information about their own lives and nature.

These pursuits, therefore, are secondary manifestations, stemming from a great internal need. Because the real need cannot be fulfilled by low-level efforts, an individual may not be able to stop reading biography; he may not be able to stop studying history. This is because he has not arrived at his goal.

It is for such reasons that Sanai and Rumi and other Sufis have called man's activities, however serious he thinks them to be, 'a game'. A game is a diversionary equivalence of something. Games are pleasant, even useful. They are horrors if they are thought to be real life, but not games.

Most organised religion, and all experimental religion, is a game. We do not talk much to people who are engaged in these games, because to do so would be to take part in their games, and make us neglectful of the origin and destiny of man.

Why not tell Me?

People ask: 'Why not tell me at once whether I am acceptable for teaching or not?' Or, 'How long will I have to study?'

The answer is extraordinarily simple. Take this parallel. If, as an employer, you say to a new recruit: 'You are going to become the head of this department eventually,' you will alter the condition of his mind. He might well have become head of the department in due time, starting from the state in which you found him. But once you have told him, his attitude may become such as to prevent him from achieving this aim.

As soon as anyone is told anything, he is not the same as he was before he was told it. In order to help the man become head of the department, you may have to tell him something completely different.

That is why we say: 'I cannot tell you what you want to know – only what you *need* to know.'

164

In order to understand how one factor can completely alter a whole situation, study our tales and stories. This will help to fix the understanding effectively in your mind.

Working within Limitations

All work takes place within limitations – all work, that is, which can be thought of or described in the ordinary way. In order to do anything, you have to have the means to do it – the facilities of materials, people, possibilities of time and place. You also have to accommodate the work within a framework, within limitations. If you want, for example, to furnish a room, you are working within the limitations of that room. Your objective is to do something within the possibilities of the situation. The limitations are another word here for your obedience to something. You want to heat a room. The room has certain dimensions, a certain volume. In providing heat for it, you are subordinating yourself to its requirements – 'obeying' the room, which says, 'in order to heat this space, you must have so much coal, electricity, gas'.

All human life with which we are concerned is a matter of doing the best within limitations. Limitations are the commanding elements which we 'serve'. The fact that we pretend that we do not serve our environment does not alter anything. Even in 'overcoming obstacles' you are serving those obstacles by recognising them and taking them into account. You cannot be indifferent to them. Man's 'conquest' of space is carried out within the restrictions imposed by his environment. He designs spacecraft in accordance with the conditions which they have to meet, not to *replace* these conditions. In so doing, he is subordinating himself to an order which he already finds fixed for him.

165

In our work, too, he serves the work, abiding by the conditions which it brings to him. Initially, at least, he is in a condition of service, and he must recognise it.

What Self-Examination is

Keep a journal. Write daily about the things that happen to you or strike you as significant. Start studying it after a lapse of time and see how your behaviour was partly due to a desire for self-inflation. Also try to see what useful or interesting concomitants there were to each event.

Why no No-Book Teaching?

We accept everyone who wants to study without books, providing only that such people have reached the stage where they cannot learn anything from books. If, therefore, you ask no question not answered in books, you can study with us in the bookless area. Providing that you perform no actions which are seen from books to be superficial (and therefore capable of being corrected through book-information), we will teach you in the bookless manner. We are, in fact, always actively looking for people who *can* study in this manner. They are hard to find. Instead, of course, there are many thousands, probably millions even, who *want* to study in this manner.

Warming Water

A problem of launching a fresh phase in the teaching is found whenever we project higher ideas into a community which is ready for them but which is attached to the lower, preparatory ideas.

You might put it this way:

If water is warm, and has been cold, it might regard its highest aim as staying warm and not getting cold. Any cold water would be looked upon as bad and all warm water as good, while water-in-between would be considered as in a state of struggle, to avoid coldness and achieve heat.

However if the possibility is that 'warm' is a stage on the way to 'hot', the whole picture shifts, and the emphasis has to be given differently.

With our kind of water, you cannot simply increase the heat. We are in a situation where the water may have to be transferred into another vessel for the warming process to continue further with any possibility of success. We are dealing with people, not water.

People in most present-day cultures regard certain principles and certain qualities as not only essential for the continuance of their communities, but also as something like talismans, which will work if they are used in the right way or energetically enough.

The fact is that this is primitive thinking.

Dedication, honesty, effort, eagerness and so on are qualities which prepare for higher efforts, higher understanding, greater being. They do not produce any of these things automatically if pushed to their limits. In fact, when pushed to their limits, they produce a static situation, in the person and in the group.

These qualities are essential in social and community areas. Their results, not they themselves, are vital for further steps.

Why People Escape Learning

Modern man, like the primitive variety, is trained (far more than he suspects) to identify things by means of labels.

The result is like a trained dog which would bark at anything that looks like an enemy, and yet eat a leg of lamb injected with arsenic, placed in his way by a burglar.

Some of the most important higher teaching, therefore, is not identifiable by such people as being in the realm of transcendent studies at all.

It is no wonder that they are confused.

This is why it is stated: 'You may need information before you need knowledge.'

Ways to Understand the Teaching

People frequently bemoan their inability to understand the Teaching, or this or that part of the Teaching.

Their problem is in reality simple: it is *they* who make it complicated.

These are the two major complications which these people introduce, and which can be resolved only by the right kind of contact with a real Sufi group:

1. You must know whether a given thing is comprehensible at your level, and whether you are trying to understand something out of due phase and relevancy. To assume that you should always be able to understand everything without the preparation necessary for it is an absurdity.

2. You could understand almost infinitely more than you are at present capable of understanding if you would

only surrender your taste for minor satisfactions or bring this taste under control. By this I mean that man has to be able to detach from greed for knowledge, greed for such things as attention by others, greed for being thought something or somebody. Man must detach, if he is a real student, from playing psychotherapeutic or social games and calling these 'trying to learn', or 'associating with people of wisdom', or 'performing initiatory rituals'. Students can start to understand esoteric matters when they stop feeding their superficial 'selves' omnivorously with superficial materials and calling them significant ones. People can start to learn when they are willing to accept the possibility that the very evidences of 'something higher' in themselves may in fact not be reliable, and may even be screening them from real perceptions.

If you want to learn, and not just to play at it, start to conceive the possibility that the foregoing remarks may be true, and could be as reliable as, or more reliable than, the simplifications of the systems with which you are familiar.

Virtuality

What is the use of a ruby in a mine?

It is, functionally, a virtuality.

The difference between an unused ruby and a man is that when the ruby is brought out it can be used, after polishing. The man, however, who thinks that he knows something and does not put that knowledge into action does not really know at all. If he did, he would be impelled to act.

Views on Incongruity

Spend a little time thinking about incongruity; about deliberate incongruity.

First consider the little-recognised fact that exposure to deliberate incongruity enables one to become used to new and unfamiliar things rapidly. New things often seem incongruous, however important they ultimately prove to be. The capacity to see beyond incongruity can be equal to the ability to adjust.

Second, realise that incongruity, if you can become accustomed to encountering it, may stimulate your inner senses, and help them to work on a higher level. Most people do not allow themselves to face incongruity when it appears at random in their lives. They avoid it and thus rob themselves of the stimulating effect which it can have.

Remember that incongruity causes the useless man annoyance, whether it is really the outward face of something useful or not. Extreme cases of this are figures of fun. But what about the millions of cases where we refuse to see something useful just because we cannot stand the untidiness which it seems to show?

Incongruity, too, causes the covetous to be impressed by it. This is not the fault of the incongruity, but the fault of the covetous. Because of this as much as for any other reason, people have been exhorted to shun covetousness.

People whose behaviour, words or outward aspect are incongruous with their surroundings may soon become surrounded by others who merely value this incongruity. This factor, operating with such regularity as to be equal to a rule or law, is observable by anyone who is not in the grip of a contrary imagination.

Incongruity, there, could be used as a means to an end.

In the past, many people have regarded incongruity itself as a manifestation of inner qualities. Its presence, however, is no guarantee of that. Such people have inferred a fact from its occasional manifestation.

When and Where?

For more than a thousand years, Sufi thinkers have pointed out such facts as these:

> 'Scholastics think in such a stilted manner that they will never allow themselves to understand the Sufi concepts, and are instead obsessed by attribution and chronology.'

When they hear or read such words, scholars say: 'Yes, yes, that may be; but what interests us is who said it first, and when was it said?'

What have you Got?

When a man thinks that he has everything, he may be able to gain what he really needs.

When a man thinks he has something, he has nothing at all.

When a man thinks that he has nothing, he may be able to get something.

When he thinks that he must give, he must not try. When he thinks that he cannot give, giving – and gaining – are coming closer to him.

Withdrawing from the World

The inner work is done in the ordinary world – but it cannot be done by anyone who is merely attracted by this idea, and who cannot really withdraw from the world, as well as participate in it.

171

Withdrawal from the world is useless to those who are attracted by withdrawal and solitude.

There are hardly any real monks. These have to be people who are equally at home in solitude and in company.

Studies and Exercises as Variables

You may forbid a child to cross the road. You make it hold your hand. You might call this a ritual and an exercise.

But a time comes when what you have imposed as a safety-device and training has to be replaced (because of the growth of understanding in the infant) by a different, even seemingly contradictory, set of rules:

'Now cross the road alone.'

So it is with studies and exercises in a real school.

The reverse is true in sterile traditionalist systems of all kinds.

Familiar religions and systems of thought come into the latter category.

More real teaching is preserved – and applied – in fields unrecognised by the shallow as 'esoteric' than any outsider even suspects.

Technology

Q: *Is there any analogy between the use and failure to use technology and the fact that Sufi studies have been cultivated by some peoples and neglected by others?*

A: The analogy is indeed close. Briefly, we can say that in the East certain ways to knowledge have been used as a specialisation, while in the West different priorities have been uppermost in people's minds. Roughly speaking, too, in the West emotion has been used as the fuel for the endeavour, while in the East more attention has been given to the drawbacks of emotion in the enterprise. Spiritual activity in both areas has been patchy. A paper by Dr. Jean Gimpel, an eminent medieval historian, has highlighted the amazingly random development of technology in the world in the past, and gives us real analogies with the same sort of phenomenon in Sufi study and application.

He noted that the camshaft was known in Alexandria very early on, but was not used in Europe until something like a thousand and a half years later! It never reached Bangladesh at all: and was recently exhibited there to simple country people, who readily understood its operation and how it could help them today. Again, the Archimedes Screw, dating from the third century BC, is now in use in the new English town of Thamesmead, for draining marshes.

Ancient and 'appropriate' technology – as distinct from elaborate and highly industrial technology – has uses both in the West and in the Third World. Similarly, we have reintroduced Sufic ideas and developments in the East and West where they have been greeted with quite unnecessary amazement, probably due to the unconscious assumptions that everything that is not in use is no use, and that if something was of use it would have been manifested through the immensely complicated and cumbersome structures which pass for advanced technology in the one field and human thought in the other.

Imitation in Techniques

It would be of less moment if imitation were the only misuse of vital human techniques. Unfortunately, the conscious performance and misapplication of prayer and exercise and observances, mental and physical, has frequently happened and it continues.

The more obvious hazards and products of such behaviour are, in fact, the least dangerous of those which are present in such mimetic situations.

Observances without specific knowledge are like taking the hydrogen without the oxygen and hoping for water, or sodium instead of sodium chloride, which latter makes salt. Don't do it.

Infantile Desires

The more advanced and mature man becomes in intellect or in material organisation, the more insistent become his infantile demands. He wants what he wants, when he wants it, and loses the sense of needs and wants being distinct.

Everyone wants stimuli, exercises, meetings and so on in philosophical areas. What proportion of people want what comes before: the preparation which makes sense out of experience, and which can make permanent the results of experience?

Ignorance and Hate

Some of the greatest damage to man is done through ignorance.

As soon as you know this, you cannot hate.

When the 'worst' people are ignorant, not malicious, how can you dislike them, or hate them, or hate the lesser malefactors, those who are deliberately destructive?

The only thing that should be hated is hatred.

Information and Experiences

If you have certain kinds of information, you may not need experience.

If you have experience, you can obtain information.

But if you have certain kinds of information alone, and it has not been made effective, you may need experience to unlock it.

As in a recipe, people need information at certain times, experience at others. It is impossible to pronounce for everyone, once and for all. Therefore the question as to who needs what and when, depends upon real people, real situations – not upon theoretical ones which can be enunciated as laws.

Imagination versus Understanding

Understanding the verbal form of a higher teaching expression may or may not be necessary for a person at any given moment. The maximum required of him may be that he familiarise himself with certain materials.

What *is* necessary is that when he has understanding it should be the right kind. There is no certainty that he can be brought from imaginative 'understanding' into true realisation of meaning.

It is characteristic of the imagined understanding that the victim, convinced that he 'understands', has effectively blocked his own way to knowledge.

'I do not need it,' he says, 'because I already have it.'

Information and Knowledge

You may need information, basic or advanced – certainly appropriate – when you can only think that you need higher consciousness.

Don't laugh at the woman who said to me the other day:

'If I don't get higher consciousness before I die, I'll be *so* mad,' because you may be the same as her, just using different words.

Everyone must move phase by phase.

Unless a person's needs have been determined, his mere *wants* are of no account.

Unless he is aware of his needs, his desires will seem – but only seem – to be the most important thing to him.

Ideology's Effect

Ideology, as ordinarily active, drives people into absurd forms of thought and behaviour. Beware of it, because it attempts to apply mechanical concepts to human development.

In the end, ideology is compelled to indoctrinate, condition and do violence to human minds, when its predictions are about to be revealed as unreliable.

Ideological thinking is, however, self-destructive in the long run.

Look at the history and fate of all communities and individuals operated on an ideological basis.

The tragedy is that although the ideology will in the end defeat itself, it may be too late for you to benefit.

Importation of Technique

In technological and scientific experience bizarre behaviour on the part of people with a strong local culture often produces amusing situations.

An example is the widespread habit, often reported in recent years, of people in Africa and Asia submitting to vaccinations and then having them 'blessed' by a practitioner of their local medicine. It is believed that this ratification by their own authority-figure will remove dangers and make really effective the new technique.

The same process, as amusing and as useless, is visible to the experienced observer of unknown techniques imported into the West from the East. A series of ideas or practices which may depend for their efficacy upon a certain kind of usage, are modified sometimes out of recognition, sometimes out of function.

In religious usage, for instance, what was originally an exercise may become a prayer. Because people were known to press their hands together, all prayers, almost, are accompanied by this gesture, which is, in ancient tradition, a part of something else. References to similar instances could be multiplied to almost any extent.

Then there is another kind of importation: where physical, psychological and other techniques are literally 'lifted' from the culture for which they were prescribed, and imported, then practised, in communities which cannot benefit functionally from them. At most these patterns train, 'condition', people to feel a sense that something significant is connected with them. It may be, it may not be. All will depend upon the specific case.

I Can Teach You

If you can be taught, I can certainly teach you.

But whether I can do it on your terms – that is the uncertainty. Learning is the reverse of choosing your own time, place and manner of instruction – and your own vacations.

Under these circumstances, entertainment and social activity which are believed to be study can take place. They can even *feel* like study.

Never, however, under these circumstances, can teaching and learning in our field take place.

In this field, as in more conventional education, the institution must be allowed to stipulate the course.

It must also be allowed to choose the pupil. It is concerned, too, about how the student employs his energies.

'I did not come here to be Insulted!'

There was a man here the other day who did not like the way he was spoken to.

His reaction, in his words, was to say: 'I did not come here to be insulted!' I almost felt like saying: 'Oh, where do you usually go?'

What he had not allowed himself to see, but what was more than evident to the other people present, was that he could very well have been described as having come exactly for that.

If you go up to an electric socket, place your finger in it, and are thrown across the room, the appropriate remark is not: 'I did not come here for an electric shock!'

People can only be insulted if they decide – consciously or otherwise – to be insulted. An insult is not an objective thing, like a piece of rock. If you call some men women, they will be insulted; if you call women men, some of the women will feel themselves insulted. And so it is with a million other things.

What is more to the point is that people who have this kind of reaction mechanism – and, in the culture in which we are living, people who have not absorbed enough of the culture's information about neurosis, about conditioning, about attention-desire and the annoyance caused by its frustration – all such people are to us like people who have not learnt the alphabet yet want to become writers. There is a small formality first: you have to be capable of understanding more than you do at present. And it is not necessarily *our* duty to teach you these elementary things. We may have the time, we may not. Learning the alphabet may be a step towards becoming a great writer. But at the level of learning the alphabet, its connection with literature is hardly to be dignified with long words to describe it. First things first. First things may be absolutely necessary. They are not, however, to be looked at as being of a higher nature thereby.

Information and Expectation

Q: *Two statements which seem to be repeated a lot are that we need information before we need knowledge; and that truly higher learning is generally 'contrary to expectation'. I have difficulty in understanding these thoughts.*

A: I can easily answer both in three simple examples:

1. You need the information that: many true teachers do not look like what you imagine teachers to be. Their appearance will therefore be contrary to your expectation. This expectation is based upon your

179

imagination, upon cultural transmission or upon other people's pictures.

2. You need the information that: you are surrounded by teaching materials which you would never dream to be such, because they are not associated in your brain with teaching materials. Hence when you do have them pointed out to you, they appear to be 'contrary to expectation'.

3. You tend to expect teachings to be put in a manner similar to the way in which higher teachings have been put in the past. You imagine that ancient teachings, in their traditionalistic form, are somehow superior to the same thing put in today's terms. You need information about this. If your expectation is that you may be able to torture concealed meanings, say, out of ancient texts, when you come across the manner of true contemporary learning, it will be 'contrary to expectation'.

Judgement

Human analysis systems are at an interesting point. Psychologists have shown that one cannot rely upon what people believe to be the causes for their behaviour.

Comparison of the psychologists' work shows that various schools will put up equally persuasive but mutually exclusive reasons for human behaviour, cancelling one another out.

What remains to be done is to find the real reasons for human behaviour: something which the patient has been taught he cannot do, the psychologist has shown he cannot prove.

The time will have to come when a third manner of determining human behavioural origins will be rediscovered. The only problem about this is that it will involve a return to concepts which current thinking finds difficult to accept.

Keeping On

People are always asking me to tell them how to keep on keeping on.

But if persistence were not already their main characteristic, they wouldn't keep on about it, would they?

Hardly anyone knows what he really needs.

That is why he will insist on being given what he imagines he needs.

Even if he gets that, you will notice, he imagines that he has not got it.

Someone has to step back to get perspective on this, because the world is littered with two kinds of exhausted people: those who try to get what they imagine they need, and those who have been worn out trying to give it to them.

Knowledge and Behaviour

'Which is better: knowledge or good behaviour?'

We might answer with usefulness: 'If you have knowledge, you do not need behaviour.'

The fact is that these two things are not alternatives. Behaviour may be a substitute for knowledge, because the person 'behaving' does not know what else to do.

Behaviour, of course, is never really good nor bad: it is only comparatively so.

If you have knowledge, you have *right* behaviour.

Right behaviour in any situation may or may not be entirely different in appearance from either 'good' or 'bad' behaviour.

SECTION VI

Liking and Disliking

First comes the real reason for liking or disliking.

Then comes the exposure to the person or thing liked or disliked.

Finally comes the supposed reason for liking or disliking.

Only when you know the three elements do you know what is really happening.

The fact that most people know these facts theoretically makes it all the worse that hardly anyone applies this knowledge either to himself or to his observation of what others are really doing.

Psychological theoreticians have done us little service in pointing out the way things work in this regard; because they have enabled people to say, airily, 'Oh, yes, I know all that!'

The grave defect has been not to devise and operate situational frameworks in which awareness of the mechanism is unavoidable.

Labels and Ancestry

People quibble a great deal about ancestry.

But what is the difference, in effect, between pride in political, literary or spiritual 'ancestry' and pride in physical descent?

It may sound different, because we are told that it is; but when we examine those who say 'my blood is superior', and those who say, 'my system is better', we rarely find as many differences between them as we do similarities. Have you ever thought about that? And you don't need my word for it – do your own research.

People claim that the difference is that you can change your beliefs but not your blood. But what does it matter whether there is or can be a change when the product is so generally useless?

Listen

Listen to a friend, and hear a distorted idea of yourself.
Listen to your enemy, and also hear something distorted.
Friendship is to help us survive and to strengthen us.
Opposition makes us stronger.

When we have survived and have been strengthened – there
is another version than that of the friend or of the enemy.

This is the Higher Vision.
The value of the Dwelling lies in the Dweller.

Last Resort

In some countries there are forms of folk-medicine which have,
as is well known, deteriorated. The result is that procedures
which were initiated for one ailment are thought efficacious for
all of them, and they only make things worse when applied.
Small quantities of stimulant substances, which might have
helped the system to increase its effectiveness in overcoming
an illness, are applied in such quantities as to weaken the body.
Cauterization, useful for killing bacteria in certain cases, is so
extensively used – and without the additional caution of
hygiene – that wounds are caused which suppurate. There is
also an admixture of magical or otherwise ineffective 'cures'
which have been amalgamated into the body of supposed
knowledge, which are equally bad, or even worse.

Almost exactly the same sort of thing has happened in what
are called spiritual studies, especially in the West and in many
circles in the East. Exercises designed for one person are given
to another; teachings are mixed up and applied like ignorant

cauteries. When people who have been exposed to several 'schools', 'systems', 'teachers' and so on, are interviewed, however, their version is, more often than not, 'all these things have helped me and deepened my interior life' . . .

Look at Me

People constantly approach me to see whether I will help them develop themselves. When I tell them that I have recorded their desires and that I will do what I can, they are not satisfied. They continue to call, to write letters and make telephone calls. They imagine problems, make all kinds of excuses to see me.

When this happens I say:

'If you believe that I am doing my job, then you should not be here unless I ask you.

'If you believe that I am not doing my job, you should have nothing to do with me.'

Nothing can be done for such people until they realise that we are not running a business from which they can obtain emotional stimulus at will.

We have no duty towards such people when they are seeking attention and emotional satisfactions, not knowledge and ability.

When you stop listening to what people say and observe what they are doing, you will be able to see what they really want. When they observe their own behaviour, they can correct it.

187

Metaphor of the Kaleidoscope

Metaphors are most useful for fixing, for a time, in the mind, concepts which otherwise have too fleeting a life to be of practical use.

When people use metaphors to illustrate situations and induce others to take them literally, or take them too far, we get the fossilisation of doctrine and consequent loss of understanding.

If I say, for example: 'Man is like the sea, with his emotions ebbing and flowing' I have to qualify this and harvest the value of the metaphor as soon as possible. The alternative is that people might start to imagine that man is like the sea in a far-reaching and complicated analogical system. They then tend to spend their time looking for as many correspondences as possible between man and the sea.

Our use of metaphors is designed to supply the minimum impression. The hearer must not try to elaborate it too far.

I am now going to refer to the situation of man and his perceptions as if he were someone looking at objects through a kaleidoscope. He can see colour, form, pattern. These factors operate consistently, giving him an impression that visual perception is always the same, and that it is always – what you can see through a kaleidoscope.

A similar situation obtains with human beings in the ordinary state. Their ordinary perceptions are subject to a restriction comparable to the looking through a kaleidoscope.

Many have suspected this, and as a result have tried, by drugs and exercises, to alter their perceptions. Few have succeeded, because they do not understand the nature of the systematic 'warp' which disables them. In consequence they alter perception inefficiently, incorrectly, uselessly.

The majority of people, of course, prefer to continue seeing the comfortingly consistent kaleidoscope-images, and they regard the experimenters as stupid or irrelevant. They are right in the majority of cases in their assessment of the experimenters, but for the wrong reasons. They think that alteration of

188

perception is not to be attempted because it is always useless. They have made the characteristic mistake of imagining that because a thing does not work if it is attempted in one way, it will never work. This is like saying: 'You cannot cross the ocean because boats made of sponge always sink.'

This reaction is standard where technical information is lacking.

The experimenters, on the other hand, make another characteristic mistake: they glamourise and mysticise their effort. In the absence of technical information, they believe that what they are attempting is supernatural. They are like the people who say: 'Making fire is an esoteric activity, and I must always attempt it in a ritualistic and emotional manner.'

They go further, and fuel their desire for mysticism from a domain where it does not exist. They say, in effect: 'If firemaking is not derived from the fire-god, I don't want any part of it.'

Some, however, are almost worse when they say: 'We don't believe that firemaking can be reduced to such mundane terms as friction and organic fuels. People who tell you so are lying.'

A woman, here in the twentieth century, belonging to one of the major current religious persuasions, actually said: 'If man ever goes to the Moon, the bottom will have fallen out of my religion.'

We are concerned with knowledge. If knowledge is incompatible with religion, we are without any doubt not engaged upon the same area of interest and effort as those who think that it is.

To us there can never be any question that there is a striking and inescapable difference between the 'religion' that consists in appealing to primitive and infantile hopes and fears, and the enterprise which requires for its fulfilment information, knowledge, experience.

We postulate the existence of the kaleidoscope, true enough: because something must be postulated before it can be investigated.

But our main object is its experiential verification.

Following this purpose, we stipulate certain conditions of

189

study, and we have little time for people who want to imagine things or to study along lines which, according to us, are atavistic.

Man Becoming Something Else

Man is becoming something other than what he was. This is true of each individual, as well as of communities.

It is because of the inner awareness of this becoming, which he does not understand and therefore fears, that man always seeks to halt and develop himself into some sort of protraction of what he is or thinks himself to be, or thinks others to be or to have been.

It is because this standpoint is fruitless that man has been adjured to know himself.

'Man Hates what is Good for Him, Loves what is Bad'

It is because of this tendency that man must strive for certain improvements of the self which is not the 'man' referred to above.

Without these improvements man harms his future far more effectively than anyone else can harm it, or than he can harm society.

It has been largely forgotten that people do not only maintain morality because of society, but because of the best kind of selfishness – self-protection.

The belief in indoctrination, emotion and intellect as the

sources of 'good' and 'bad' is an invention, a substitute for truth devised by the superficial populariser.

It is no part of higher study.

Men of Learning

There are men of learning who have not been transformed by their studies. 'Knowledge' may be carried about by them as a virtuality, awaiting development.

Almost everyone who has not been in a real school has something of this in him: undigested learning.

There are people who have not even acquired undigested learning after being in contact with it. They confuse others because they give the appearance of being learned.

But far more unpleasant is the fact that there are people of learning who have learnt at wrong times or in incorrect circumstances.

One can only hope for protection from them.

Morality and Culture

In the name of all that is just, when and where did this superstition start:

'A man of culture is a man of moral worth.'

The refutation of this strange assumption, illustrated almost every day in ordinary life, hit Western civilisation a blow not long ago from which it has not recovered. People still reel from this blow.

It must have been very much the same effect as when it was first realised that the thunder-god was not after all the source of all power . . .

Merit

People are full of ideas about merit. There is the merit in following rules. There is the merit in not following others. But do you not know that the more knowledge you have, the less is the meaning of merit?

You cannot be meritorious or the reverse if you are doing and being what is necessary: if you have the knowledge of that. Merit and demerit – good and bad – are stages on the way to the state when they vanish. If a person has the knowledge, the power and the ability to act in a manner which is necessary, you do not call that merit. You must pass through merit before you can transcend it. Do not discuss it until you have got beyond it. Then you will know what to do.

There are many other things, too, on the higher level, which you are trying to discuss which you could not understand because of lack of the first stages.

Meditation

Meditation is the first exercise of the triad:

Meditation-concentration-contemplation.

Any one of these indulged in isolation, (not as a part of a threefold operation) produces fixity of opinion and illusions of certainty.

Such a result is a psychological, not a spiritual one.

Ignorance of this fact has led people to adopt one or other of these procedures assuming that the results that they feel are 'higher' ones. It must be admitted that there is an element of greed in the choosing of one 'simple' technique rather than seeking further.

Although not constantly aware of this greed, the practitioner can find in himself, on careful examination, the sense of greed, probably disguised as a desire for fulfilment.

Specialist teachers exist to pilot students as much because of their difficulty in perceiving this as for their specialist knowledge.

People who 'teach' single techniques as methods of arriving at 'harmony', although always numerous and using the vocabulary of spirituality, are in fact only 'conditioners'.

No Accident in these Studies

In social groups, schools, political, religious, national and other groupings, one:

1. Chooses people who can be instructed;
2. Works with people whom one already has.

In both cases there is a laudable presumption that most of these people are suitable for the objectives of the group.

One always works selectively in mundane affairs.

How much more, in a highly sensitive operation like ours, do we work selectively.

To use metaphysics as a place where one can abandon selectivity and act like a rabble is the height of irrelevance.

Needs, not Fantasy

A concept, process, technique, curriculum, does not have to be attributed to authority, recorded in prestigious literature, or capable of affording emotional stimuli.

Its requirement shall be that it is effective: apt for the individual and the needs of a group.

Not, therefore; 'Is it new, does it resolve, or seem to resolve, my psychological problems, does it seem like something which I can believe . . .'

But, imperatively: 'Does it work, and do I have the basis of preparation necessary for it to have a chance to work?'

A major purpose of metaphysical schools is to select and to apply the processes, techniques, curricula, concepts and materials which shall apply to a given community, without regard to the superficialities of mere taste, personal inclination and popular demand.

It is for this reason – the need to work without compromising with irrelevancies – that so many serious endeavours of the past and present are carried on in privacy, even in secrecy.

'Nothing is Happening'

Anyone who really thinks that 'nothing is happening' has, in fact if not in appearance, already left our studies, because such an idea in the mind of a pupil means that he has taken too long to learn a basic lesson. He can start to study again, but he must know that he had stopped learning.

He might note that a child or a peasant being told that he is revolving with the earth would deny it, saying 'nothing is happening'.

To such a person, something happening is not really something happening. It is something happening which he can himself feel and decide to be such. It may be utterly unimportant, it may actually be dangerous to him: but if he can feel that it is happening, he is happy or interested.

To feel something of real value taking place, you have to be farther advanced than a savage who looks for crude symptoms (which only mean crude happenings).

News

People don't notice that they are, nowadays, reduced to getting their information from sources which specialise in providing it, not by thought, observation, informal contact, or instruction.

Only the other day I met someone whom I hadn't seen for some time.

I said: 'What's the news?'

He said: 'I don't know; I haven't read today's papers yet.'

Observation

The advanced value of observation is to show one the gaps in ordinary observation.

Using observational capacity to observe how well one has observed something is a practice which the mature outgrow. Those who have not grown out of it may still have chances, but they are immature.

Organisation, Study, Belief

Traditional usage of certain important materials in special teachings, the higher levels of what is known as religion, and in psychology, has produced methods of study and has used materials which cannot be improved upon.

Unfortunately, in response to what operates in effect as a 'law' among humanity, these materials have become misused, misunderstood, frozen into symbol, ritual, emotional and intellectual usage.

In legitimate traditions certain word-arrangements, called prayers in some circles, are artefacts which are intended to be used as exercises. In ordinary usage these have become little more than incantations. This is because of the loss of the knowledge upon which they are based, and because of the ridiculously random grouping of the devotees.

Certain items generally known as 'holy' or 'religious' objects, which have been adopted, chosen, made and devised for inner functional purposes, have become fetishes. At best they are used to elicit 'Pavlovian' conditioned responses on the part of the worshippers or students.

This adds up to the fact that such 'religious', 'work' or 'teaching' attempts as are carried out in this manner are next to useless. Worse still; the 'believers' do not realise that they are in fact being worked upon, while the scoffers who deride ritual and tradition are almost more right than the 'believers'.

We have to reclaim the correct employment, the conscious use of objects, procedure, oration and exercise to rescue these things from theatre, mime and absurd fetishism.

In order to do this, we have to decondition our own students from the conditioned reflexes implanted in them, so that they do not see holy symbols as things which give them an emotional thrill; or ritual as something which they enjoy; or certain garments as evidence of the initiation of individuals. All ingredients of real traditions were chosen and employed originally for specific purposes.

196

Some such ingredients have outlived their usefulness; some apply only to the culture in which they were projected. Others are among our most valuable possessions.

Unless these facts are known and certain procedures practised in order to reclaim this heritage, no real study of the operation of the interior function of these elements can be made.

Original Function of Practices

The blind performance of practices handed down from real teachings is not only ridiculous: it can be harmful.

You have to be a real teacher, or be directed by someone who has already travelled the road to the end, before you can say that you are not working randomly.

A serious danger in random work is that the student may become captured by a cult.

Pure Water

Did you know that you could not tolerate absolutely pure water?

When water is purified from contamination, it has then to be made slightly brackish before it is palatable to the human being.

Similarly the very greatest spiritual masters and the most advanced individuals are imperceptible, in their real greatness, to the ordinary man.

In order to communicate matters of a higher level onto a lower one at all, some adjustment must be made by the communicator.

It is interesting to note, in ordinary human affairs, how the equivalence works. People are always saying, for instance:

> 'You would never guess that such-and-such a person is so important, from his behaviour; he looks and talks just like an ordinary man.'

But, instead of trying to make some part of him perceptible in relating it to the ordinary man, people instead work at inventing or dilating aspects of his personality. That's why gossip columns are full.

Pupil and Teacher Interchange

A teacher gets much communication of higher materials from other people.

They are rarely 'advanced' people.

This form of communication is always operating. Most people cannot benefit from it because there is so much irrelevant mental activity in them.

When they can suspend subjective ideas, or keep them in their own time and place, they can:

1. Perceive the vibrations which constitute messages suitable for their own development and sometimes for further transmission;
2. Become aware of special and characteristic roles which they can fill in the service of higher needs.

The mutual-concentration exercise interchange between teacher and pupil enables, among other things, the teacher to provide both the means of 'stilling', and also the necessary range of subtle stimulus to help the pupil in his development.

Payment

From almost his earliest days, man is constantly informed that he will have to pay for his own carelessness, stupidity and ignorance.

There is a widespread convention among professional men everywhere that their charges are not based upon the time spent on a case, but upon their years of study and experience.

We pay, the notion goes, for their knowledge.

Yet any ordinary experience of life, let alone a reading of the daily Press, will show just as surely that what we frequently pay for is not the knowledge of experts, but their ignorance.

How interesting that all human cultures still retain this unbalanced view of the expert: still believing in his infallibility, without having caught up with the abundantly available and frequently demonstrated evidences of his limitations.

We cannot help the expert to grow up if we do not grow up ourselves.

Purposes of Experiences

I have said that in the final analysis we are teaching something which can be likened to a new perception, carried out by an 'organ' which has to be developed.

This development, people will immediately assume, is made possible by exercises and specific studies.

Such studies are indeed available, and we do carry them out.

But there is another factor which is equally important: it is context.

In addition to deliberate study and effort, we have to have right conditions and experiences. People must enter circumstances in which they are more powerfully surrounded by the substance which their emerging organs of higher perception are to perceive. This is analogous to saying that, if you want to teach someone wine-tasting, he has to have the chance to taste many wines.

This causes much confusion when people are always looking for a simple or easily understood or practised exercise in an 'experimental training period'.

Prescience

Why is it so important to be able to know the future, or at least something of the future?

Because the man who knows the future cannot be bad.

The bad man is bad because he can always pretend that things will not necessarily be so bad as a consequence of his actions.

If a person has a scheme, or a doctrine, or a set of beliefs of any kind, and he does not know anything about the future, he can easily assume and tell himself that 'it will work out for the benefit of everyone'.

If he knows the future he will be able to tell whether it will harm anyone – or even everyone.

Ignorance of the future makes man bad.

This is why people have tried so hard to penetrate the future: so that they can act correctly, not just as they imagine might be correct.

This is why so many good people and saints in so many cultures are credited with this power of prescience. They can see what is going to happen. That is why they do not do destructive things. That is why they can do things which are likely to be good.

Knowledge of the future makes man good.

Idealists, who hope for the best and try to act for the good, must admit that they do not know what the good of all really is. 'The road to Hell is paved with good intentions'. But such people are not really idealists.

Real idealists are those who are not only prepared to do good, but are prepared to fit themselves for doing good. The most important step in this direction is to develop the capacity for prescience.

Possible Functions of Studies

Each inner exercise has seven major functions.

The very lowest and truly least useful are those used in systems familiar to us in the current world.

By practising an exercise in an incorrect place or at the wrong time or in the wrong company for you, for instance, you may indeed feel something pleasant or 'significant'. It may, however, actually hinder your possible development.

It is obvious from the large number of people who prefer the minor stimuli of exercises (although they may have a capacity for greater experiences) that they long ago made their choice. They are not experiential philosophers, religious people or mystics. They have arranged their 'studies' as a means of self-gratification.

Something in them knows this. They combat its realisation by keeping themselves occupied, sometimes even by idleness.

Patience

Those who encourage the development of patience in others without also instructing them in how to avoid elevating negativity into a virtue instead, are in fact unable to teach at all.

Better to say nothing about patience than to enjoin patience and instead produce an excuse for laziness.

Practice of Virtue

To practise virtue for the sake of virtuousness is inconclusive, to say the least. It may even be deleterious to the individual, taken on its own. This is because the person feeding on this emotion is consuming its yield, while at the same time he imagines that he has acquired merit, credit or gain somewhere. He is self-satisfied, often without realising it.

It is easier and more instantly profitable to preach only the value of virtue. The drawback in so doing is that it is untrue. Yet most well known human institutions at least give lip-service to virtuousness as an end in itself.

The fact is that such virtue is a vice.

Generalised moralism, masquerading as higher teaching, mistakes through technical ignorance, fixation and obsession for real, productive attainment.

The latter can never be learned from books, nor from lower-level, boy-scoutish indoctrination.

BUSINESS REPLY MAIL

FIRST CLASS   PERMIT NO. 2788   BOSTON, MA

POSTAGE WILL BE PAID BY ADDRESSEE

ISHK Book Service

P.O. Box 1069

Cambridge, MA 02238-1069

ISHK BOOK SERVICE

If you are interested in our books and tapes and would like to be on our mailing list, please complete and return this card.

(Please type or print)

Name _____

Address _____

_____

(City) _____ (State) _____ (Zip) _____

'Prescription' versus Mixing

In real teaching situations, as in therapeutic ones, studies are 'prescribed' for the needs of their beneficiaries.

If you mix someone else's medicine with your own, don't be surprised at an unpleasant, even harmful, result.

If you try to make sense of several 'prescriptions' while ignoring the possibility of a reason for their apparent diversity, don't be surprised if you get a headache, or worse.

If you think you can find the real common denominator, I do not know what you are, but you are not a student.

Purpose of Regular Meetings

The purpose of regular meetings is to maintain the special contact already established between numbers of people, each body of people being in a sense distinct.

This special contact is inhibited by an over-development of the social element. These gatherings should be harmonious, but should not be allowed to become 'clublike' or gossipy.

The special relationship is harmed by the assumption of status by individual members of the group. Each member should discharge the functions for the time being allotted to him, if any, as a communicator of material, as an organiser, or whatever it might be. The community has to develop a sense of unity of purpose – learning and development – in which each member is to be regarded as important for the success of the whole.

The special relationship is crippled by the exploitation of one member by another, so that co-operation between individual members must be kept within reasonable limits. The development of smaller, informal relationships between small numbers of people from within the grouping must not be encouraged, as such 'sub-groups' without official sanction start to cause the group to operate in an unbalanced manner. The group will in such cases operate as an ideological, social, intellectual or other entity, of which in any culture there are enough already.

Each group is a sensitive organism.

Members of the group meet:

- As if there is a special current passing through them. They have been chosen for the group in order to be able to function in this manner, and people leaving or joining the group altering its composition must maintain the same capacity of the group to be an instrument.
- In order to observe their own reactions to meetings. They have to realise that great enthusiasm or any degree of dislike of meetings are symptoms of insufficient integration into the sensitivity of the group, and not bases for decision about the group, the materials or its members.
- In order to be exposed, under correct circumstances, to materials which suit that group and from which they can profit. These materials may be written, recorded, handled, experienced in a variety of different ways.
- In order to realise, through practical experience, that there is an almost inevitable tendency for groups to become ossified or mechanical, and to observe that there are possibilities in this specific group for a current to enter and be maintained which is manifested by a relationship between members which is quite unlike customary groupings.
- In order to prepare themselves for selection to carry out more advanced studies.
- In order to maintain their contact with the Teaching, and their ability to profit from it, so that the Teaching may be able to select them for special activities and higher understanding at the proper time.

- In order to shed the emotional and intellectualist approaches which constantly creep into all studies, our own included, when carried out without due regard for time, place, people and also the statement that there is 'another way'.
- In order to see and sense the special flavour in our kind of relationship and work, for the purpose of recognising it instantly, just as one can recognise more customary atmospheres.

Qualitative Perceptions

All experiences have content, in layers and otherwise.

An orange, say, has layers and parts: rind, juice, seeds, skin, pulp; minerals, sugar, vitamins.

You are trained to devour experience as a whole, and evaluate it quantitatively, like a greedy man gobbling down an orange.

This would be good enough if the prerequisite were not to develop digestive organs. The palate can say what it likes, if the stomach is there to do the work.

Part of the studies which cannot be telescoped is to make sure that there are digestive organs for a certain nutrition, and that they are working correctly.

Questions and Desires

If you think that every desire for knowledge which you have can be satisfied in exactly the same form as that in which you put it, you still have a great deal to learn. I do not suggest by this that you need a great deal of time, but you need breadth and nutrition, and another way of looking at things.

Real Teaching

The teachings passing under the names of the ancient teachers do not represent their real teachings.

They consist, at best, of those parts which it has suited others to pass on.

The result is a system of imprisonment.

This is the reason for the constant need for real interpreters and men of insight who can scrape off accretions and add missing elements. Not to speak of the need to suit the teaching to the requirements of the locale.

⋆   ⋆   ⋆

Simplification and systematisation of ideas can only be done by people who are capable of it. These tasks are, however, almost always attempted by people who are not capable of it. The basic qualification for simplification is a complete knowledge of the materials.

Random and Real Seeking

A most important principle is emphasised in what I am about to tell you. A certain man, passing through London on his way to the East, contacts me and asks to be put in touch with what he calls teachers in the East. He has a travel plan, and wants to combine it with his search, as he calls it.

You might think that this is all very convenient. Why should he not visit people of knowledge or sanctity, and profit thereby?

Yet this kind of thinking is based upon one of the most disastrous of all assumptions, and is motivated by the Commanding Self. The assumption is that the man can always make his own choices: that he can drop in on a mystic and get something out of the contact, just as if he was smelling a rose or buying a pound of butter, or looking at a tourist sight – 'on a higher level, of course'. He says to me: 'Have you anyone in Chittagong?' Not, mark it well, 'I have to go to Chittagong,' and leave it at that, so that one would have the opportunity of saying: 'Yes, there is someone whom you could profitably meet there.' And, strangely, because he is like this, we have to say, just as we say to someone whom we cannot introduce to our best friends, 'No, sorry, there is nobody in Chittagong.' And he becomes importunate, so you have to say, perhaps: 'Nobody you could benefit from is in Chittagong.'

The Commanding Self tells the man that he can benefit, at any time, in any place, from a contact with something higher. The assumption, made from ignorance of simple facts, tells this man (a student of many years' standing) that he is in a state suitable to picking up advantages, just like someone without eyes who tells you that he wants to see something.

The amusing dichotomy here between what is real and what the man thinks is real is this. He believes that, by going somewhere and seeking out someone who will tell him something or instruct him in some way, he is acting purposefully. In fact, he is acting randomly, because there is no chance that he will be able to find the right man at the right time in the right place to answer to his special needs. Remember that we are all individuals, and that our development can take place only under conditions which make it possible. That is the difference between a quest carried out randomly and one which is really efficient.

Now, how to inform such a man? All his life he has been

207

fed on the pap that says: 'All you have to do is struggle.' And, 'be selective,' without giving him the capacity to be selective, or teaching him about struggle.

Our job is to help this person to become selective. It is not easy, because he assumes that he already has this faculty. This is a man who once complained to me that I had sent someone else to see someone in a remote place, and that I had not allowed him to go. The other man, in contrast, complained that when he met the man I had sent him to, this man did not speak of mystical matters. In fact he was a bookbinder, absorbed in his vocation. To make it all worse, from the viewpoint of the man I sent, this latter did not even feel a sense of mystery from the bookbinder. Looking for the wrong thing, he sacrificed a chance to find the right thing. I sent him to a bookbinder. That was not enough.

Reinfection

Though self-esteem is born into you, you can still be re-infected with it by almost anyone until you have become immune.

You do not become immune through seeing its frozen manifestations here and there in your actions and reactions. You become immune through carrying on the art which prevents it from over-developing.

Ritual

Ritual can be important.

The last people to be encouraged to take part in ritual, if the intent is genuinely to help raise mankind, are the ritualistically-minded. Real ritual, you see, is functional, while ritualistic individuals, whatever they imagine, in reality live for the vehicle, not the content.

When you hear their eager and sometimes persuasive explanations – that they do not feel ritualistic at all – know that you are hearing automatic self-justifications seeking to protect an acquired taste.

It is a major task of real learning to understand the 'idolatrous' processes which, however hallowed by 'tradition' (repetition), are inimical to the true development of man.

Nitrogen

People are always hoping that they will be able to extract and concentrate something of great value from available materials. There is no doubt that this can be done. But what distinguishes those who *can* do it from those who merely believe it, is – the ability to do so. Ability doesn't only mean capacity to do the concentrating and the extraction. It means knowing what to extract and what to concentrate. The teachings of all wise people, suitably concentrated – or should I say unsuitably concentrated – become poison. Take one thing without the other and take too much of it – and you will suffer for it.

You are surrounded by air, a mixture of gases. Suppose you extracted only the nitrogen. Then suppose you concentrated it in one place, and then breathed it, and only it, in. You would die in minutes: and most unpleasantly.

Identifying, concentrating and increasing the quantity of oxygen, even, would not always have the effect you need.

Do you still prefer faith to knowledge?

Reason for Exercising Sincerity

Man possesses a deep capacity to recognise truth, even in written materials. But greed and comparative laziness (which can render him much more superficial and immature than he thinks) make him blind to what he should do once he has perceived it.

This is a major reason why he has to cultivate sincerity.

> 'Sincerity is the true self-interest; compared with it all else is spurious.'

Reviews

Today I read two book reviews. They were about the same book, criticised by two different people.

One said:

> 'This book will live for many years. Its author is a genius.'

The other:

> 'Seldom have I read such nonsense.'

There are three main possibilities here:

One may be right, the other wrong. Or it may just be that

the reviewers are in fact describing not the book, but themselves, their own reactions to a stimulus, born of their personal prejudices.

I turned to another book review. I read:

> 'The author would have done far better if he had written the book in a completely different manner . . .'

Is *this* reviewer right? Is he wrong? Or is he just describing himself, what *he* would have done?

Relationship with a School

People put their difficulties back to front.

The true situation of man is that it is difficult to find and to be accepted by a real school. Even when something is 'found' with difficulty, it may not be a real school.

When it is 'found', one may not be able to study there.

Man prefers, however, to believe that if something is difficult it is automatically worthwhile. He also prefers to think that the difficulties may start only when he is in such a school. They start long before.

He may be in touch with the School. Does he measure up to its requirements?

Right Thought

To invoke a quotation, an 'observation' which seems apposite but which is not functional, is to the true teaching as playing with mud is to acquiring literacy in primary education.

You will, in dilettante circles, encounter people who have substituted imitation for function. That they do not allow themselves to realise that it is imitation is not the point. For them, the function of a word, quotation, exercise, principle is the low one of emotional or mental stimulus.

Running Before You Can Walk

This heading is an absurdity. But lack of information and disorganised desire (impatience and ignorance) can cause a person to talk and act, as well as think, in a manner which is in fact crazy, even if it is not socially objectionable. It does him no good.

Often such a person may be respected. The disease is common among people of religion and metaphysics, alternating with the special kind of pessimism which I have noted elsewhere.

Reflection Theme

If you damage the jail, you harm the captive. If you remove the prisoner, you bring the guard along too. If you touch the captor, you imperil the victim.

212

Each human being lives in a jail. The prison is himself; and he is his own warder as well.

While the warder is the prisoner and the jail, it is not surprising that there are so few escapes, and rescues are so rare.

And the process of interweaving captured and captivity, not to say dungeon, is so effective that this reflection must inevitably sound like nonsense.

But then, everyone's sense is someone else's nonsense.

Respect

You say that a lot of people do not respect me, and indeed many of the people whom I meet every day have no idea of what you say is my amazing interior worth.

But at least in the case of such people we can all know that their feelings for me are not the result of an overheated imagination.

Real, Empirical and Imitative Study

All studies have their conditions. The more advanced, the less instantly observable these are. In our study, time, place and people are essential. When these are fulfilled correct guidance can operate.

In our studies the disciplines are not of the familiar sort: stylised sacrifice, ritualised suffering, automatic behaviour, reward and punishment, threat and promise.

213

In teaching this, our curricula have been confused by imitators, however dedicated they may have imagined themselves to be. As a result, exercises which are a means towards a potentiality for another exercise, have generally become ends in themselves – or they are thought to be leading to ends. Exercises are not isolated things.

Only accepting this and experiencing it in a real school can resolve this muddle.

Without the results of much sacrifice by others, you cannot be helped to overcome the conditioning which you have connived in implanting in yourself, by seeking to choose, through shallow self-esteem, an easy way.

Reasons for Discipline

Our Way requires of its followers discipline, humility, co-operation and many other things primarily because they are essential to the survival of the true self of the individual: and only secondarily because they are of social value.

These factors are never properly active when they are, or have become, sources of either self-satisfaction or rejection. Even opposing something is generally caused by an attempt at self-gratification.

Remember the statement:

> 'Oppose nothing if opposition pleases you;
> Approve nothing, if approving pleases you.'

The Loaf

People often ask how it is that Sufis can bring something as ordinary as words and cause spiritual effects with them. They also wonder what might happen to those who do not listen to what Sufis say. The ancient Tale of the Loaf is an illustration, an allegory, of the ordinary made extraordinary, and the result of heedlessness.

There was once a baker, who had heated his oven and prepared a large quantity of dough, ready for the day's baking.

As he was about to start shaping his loaves, a man, a Sufi who looked no different from anyone else, walked into the bakery.

He offered a small coin, and asked the baker for a piece of dough.

'Very well', said the baker, 'but you can only have a very small piece for that.'

The man took the dough, and then said, 'Please be so good as to bake it into a loaf in your oven.'

'All right', said the baker, 'but you won't get much of a loaf out of a scrap of dough the size of a walnut.'

He put the dough in the oven and, when he took it out a few minutes later, it had turned into a loaf the size of a pillow.

'This can't be your loaf,' said the baker; 'yours must have slipped down into the fire and got lost.'

The Sufi smiled and said, 'Here is another coin. Please be so kind as to bake another piece of dough.'

The baker did as he asked: and again a huge loaf was produced.

'I must have put some of my own dough in, instead,' thought the baker. To the Sufi he said, 'Your dough is lost again, I am afraid.'

The third time that this happened, the Sufi said, 'Do you not see that the dough you put into the oven has turned into a large loaf, and that you should give it to me?'

'Such a thing is impossible', said the baker. 'I can only

conclude that you are trying to fool me with some trick!'

The Sufi smiled again. 'Give me the loaf. You have gained two through my presence here. I need the third for someone else.'

But the baker, now thoroughly confused, shooed the man away.

The Sufi went off, down the road. The baker, in less time than it takes to tell, decided that he had fallen asleep on his feet for a moment, or imagined the whole thing, and so – nothing happened to him at all.

Sufi Sayings and their Application in Teaching Situations

1. To whomever has sense, a sign is enough. For the heedless, a thousand expositions are not enough.

Haji Bektash

Sufi materials, experiences, explanations may be registered in the mind on one level, and may have to wait for their full understanding until 'heedlessness' is removed. The main source of this is the 'Commanding Self'.

2. Those things which are apparently opposed may in reality be working together.

Jalaluddin Rumi

This has to be experienced. It is a sign of the shallow to cleave to something obviously opposed to Sufi ideas and then invoke this saying.

3. The apparent is the bridge to the Real.

Again, superficial thinkers and emotionalists will choose something apparent and decide that this is the bridge to the real. Only certain parts of the apparent are such a bridge.

4. Be **in** the world, but not **of** the world.

One must be able to detach from things of the world, without having cut oneself off from it: which is a pathological condition.

5. The Path is none other than service of the people.

Saadi

Sufi service has to be the right kind of service; neither servitude nor hypocrisy.

6. None attains to the degree of truth until a thousand sincere people have called him a heretic.

Junaid

Sincere people include those who sincerely hold mistaken, shallow or untrue ideas.

7. Whoever knows God does not say 'God'.

Bayazid

The meaning of 'God' in the hearts of superficialists is someone or something to be bribed and asked for things. So whoever knows more cannot use this term, which contains unworthy elements such as those.

8. If you split a single drop asunder
   From it emerge a hundred pure oceans

Shabistari

A very tiny impulse from the Sufi reality will be able to unlock great understanding. But people seek stimulation and noise.

9. He who is the Completed Man is he who in his perfection
   Does in his mastership the work of a slave.

Shabistari

Think about it.

217

10. A man concealed in a blanket is the world's ruler
     A sword asleep in a scabbard is the guardian of the realm.

Amir Khusru

Are things what they seem?

11. Die before you die.

For contemplation.

12. Pagoda and Kaaba are houses of servitude
     Ringing bells are the melody of slavery
     The (sacred) thread and the church,
        and the cross and rosary
     Truly, all of them are the mark of servitude

Khayyam

Attachment to externals, to ritual and symbols, automatism, conditioning: these are what people too often mistake for faith and religion.

13. The touchstone it is which knows the real gold.

Saadi

The Commanding Self, the subjective mind which is a compound of instinct and training, of intellect and emotion: these are the factors which stand between the 'gold' and the 'touchstone' in everyone.

14. One pull from Truth is better than a thousand efforts.

Rumi

People think that they can 'storm the gates of heaven'. In reality it is a matter of 'time, place and people', so that the higher impulse can act upon the suitably prepared individual.

15. The bird which has no knowledge of pure water
     Has its beak in salt water the whole year round

Akhlaq-i-Muhsini

People are trained to think that certain things are useful, sublime, real and true. Have they anything to compare these with?

16. Tranquil the person who did not come into the world.

      Khayyam

   That is why the one who did is anything but tranquil . . .

17. If the donkey that bore Jesus into Jerusalem went to Mecca
    Would it be less of an ass when it came back?

18. You did not exist when your work was created;
    You were created from a sea of work.

      Shabistari

19. To be a Sufi is to maintain states in relation to
    Objective Reality.

      Al Muqri, in Shabistari

   In the Sufi state, the perception of Reality becomes possible.

20. In cell and cloister, monastery and synagogue, one lies
    In dread of hell; another dreams of paradise.
    But none that know the divine secrets
    Have sown their hearts with suchlike fantasies.

      Khayyam

21. Gold needs bran to polish it . . . But whoever makes
    himself into bran will be eaten by cows.

   Do you use it, or does it use you?

22. The mind large enough for ultimate Truth
    Cannot be narrowed to the world: do you understand,
       listener?

      Ibn el Arabi

23. The Sufi is one who does not own and is not owned.

      Nuri

24. A man has seen the mountain, he has not seen the mine within it.

Rumi

25. Love is bestowed, not earned.

Hujwiri

26. Real love is neither diminished by unkindness nor increased by kindness and bounty.

Yahya ibn Mu'adh

27. Unification is silence and, always, thought;
Discussion comes and unification goes.
Once, 'Thou' is said, duality is established;
Unification departs from the point where you take its name.

Dara Shikoh

28. Wealth reveals bad things previously concealed by poverty.
One places a seed in the earth
So that, on the day of distress, it shall give fruit.

Saadi

29. Whoever is without impressions and is made polished
Becomes a mirror for the impression of the Hidden.

Rumi

30. Do not twist the reins because of the difficulties of the
Path, O Heart;
For the Man of the Path does not concern himself with
ups and downs.

Hafiz

31. What freewill have you, O heedless man
A person who has a void, illusive essence?
Tell me where this freewill of yours comes from.
Someone whose essence is not of himself:
Has no good and bad in his essence.

Shabistari

32. Speak to people in accordance with their understanding.

33. You yourself are under your own veil.

Hafiz

SECTION VII

SECTION VII

Systematic Study

Q: *People always want rules and directions: not always to be dominated by them, but so that they can follow a coherent course of study. Reading about traditional stages of study among the classical Sufis I see that they vary a great deal. Reading your writings I do not see a clear succession of practices and stages. Is there no organised course among the Sufis?*

A: When you read about different 'systems' among the Sufis, you are seeing studies which have from time to time been prescribed for people in accordance with their possibilities, like a doctor prescribes according to the hopes he has for his patients. People adopt these and imagine that they should be applied to any and all students, regardless of the flexibility which, in the first place, demanded that courses must be scripted for the prevailing conditions, and taking into account many other factors.

Q: *But other systems do not assume this about man at all – that there is a variation in people and conditions. Why is this?*

A: You will have to ask the people who are promoting those other systems. If they answer that man is always the same, that conditions are always the same, you will have to decide which contention – ours or theirs – appeals to you most. We cannot answer for them.

Q: *But if we find the same principles and practices repeated in a so-called Sufi grouping, what does this show?*

A: This shows that you are not dealing with a Sufi grouping, but with a system which has become automatized. Due to imagining that learning is mechanical, and due to a desire for stability (which leads to atrophy) such people are merely imitators.

Q: *Why do study groupings become automatized in this way?*

A: There are two very good reasons. First, where the desire for reassurance and repetition is stronger than the desire for knowledge, rules and repetition become the most important factor. This occurs when people try to learn without proper preparation. Proper preparation is to make sure that the people have a balanced mind into which to feed the seeds of knowledge. If the mind is not integrated, it will, naturally, seek to use whatever is fed into it for the purpose of balancing it. You may try to feed something into the stomach because of its taste, but if you lack nutrition, the stomach will process the delicious food as nutrition. The most pressing need always over-rides everything else. The second reason is that it is easier to organise and manipulate large numbers of people by using a small number of factors (exercises, beliefs, etc.), rather than by giving them proper attention. Consciously or otherwise, leaders of thought and of groupings always seek the most effective methods of mass organisation.

Q: *But why is this not better known?*

A: Merely because the history of teaching enterprises does not start at an early enough stage. People have only looked at the over-organised phase and assumed that this was the school or the teaching.

Strange Literature, Odd People

Q: *I have read many books on metaphysics, and the reason why I am attracted to those about Sufis is that it is only here that I find what I would call 'normal' people. All the others seem to me to be too obsessed, or too full of flaws which only the believers or those who have not digested the materials could fail to see. Further, going to meetings held by all kinds of 'believers', one cannot but note that there is something distinctly odd about them. Among those who are called Sufis, only some groups seem to have odd people in them; and these are the ones which I suspect are imitation ones. It is for this reason that I choose the Sufis as probably legitimate, if there is any truth at all in spiritual matters.*

A: This is more like a statement than a question. But it is possible to say that, in a free society, all kinds of people will be attracted to anything. Legitimate activities will always attract odd people as well as normal ones. It is, however, up to those directing spiritual studies and other activities to see that the odd ones do not influence affairs so as to affect progress adversely. Among the things which affect human groups adversely is the presence of too many odd people, for the reason that this keeps away the normal ones, quite apart from interfering with the normal running of the enterprise, as with any other human endeavour. But I am not sure that the matter, especially where literature is concerned, is as simple as that. For example, odd literature can not only appeal to odd people: it can also make normal people odd, and for that reason it certainly is to be deplored. One cannot just take no notice at all of it, saying, 'the odd will be attracted to oddness'.

Q: *Then how do you deal with oddness, if not only by shunning odd people?*

A: Simply by having a 'department' which helps to make oddness more visible. This, however, is not a part of spiritual teaching, but a part of human duty. In their own way, all people who are healthy-minded will point out oddness, and this 'department' will help to strengthen them.

Slaps

Q: *I have seen Sufis apparently angry, or talking severely to people who have not even spoken a word to them. Since there was nothing to arouse their ire, why was this done?*

A: A Sufi is not one who has ire. The Sufi is like the man who slapped the boy before he broke the pot, without anger, to prevent him dropping it; rather than like the man who, in anger, punished the boy after he had broken the vessel.

When a Sufi knows what a person is like, that person does not have to 'speak a word to him'.

He will know an individual's inward state and he will, if necessary, signal his disapproval of it by a show of reproach. He is not talking to the outer personality, and so he needs no pretext. He is signalling to the raw inwardness of that individual, saying in effect, 'I know what you are like'.

It is this ability and its usefulness which indicates a real Sufi.

The individual who is being dealt with is like the blind man of the saying, who 'fouls the pavement and thinks that nobody sees him'.

Teachers and Pupils

Q: *There are a lot of people who claim to have studied under you who have now become 'Sufi Teachers', both in the East and in, for instance, the USA. How do we know whether they are genuine?*

A: The number of people who claim to have studied under me and to be teaching what I communicated to them will soon, I fancy, equal the number who say that they taught me. They, in turn, may be as numerous as those who say that they have improved on what I am doing, and those who insist that they would not have anything to do with us at any price. This is a sociological phenomenon, common among people who know very little about something but imagine that they know a lot. This is the kind of person who thinks in 'transactional' terms: he accepts, rejects, 'improves', avoids things: treating all things, from cornflakes to Sufi knowledge, with the same low-level lack of perception.

Q: *Then how are we to know which of these people to heed?*

A: You will instantly know as soon as you get rid of your own transactional mentality. Until you do, you cannot know; you have to depend on opinion and what you can evaluate of what you are told. This is why we have organisations providing that information. Virtually all specialisations have to have such organisations. On its own level, this is similar to the Automobile Association telling you whether a certain garage is affiliated to it or not: this is a shorthand for 'we approve and endorse the level of competence of this garage'. If you doubt the garage, so to speak, check the individual garage with the Association.

The Sheep's Ear

Q: *What is the meaning of the Sufi saying:*
  'The disciple takes the sheep's ear'?

A: Someone who has no idea of the value of, say, a sheep, will covet its ear, one of the most attractive but perhaps the least useful of its parts.

When someone does not know what is useful to him, he may imagine that something irrelevant is a necessity.

Random so-called spiritual exercises, self-absorption, irrelevant questions – these are among the things which the Sufis refer to as 'Ears of the Sheep'.

Love and Fear

Q: *Sufis may treat spiritually-minded enquirers harshly, and this disappoints them, even makes them turn against the Sufis. Surely this is counter-productive, for it not only means that recruitment is slow, but also that enemies are made?*

A: If Sufis behave thus, it is because these people are not really spiritually-minded and have been recognised as such.

If the people are indeed spiritually-minded, it means that the people to whom you refer are not in fact real Sufis.

Most often these people are sentimental but not spiritual, and come from an environment where the distinction has been forgotten.

They are the people of whom it is said, in an analogy:

'They love war but fear battle.'

As to the 'recruitment' of such people: it should not be slow – it should be non-existent.

The Sign of a Master

Q: *How would one know whether a devout person is in reality Sufistically a Master? Surely, anyone who is deeply religious and totally or mainly absorbed in spiritual observances might well be such a person?*

A: This may at first seem a difficult question. However, you should remember that when a question has already been adequately answered on impeccable authority, it is necessary only to quote the answer. To do so is the equivalent to displaying a wheel instead of trying to re-invent it. So we can turn to the question and answer in this regard which featured no less a Sufi than Bayazid Bistami.

According to the *Risalat-i-Malamatiyya*, Bayazid was asked what would be the most important indication of a master who knew the secrets of the Sufi Way.

He answered:

'When he eats and drinks, buys and sells, and makes jokes with you, he whose heart is in the sacred domain – this is the greatest of signs of his being a Master.'

Those people to whom you refer, who are devout, religious and absorbed, if they are incapable of detaching from these things – if, in fact these characteristics are obsessional – then they cannot be teachers of the Path.

This, in fact, is the chief difference between the indoctrinated person and the spiritual one, according to the Sufis.

It is indeed odd that this question still has to be asked today: over one thousand years after it was answered by Bayazid. This fact should make us realise how long it takes for knowledge to penetrate from being specifically targetted to being understood by people in general.

The Guardian

Q: *Why is it that so many religious people and institutions are so heartless? Dogmas so often mean that people have to suffer, or at least to comply, with instructions which seem to cause them harm. People object to minority cults on this basis, but we can see the ill-usage of humanity by some of the apparently respectable religions.*

A: Such individuals and organisations as you speak of are now operated by rule and not by knowledge and understanding. They are bound, therefore to create difficulties and injustice.

Unless you understand people, you will always, in such circumstances, be 'putting a cat to guard a hen', and some part of the individual or society will be correspondingly despoiled.

The Mad Rabbit

Q. *A shepherd is for the care of the sheep; his love is what protects them from the wolf. Is the Sufi teacher not just such a shepherd as we hear of in all compassionate spiritual traditions?*

A. This question could be answered by repeating platitudes, and this would clearly please the questioner, for that is why it was asked. On the other hand, answered in another way, it might help us to clarify the limitations of analogy, and to stress some of the banalities of unexamined truisms.

Have you ever thought, for example, of your 'shepherd' in a wider perspective? Did you not know that the shepherd as we know him is, effectively, the employee, and therefore the agent, of the butcher? Why is he looking after 'his' sheep? Mawkish over-simplifications are useless; however beneficial, at a low level, the simplistic may be. One must learn to perceive the value of gentleness and see the absurdity of the shepherd's role beyond a primitive and unthinking observation of his immediate actions.

Human capacity to understand compassion does not have to be imprisoned within such a fallacious analogy as that of the shepherd, unless you are dealing with fools or small children.

There is a saying in the West:

'It is a mad rabbit which is caught by a drum'.

The Hammer

Q: *People who have been through Sufi training often say that it is hard and that they do not see why they should have to endure so much. How can something which is difficult or long-drawn-out be better than something which is not?*

A: In the first place, the people to whom you refer have never been 'through' Sufi training – they have perhaps been in it for a time; through it, no. People who have been through it know the answers to the questions which you put.

The overall picture, understood at a certain stage, enables one to perceive what place each experience takes in the process, but it is not easy to describe it in advance.

There is a saying, though, which may help:

> 'The hammer hits the nail; it is the nail which fixes the plank; neither knows its function, nor the advantages which will eventually accrue – this is unknown even to the man with the hammer.'

Unaltered

Q: *Religious training, all over the world, makes much of the need to provide people with habits which make them both good citizens and also followers of the precedents, the patterns, laid down by great figures of the past. Why is it that the Sufis seem to place so little importance upon precedent and upon rules laid down over the centuries?*

A: It is not the rules or the precedents, it is what people make of them. If a rule becomes a way of self-deception, it is not a rule, but a shackle. Habits are no use unless the person with the habit is such as to benefit from it, and to benefit others with it. More often we have merely servile imitation grafted onto undesirable inwardness.

Remember the proverb, created for the purpose of pointing this out:

> 'A blind cat still desires mice.'

Unwitting Knowledge

Q: *Is it possible for people to have higher knowledge without knowing it? What can make it stronger or weaker?*

A: Everyone has got higher knowledge, whether they know it or not. Some people have more than others. What weakens it is to take pride in it. What strengthens it is to disregard it when it is weak, so that it may grow. It can be matured under the right conditions: and that is what the School is for.

A great deal of higher knowledge is incipient, and becomes perceptible in its own time.

Withered

Q: *Traditionalism for its own sake is now very well understood by many people to be useless for learning, however attractive for experiencing. But how are we to know when we are experiencing and not learning, when the vital element in a teaching is exhausted, and where to look next?*

A: This is not a new problem, and it has been alluded to in these words: 'A bee knows when a flower is dead and shuns it. But a man or woman alone will not know when a teaching has withered.'

The bee, you see, possesses the faculty of recognising the nectar and its absence. But the human being, to become as efficient as the bee in the parable, must rely upon those things which develop his 'nectar-perceiving faculty'. His only problem, generally, is to assume that he has it already.

Why some Stay and some Pass By . . .

Q: *People go to listen to spiritual teachers, and then they either stay or they pass on. Why do some stay and some pass on?*

A: In the case of true teachers and true learners, they stay because they should. In the case of true teachers and untrue learners, it is because the former are following the injunction: 'Speak only to those who will listen: but remember that you must tell them what they do not want to hear!'

The people who hear or understand little are always those who in reality (whatever they imagine) have very shallow expectations. They ask for little, but it is not the 'little' of humility, but the 'little' of pettiness.

Those who can learn are rewarded like the old couple in the fable, related by Saadi, in his *Bostan*:

> The man had asked for ten pieces of silver from Hatim Tai, remembered as the most generous man who ever lived.
> A whole sackful of silver was delivered to his tent.
> His wife asked:
> 'Why so much when our need was only for ten?'
> Hatim, when this remark was reported to him, said:
> 'Their need was ten: that is their measure. And I, for my part, gave according to my own family's tradition!'

What is the Sufi Enterprise?

Q: *Is the Sufi effort a church, a sect or a cult? If it is none of these, what is it, and how can you establish this?*

A: Without intending any discourtesy, may I first ask whether you know any established difference between these things, and also if you can define each one of them, so that I might be as specific as possible within your dimensions?

Q: *I don't take offence. I must admit that, thinking about it, I have no definitions for church, sect and cult. Perhaps a church is respectable, what we believe in, a sect something which diverges from our idea of what is right, and a cult something of which we disapprove.*

A: If we assume these are accurate definitions, we at once see that one man's church is another's sect, and so on. So we cannot answer the question if we admit that Sufi effort is one of these things. Can anyone else give us a definition?

(Another speaker): I am a sociologist, and can give you the standard contemporary idea of these three things. A church is the custodian of the standard values of a community; a sect is a group partially withdrawn from society to intensify or purify doctrine; a cult is detached almost completely from the surrounding practices, whose members are committed to authoritarian figures, alive or dead . . .

A: Excellent though this rendition is, it still means that the true church for the people of New Guinea is one where heads have to be hunted; that a sect may become a church; that – say – the associates of a pioneering psychologist or even a scientist might be regarded as members of a cult. Luckily we can say that Sufi activity is not characterised in its accepted form as being similar to any of these things; Sufism is education. Sufis have been called a church, a sect and a cult precisely because the most visible distortions in the form of deteriorated communities have indeed behaved like churches, sects and cults. So you might say 'Sufis are those who do not appear like the sociological definitions of churches, sects and cults.'

234

Wind and Water

Q: *I read books and listen to talks, and yet I feel so often that this is just like trying to catch wind in a cage or water in a sieve. I know that the wind and water are there, but I have not got the means to collect them. Should I not give up this hearing and reading, and try something else?*

A: You look upon yourself as a cage or a sieve, which should therefore not be trying to catch wind or water. Your analogies have only one thing wrong with them: they are inapplicable to the situation.

A Sufi would not allow that you really do have a sieve or a cage, though he would accept that you need them. He would say that the books and the talks are there for the specific purpose of helping you to make these items to use them; because what you need is not wind and water at all.

The cage you need to catch that which would otherwise fly away, and to keep it in. The cage must be built and baited, and made a fit place for the bird which you need. The sieve has to come into being, so that you can sieve out the fine from the coarse.

The wind and the water which you are trying to catch are not for you, and will not help you. Why should you have given them such importance?

Wirewalkers

Q: *Why is it said that the Sufi first trusts in God, then he does not trust in God?*

A: Because trust is something that has to be done by someone who is ignorant. You trust someone if you do not know whether he is to be trusted or not. If you knew that he would never fail you, you do not call this 'trust' at all. You do not, for instance, trust yourself to an iron bridge, but you do to a rope which might break. When you know that you can trust in God, you do not think of God in terms of trust at all.

There is a saying which illustrates this:

'He walked a tightrope and cried out, "I trust in God!"'

Why do we not Get More?

Q: *I wonder why the devout, the people who really have worked for higher consciousness, and — indeed — all who believe in the truth of higher things, are not usually benefited by all this effort? Why do they not get any visible reward?*

A: There was once a dervish (as Rumi reports in *The Masnavi*, Book Five) who looked with envy at the splendidly-equipped slave of a certain gentleman.

The dervish was indigent, hungry and freezing and overcome with the feeling that he should have attained something in spiritual gifts.

He started to cry out:

'O God! Why do you not learn from the owner of this slave how to treat one of your own?'

In this way the dervish's feelings continued, until one day he heard that the King of Herat had had the slaves of the gentleman seized and tortured, to discover where he had hidden his treasure.

For a month, day and night, the slaves were made to suffer. Because of their loyalty, not one of them gave away the secret.

And the dervish, in a dream, heard a voice from Heaven. It said:

'You, too, learn to be a slave, and then apply to be mine.'

236

Q: *When there is an incorrect reaction to Sufi materials or experiences, does this not produce any kind of imbalance in the personality of the person?*

A: The worst kind of development, if we can use that word for it, is when people effectively turn into wiseacres. What happens is that people start to imagine that, using their wits instead of their brains and feelings, they can excel or advance even in Sufi activities. So they learn how to be glib; either repeating sayings, or working with association of ideas, and so on. The end result is the sort of odious personality that one often meets in superficial followers of anything, anywhere.

Human Identity

Q: *How concerned are people, really, about their identity, about who or what they are, and whether what they think and do is real or just habit and instinct?*

A: They are so concerned about this, that they think of very little else, though they do not realise it. It is very easy, however, to observe that this is what is happening, if we only examine what people say, think and do from the point of view of whether it is connected with their identity and/or their perception of themselves and of others. The interesting thing is that they seldom suspect that this is their obsession.

Anyone can check this – the fact is that few people do. Take, as I have, the current issue of a magazine with a monthly sale of over thirty million copies in thirteen languages. List the articles and other items. Before you have got through half of the pages, you will find no less than a dozen items about identity. There is the British Ambassador in Washington worrying about his identity, a rector's wife feeling that she had lost hers, a piece on what the relationship of computers should be with humans, two others on the position and identity of immigrants, one on twins and how their identity is affected, a joke about identity through appearances – and so on, through a long catalogue. In the first hundred pages of this same periodical, there are no less than twenty-five pieces on personality perception. They include how Pablo Casals feels when playing, how Onassis projected his personality onto entertaining, a piece on identifying oneself by how one speaks, and much, much more: all adding up to how people feel about themselves and about others.

Compared to this, there is hardly anything about other subjects. You could have answered your own question by looking at people and their media intake.

The Spice-Market

I get letters all the time from people who think like the monkey with his clenched fist in the bottle.

The fist, in these cases, is the rigidity of their thought, imprisoning scraps of real or supposed religious or esoteric lore, picked up from here and there. The 'lore' is usually useless, or inapplicable to them: but even if it were useful, the fist is fast clenched. The 'monkey' can't get free.

'I have this,' they say, 'and I just want that or the other.'

In the fable, though the monkey possessed a cherry, or a nut, or something, he could not do anything with it because of the bottle. In some versions a hunter creeps up on the hampered ape and captures him, cherry and all . . .

Although the letters are frequent enough to keep my mind on this subject, I have just had another one, from a man to whom something similar actually happened, and I want to share the story with you.

This man, as he freely admits, is and was rather a miser. He lives in a Middle Eastern city, which has a spice market.

Too stingy to buy spices to flavour his rice, the man used to go out and trail his cloak near the open sacks of ground spices, so that enough of the powder would adhere to it for him to dust off at home and put in his food.

He did this for something like a quarter of a century, and nobody ever suspected him, although the shopkeepers knew his face well enough.

One day recently, there was a robbery, and a large quantity of spices were stolen. The police, looking for suspects, were told by some children that the miser always smelt of spices, though they had never seen him buying any.

He was interrogated, and at first refused to say why his clothes smelt as they did. When arrested on suspicion and taken to court, the miser confessed the truth. Nobody believed him, and he was fined an enormous sum: more than he would have spent on spices for the whole of his life, if he had got them in the normal way.

Now he writes to me. Guess what he says? 'Is there no justice in the world, that an innocent man can be convicted on circumstantial evidence?'

He hasn't even realised that he is a thief.

Now here we have nature imitating art, a true event paralleling fiction in the real world.

Of course, you aren't a thief and a miser, but if I were you, I'd think carefully whether there might not be a corresponding parallel, somewhere, in the case of people who 'steal' bits and pieces of supposed spirituality . . .

Understanding Sufi Study

The Sufis speak of 'the world', and how it causes a barrier to be erected between humanity and reality.

What is this 'world'?

It is the amalgam of natural acquisitiveness and social conditioning which have gone too far.

All organisms, including human ones, try to extend their acquisition of all kinds of things. Human beings are taught, by society, to restrain this tendency. This restraint, among other things, enables the human being to perceive more than would otherwise be possible.

The degree and kind of restraint has to be taught and learnt. One aspect of Sufi activity teaches the balance which enables other things to be acquired than social harmony or a mere sense of emotional well-being.

Much of what passes for spiritual teaching relies, in reality, upon increasing greed, emotion and acquisitiveness. Of course, this is not understood by those who carry out such teachings. They imagine that emotionality is the same as spirituality.

Sufis have, in the past, been accused of encouraging emotionality. But the fact is that such Sufis have only been stressing some degree of emotion when faced by pupils who needed it through excessive coldness. Naturally, emotionalists who have studied only a part of Sufi activity (usually from books) have selectively chosen such emphases. As a result, they have misled others, and themselves. The result is Sufic cults which are, in reality, not Sufi at all. Many, because of the large proportion of emotionalists in any population, have become very well known. Some have even been considered classically Sufi.

Are you one of the people who, unknowingly, seeks from Sufi study some form of emotional stimulus, and who feels a vague discomfort when Sufis deny you this?

Any ordinary psychologist will tell you that people have expectations from anything in which they interest themselves. They will have a preconceived (though not always conscious)

240

picture of what they will 'get' from anything. If they do not feel that they are 'getting it', they will react. The sensible person, whenever experiencing this unease, will seek the real reason for the sensation. Unless on one's guard, however, the conclusion will tend to be flattering to oneself. The individual will think, 'This is not for me; it does not give me what I want.'

The contemporary world, which is largely based on advertising, on transactionalism, on exciting greed and on the stick and carrot, conspires with the primitive in human beings. And this pattern, of threat and promise, is visible even in some of the most respected of spiritual traditions, so over-simplified have they become by what can only be called the current practitioners.

The Sufis are a challenge to this doctrine. In some measure, they have always opposed it. In some measure, they have always, somewhere, elicited an antipathetic reaction. This is because the stick-and-carrot people feel threatened by the Sufis. In reality, the Sufis are no threat to them: there will always be such people, and they will always have enough hearers and believers to suffice them. If they were a little less insecure, they would see this easily enough.

But the Sufis are, though not a threat, certainly a challenge. The concept that people can learn, can get to know themselves, to know others and what lies beyond ordinary perception; all this using the minimum, not the maximum, of emotional or intellectual effort: together with the right balance of each and not the extension of either or both: this is a challenge. It goes against the attitudes of the intellectualists and the emotionalists alike. It also appears to oppose the attitude of those who think that neither intellect nor emotion should be allowed to operate if spiritual perception and understanding are to emerge. But if a statement of fact is to be considered a challenge, we are entitled to ask why.

Naturally, there has to be a framework within which the Sufi aspirant will approach learning and understanding. Throughout the ages, and in varying communities and groups, Sufis have used the frameworks which will best help to conduct the learners

241

to the learning. Under present circumstances, you could take note of these important points:

Those who wish to progress should try to examine their assumptions. They should examine their reactions to Sufi teaching as well as to their daily human contacts and experiences. They should ponder the principle: 'None should be the worse off from having been in contact with me!' They should add to these three points two more, which are:

'Sufi understanding comes through right study and teaching, through right exercises when indicated, through remembering that the flaws which are not repaired are those which can make most effort useless.'

And remember, it is the Teaching, and not the individual who teaches, which is important. In the words of one sage who (because of the foregoing) does not want to be identified:

How many people have called someone great who has only frightened them?

How many people have called someone good who has only delighted them?

The Elements of the Situation

If you are trying to teach anything, you have to bring together certain elements. These include the knowledge, an assessment of the student, and the method and content of the teaching.

All three factors must be present, and present in the right order, to the right extent, and in the right manner. Any other situation will lead to partial learning, to confusion, to lack of progress.

If you are trying to teach, let us say, literature, chemistry, business studies or drama to people who have been reared in the atmosphere of the contemporary West, you will not need to give the above requirements the very greatest attention. This is because the minds of the learners already contain, transmitted by the culture, a large number of elements and attitudes on which you can build. You do not have to start from scratch.

If, however, you were starting to teach chemistry to members of a community already thinking only in terms of alchemy; or astronomy to people who confused it with astrology, you would have a different problem: and so would they.

The study of metaphysics in the modern West can be likened to an attempt to study what is in fact chemistry from the point of view of alchemy. If you were teaching in that situation, you would not simply plunge in and obey the demand of the students to give them a 'higher form of alchemy'. You would have to go to an earlier stage, and establish the framework within which chemistry could be learnt.

You would be able to USE concepts and processes, experiments and so on, which had been transmitted by alchemists. But you would have to disentangle these from all the rest: from the accretions, misunderstandings and so on which separate chemistry and alchemy.

You would also find that some, even all, of your students would have read and heard of all kinds of theories. They would have read books and even carried out experiments; and they would expect you to give them explanations which – to their minds – were necessary and interesting.

What would you say to them?

In what order would you approach your sequence of ideas?

What equipment, instrumentation and elements would you use?

What would you eliminate, postpone or ignore?

If you knew your job, you would have to start by instilling concepts which would enable the student to learn, stage by stage. You might compromise to some extent, but only to an extent which would not make learning more difficult, or set people onto the wrong track.

This is the position of the Sufi teacher at the present time.

The individual who wants to solve the problem of humankind

243

today comes to the teacher with an often enormous ragbag of ideas, impressions and theories, only some of which will be of use in this particular specialisation.

The test which the learner has to pass, first of all, is to show that he or she can study what is important and relevant. The pupil who is his or her own enemy is the one who wants to retain ideas, experiences, theories because they are fulfilling a pleasure-inducing function. So, first of all, what has to be determined is whether the student wants to learn or really (often without knowing it) wants to 'be entertained'.

This is why the Sufis so strongly emphasise the need to examine one's assumptions. The chief assumption which can get in the way is usually 'I feel that this is right, therefore it is: so I want to continue with something which continues, and preferably amplifies, that feeling.'

Knowledge does not, however, exist for the purpose of making people pleased, or the reverse.

Sufi study materials, which include study papers, have a dual purpose. First, they inform: as in the foregoing paragraphs. Second, they contain the elements which will connect, at the appropriate time, with the frame of mind which enables the pupil to progress. This 'frame of mind' is NOT a substitute for conventional thinking: it is an addition to it. The Sufis do not merely assume that people can develop their understanding by grafting their teaching upon preconceived notions. To do so would be analogous to taking a group of would-be alchemists and ladling fresh material on top of unsuitable ground.

The process by which people learn, in Sufi schools, is similar to the way in which people accumulate, in conventional societies, the basic elements which enable them to be taught more. The child or mature student in the modern world has, long before starting any organised learning programme, already absorbed a very large number of facts and experiences upon which the learning builds.

The often disastrous assumption made by people wanting to study Sufi knowledge is that they already have an equivalent to that basis. It is as if someone wanted to read a book and

244

insisted that literacy was unnecessary. Or as if someone wanted to learn farming and assumed that it could be learnt through the concepts and procedures of blacksmithing.

The basic stock of knowledge and experience at the disposal of the contemporary individual is large and extremely useful. Through it you can learn all kinds of things. To become a Sufi you not only have to acquire more ideas, experiences and skills: you also have to learn to use them.

People constantly approach Sufis and tell them that such-and-such contacts, reading, experiences 'have led them to the teacher'. They seek an assurance that they are right in this belief; they seek further stimulus of a similar kind: they often expect that the Sufi will elucidate mysteries and give answers to problems. They seldom realise that mysteries and problems are not always there for the purpose of being elucidated. Still less do they generally understand that the path which has brought them to the Sufi almost always ceases to have relevance when they have found the source of teaching.

They have never heard (or have not heeded) the admonition: 'When the donkey has brought you to the door, however admirable it may be, you have to dismount from it before entering.'

The main obstacle to learning, though not to imagining that one can learn or has learnt, is making what are (in fact if not in appearance) random assumptions. Sufi study materials are designed to help in dealing with this problem.

Impatience and vanity are deprecated in virtually all religious systems. Why? Because they reduce the human being, instead of elevating him or her.

Impatience and vanity are deprecated, too, in all moral and ethical systems. They are disliked and opposed everywhere: in the law, in social contact, in science, everywhere. Why? Because they make life more difficult for someone or something, and retard developmental progress.

Because from our earlier days, whoever we are, we are constantly told to overcome these characteristics, they go underground. People are not even aware that they are vain or

245

impatient; or else will argue fiercely that 'At least in my desire for truth, knowledge, etc., I am not impatient or vain. I want to know so that I can help other people; I want to hurry because I have achieved so little in my life'. Throughout history, Sufis have enabled people to deal with these negative characteristics.

They cannot be dealt with by suppression; only by observation and examination and finally detachment from them. The monastic systems which once specialised in illustrating these things fairly soon turned into repressive or mechanical organisations. Why? Because one factor fell into disuse: the analysis and prescribing of specific remedies. Something which started out as a flexible and interacting school turned into an automatic one: with the same prayers, meditations, litanies, tunes, activities and so on imposed upon everyone regardless of need and potentiality. Human beings were, effectively, being treated like animals being trained: with threat and promise, tension and repetition, and all the rest.

Western society has in the past few decades taken a great step forward, which gives its members a perhaps unparalleled opportunity. This has been due to the final recognition of the way in which people can be (and are) conditioned to believe virtually anything. Although this knowledge existed earlier, it was confined to a few, and was taught to relatively small groups, because it was considered subversive. Once, however, the paradox of change of 'faith' began to disturb Western scientists in the Korean war, they were not long in explaining – even in replicating – the phenomenon. As with so many other discoveries, this one had to wait for its acceptance until there was no other explanation. Hence, work which Western scientists could have done a century or more earlier was delayed.

Still, better late than never. What remains to be done is that the general public should absorb the facts of mind-manipulation. Failure to do so has resulted in an almost free field for the cults which are a bane of Western existence. In both East and West, the slowness of absorption of these facts has allowed narrow political, religious and faddish fanaticisms to arise, to grow and to spread without the necessary 'immunisation'. In illiberal societies it is forbidden to teach these facts. In liberal ones, few people are interested: but only because mind-manipulation is assumed to be something that happens to someone else, and people are selfish in many ways, though charitable in others. Yet the reality is that most people are touched by one or other of an immense range of conditioned beliefs, fixations even, which take the place of truth and are even respected because 'so-and-so is at least sincere'.

Naturally, such mental sets are not to be opposed. Indeed, they thrive on opposition. They have to be explained and contained. The foregoing remarks will not 'become the property' of the individual or of the group on a single reading. An unfamiliar and previously untaught lesson, especially when it claims careful attention and remembering, will always take time to sink in. This presentation, therefore, forms a part of materials which need to be reviewed at intervals. Doing this should enable one to add a little ability and to receive a minute quantity of understanding, each time.

The Melon

Once upon a time there was a man whose neighbour had a melon-field.

The friend gave him melons every time there was a crop. This went on for some years until, he was not quite sure why, the melon-eater became dissatisfied. He asked:

'The fruits give me food and pleasure, but I seek more; tell me the secret of melons, so that I may penetrate to their innermost being. Anything which is so exciting when tasted must surely have an origin, and an inner reality, which is even more sublime.'

The farmer, however, only said, 'Take what is given to you,

and be grateful for it. If you are grateful, something more may be opened to you. But to want more, just because one has tasted something, is not the right attitude for a good man to adopt.'

This recommendation to take what was offered and to remain patient, however, did not appeal to the melon-eater. He said, 'Then just tell me where melons come from, so that I may journey there. Perhaps I may be able to do some investigating on my own. After all, I cannot be sure that what you say is the be-all and end-all of this matter.'

The farmer smiled, and said, 'My intention was not to make you dependent on me, nor to conceal anything from you. Rather it was to save you needless labour and disappointment. But, as you ask, go to Bokhara, from where the best melons come: and then, one day, you may see whether my words were right or not. Do not, though, hold it against me if you find that you have wasted many years of your life.'

The melon-eater travelled to Bokhara, where he went from one melon-field to another, looking at the fruit and asking the farmers where the essence of melons came from. Most of them thought that he was an idle enquirer, and some thought that he was mad.

Finally, one ancient sage who also grew melons said, 'The melon comes from a tiny seed, as you will have seen whenever you cut one open. Inside it is the essence of the fruit. The seed is of use to cultivators of melons, who know how to nurture it and pass it on through a ripe fruit. To anyone else, apart from the transient and tiny kernel, it is of little use. Indeed, you would almost starve to death if you tried to use it for food.'

But the would-be seeker only listened to the first part of what the old man had said, and he tried to live on the 'essence', the seeds of melons.

He nearly starved to death but, being both greedy and determined, he just managed to survive, always eating melon seeds, and always hoping that the secret which he sought would come to him by this means. This was his condition until he died.

The Stone and the Tree

There was once a dervish at Abadan, whose cell was always surrounded by disciples, people who had come from far and near to hear his wisdom and try to achieve knowledge and spiritual fulfilment.

Sometimes he spoke to them, sometimes he did not. Sometimes he read from books, and sometimes he made them perform various tasks.

The disciples tried, for decades, to understand the purport of his words, to fathom the depths of his signs and symbols, and in every way possible to get closer to his wisdom.

Those who understood what he taught were the ones who did not spend time trying to puzzle out things. They cultivated patience and attention, and refrained from looking for verbal associations from books and from what others had told them.

The majority, however, as is the way of the world, were sometimes elated, sometimes sad: and always covetous, even if it was only for wisdom and their own well-being.

They had all kinds of explanations for this way of thinking except the real ones.

At long last, after many years had passed, one of these disciples plucked up enough courage to approach the Master directly, and said:

'There are a number of us, O Wise One, who have been trying to follow the Path of Knowledge for most of our lives. Now, as some are old and others are getting older, we feel that we have to open our hearts to you, saying that we need a further indication of how we should proceed.'

The Dervish gave a long sigh and answered:

'Come with me to the seashore, and I shall show you something which tells you everything, if you can only hear it.'

At the pebble-strewn beach, the Dervish took a stone from the water and asked a disciple, 'How long has this stone been here?'

The man said, 'It is worn smooth, so it must have been rolled

249

back and forth, under the surf, for perhaps several thousand years.'

'Now,' said the Dervish, 'Take this wet stone and crack it open, then tell me what you find.'

They smashed the stone, and saw that it was very much the same inside as it was out.

'You observe,' said the Dervish, 'that, although submerged in the sea for uncounted ages, the inmost part of this stone is as dry as if it had never been near water. You people are like the stone. Surrounded by wisdom, you do not allow it to penetrate. Unlike the stone, there is a talisman which will let the transforming quality suffuse you, to your innermost being.

'That quality is patience, forbearance, and openness, things which you call three qualities, but which are in reality only one.'

Next the Dervish took his followers onto a hill overlooking the sea, where in spite of the aridity of the place, a magnificent tree grew.

'This tree,' he said, 'can live and grow tall and fruitful where nothing else can. This is possible to it only because it has made worthy efforts, signalled by the inner quality of the seed which gave it birth, to penetrate deep into the earth to find water.

'Learn the lesson, my friends.'

The Path of Love

Think not the Path of Love
    An easy way.
Here certain senses guide the Lover's climb:
Its heights and depths defy
The plan of Matter.

Think not of this in careless terms
But bear in mind
Thy first station towards Love is nigh
    When all is blotted out
But the Beloved.

The mystic's Way – all of the Way
Is the path of the heart
    To One Beloved:
The quest of love –
With heart athrob.

The Master Sanai of Ghazna
(translated by *Sirdar Ikbal Ali Shah*)

One of the very greatest of the poets and mystics of the East, Hakim Sanai (1077-1150) was acknowledged by the Master Rumi as his teacher.

The poem above, translated by my father, is one of the Master of Ghazna's lighter works. Sanai is one of the Sufi poets who have been recognised as having influenced Dante, who lived more than a century and a half later. Sanai's *Journey of the Worshipper* is a masterwork in Persian, dealing with the experiences of the mystic on the path to enlightenment. It is almost bewildering to those who have not followed this route, in its sublime allegories and very many dimensions. But the beauty of the words and rhythm give it a haunting, unique quality for those who can read the original.

Tattoos and Soup not Spiritual?

Psychological and spiritual systems, you will note if you look at what they try to do, concentrate upon grafting behaviour patterns on top of basic impulses.

These impulses are: (1) inherent, such as those which stem

from the animal nature, and (2) learnt, such as cultural conformities.

Recognition of the action of either of these factors, according to the Sufis, can make possible the emergence of a third kind of thought and behaviour: the spiritual, as distinct from the social and emotional. The profound, as distinct from what is in comparison superficial.

It is not easy, since all major cultures are stabilised on the belief that these 'superficialities' are in fact deep. This, in turn, has only come about because it is easier to assume this than to make efforts.

The following notes, taken from actual instances, will show current tendencies, and can help one to operate in a different manner – without excising or affecting laudable elements in the inherent and learnt characteristics.

A.   Unconscious seeking of one's own advantage. This takes many forms, both 'offensive and defensive'. It is natural enough to oppose suggestions or avoid facing facts; but for such strategies to be effective, one needs to KNOW what 'one's own advantage' really is.

As one Sufi put it, 'A man with a mask on his face and a sharp instrument in his hand may not be a murderer – he may be a surgeon proposing to remove your appendix to save your life.' So the intending learner must first determine whether he accepts the 'surgeon's' role. He does not start to learn until this is clarified. If he cannot arrive at this stage, no true teaching situation can exist.

B.   Frequent discussion or repetition of a subject, instead of making a decision and carrying it through or attempting to do so.

C.   Acceptance of co-operation without extending parallel co-operativeness.

D.   Assertions take the place of actions. Brushing suggestions aside, a strategy for avoiding action.

E.   Laziness.

F.   Confusing one thing with another.

G.   Failure to observe that one's actions do not match one's words; speech without thought.

H.   Anxiety as a device to avoid action.

I.   Once accepting someone's competence to guide or advise; arguing, heedlessness or attempted modification ('negotiation').

SECTION VIII

Turnips

'Many a true word is spoken in jest,' they say in England. Having said it, people nod sagely. The ones who laugh at a joke generally think that it would spoil their fun if the other content of the joke were examined. Those who look for the moral too often lack a sense of humour. Because of that, they haven't a well-rounded enough mind to learn, anyway.

This is an interesting peculiarity of the current culture, so well-established as to deprive hundreds of millions, perhaps billions, of people of a great deal of knowledge and experience.

Let us look at a joke and see whether we can both enjoy it and learn something.

I heard this one at a party given by the Afghanistan Society of the School of Oriental and African Studies at London University. People had been invited to tell tales, and one young woman stood up and told it:

There was once a philosophy don who had had little social life. One day he had to attend a conference and wondered what would happen if he was expected to talk to a woman.

He asked a friend what he should do.

'No problem,' said the friend. 'Women are interested in two things: families and dieting. Mention one or the other and you can have a reasonable conversation.'

So the academic went to the conference and, when the time came when he found himself obliged to talk to a woman, he felt adequately prepared.

'How is your brother?' he asked, sure that the family aspect was bound to start the conversation correctly.

The woman looked at him oddly. 'I haven't got a brother,' she said.

'Well,' thought the scholar, 'there is still the second subject.' He asked, 'What do you think of turnips?'

The woman said, edging away from him, 'I do not like them at all.'

The don was not a man of the brain for nothing, and he was

now sure that, with his philosophical training, he could initiate a really good conversation on the basis of what had gone before.

'Tell me,' he enquired, 'If you did have a brother, would you like turnips?'

If you try to think of two things at once, you lose both; so one should enjoy the joke before looking for a meaning.

In the case of this one – and of most other jokes – there are lots of useful meanings to be extracted from the story. Your immediate reactions can tell you something about yourself.

I tried the joke on a man who swore that it showed up the foolishness and shallow thought-patterns of philosophers. He was delighted to find this in the story, since he had disliked such people for years. In other words, his reaction told us something about him. Unfortunately, it did not help him much, since he could not believe that his opposition to philosophers was in the nature of a fixation.

Now let us look at the tale as a structure, and take out individual parts. First, it shows assumptions: the assumptions of the university man that all he needed was a couple of points and that he would be sure to be able to use them effectively.

Split this up into the facts that the don needed basic facts, needed skill, and could gain nothing by rushing into something without these two factors. Facts plus skill produce the timing and context in which to make an approach to a problem.

I get at least one letter a week from someone or other who knows that I write books, but does not want to read them. He (or, as often, she) has read something from one of the books ('the family and diet subjects') and then approaches me asking for 'real teaching' ('the ridiculous attempt at conversation').

Why do people carry on like this? If you meet them, they do not prove to be unthinking idiots: some of them are highly intelligent, some are even spiritually-minded people.

When you have seen enough cases, the pattern becomes absolutely clear. The clue lies in the very fact that they are normal. Just ask yourself, what is it that makes normal people act foolishly? Almost always it is emotion. And the particular form of emotion involved in spurning something to seek something else? Greed. The greed for knowledge, for 'holiness', for attainment of all kinds, is every bit as ugly and reducing of human potential as any other kind of greed.

You see, I (like many others) have written books for the precise purpose of providing a basis from which people may go on to something higher. The books are there to provide an essential step. In the West people say, 'Don't try to run before you can walk'. Do they apply this to every aspect of their life and thought?

In the East we say, 'The evident is the bridge to the Real'. It is greed which says, 'I'll start with Lesson Ten, because I do not see why I should do the first nine lessons.' Greed, and vanity. That this greed and vanity are well hidden does not mean that they are not there, and active.

And there is what we could call the profit motive. People seek, usually unwittingly, a profit from everything, and an easy profit. The academic in our joke wanted a profit with little effort, and on his own terms. This problem has been with us for a very long time.

Do you know the story of Euclid, when he had just described his first theorem to a class? A young man stood up and said:

'That is all very well, but what does it profit me?'

Euclid said to someone, 'Give him three coppers, for here is a man who won't do anything unless he can see his immediate profit!'

This is not only a marvellous story. Euclid lived (in Alexandria) well over two thousand years ago. And his work was not entirely original: he taught things which had been taught by his predecessors.

We can look back over that long period of time, to entire civilisations, including present-day ones, whose people claim to be inheritors of this tradition. But we can demonstrate that they have not yet learnt what it was trying to teach.

It is not only pointless to try to teach the second step before the first has been learnt: it is impossible.

You will have noted from the foregoing that the method

adopted by the vain-greedy-impatient elements in the mind is to think and act selectively. People choose things which interest them and avoid those which do not. No harm in that. But the next step is absurd: having chosen these things, they try to use them to solve a problem. Worse, they try to make others connive in this.

If you said to an apple-tree, 'Give me oranges, and give them to me next Thursday, wrapped in plastic', you would be adopting the same kind of logic.

There is an ancient saying, 'A genuine halfpenny can be more useful than a false gold coin.' Indeed, not only might the counterfeit piece gain you nothing, it might land you in jail for possessing forgeries.

Falsely spiritual people are easily seen through, because they think, like materialists, in transactionalist terms. They want to get something in exchange for something else.

Spiritual teaching throughout the ages concurs in emphasising the folly of greed, vanity and impatience. Why? Because they blind, hamper and cripple people.

Spiritual teachings, of whatever origin, stress the need to avoid expectation and transaction-mindedness. Yet people who claim that they believe in God still offer to God things which, by definition, already belong to God. The most obvious example is when people give up things which they should not have anyway - and then expect to be rewarded for it.

No wonder materialists laugh at believers. And how lucky it is that we can feel that the 'believers' at whom the materialists are laughing are simply not spiritual people at all.

The Wise Man

'Wise' is one of those words which people have not been wise enough to define clearly. One constantly meets people who are called wise, but who seem only to have impressed others. 'Wise' is evidently not an absolute; someone can be wise about some things and not about others.

So, how wise is wise? How relevant is someone's wisdom to your own life? How clever, for that matter, is clever?

I think that it is worth looking at the story of the clever bird.

This is a very old tale. What it tells you will depend a great deal upon where you are at the time you hear it:

Each year a peaceable bird laid a clutch of eggs. Just as regularly, a fox in whose territory she made her home appeared and made her throw down two of her chicks, which he then ate.

'This is my right,' he would say, 'and if you refuse me I shall climb up and eat all your little ones.'

One day, when the miserable hen was sitting with her fledglings, waiting sadly for the fox to come, a wiser bird flew down and perched near her. She told him her troubles.

'The solution is easy;' said the wiser bird. 'Foxes cannot climb trees. Call his bluff!'

Although frightened, the mother bird did as he advised. The Fox was furious.

'Who told you I can't climb trees?' he asked.

'The clever bird. He's very wise.'

The Fox went off and prowled around until he found the clever bird perched on a branch, and engaged him in conversation.

'Tell me,' he said, after exchanging some general observations, 'what do you do in Winter? Foxes have burrows to shelter in, but birds don't seem to have proper shelters.'

'That's easy enough,' the bird told him, 'we go down into hedges and put our heads under our wings.'

The Fox shook his head, as if perplexed. 'How exactly is that done? It must be a very clever thing to do . . .'

'I'll show you, if you like,' said the bird.

He flew down into the hedge which, as it was Summer, was very thin, and sat there with his head under his wing.

The Fox leapt on him and gobbled him up.

Everyone can be clever when it is a matter of other people's problems – so says one interpretation of this story – but it is not so easy to apply wisdom to oneself.

After a Swim

Once upon a time there was a cat who lived in a field beside a river. He often wished that he could swim, for across the water was a large pigeon-house, full of tame and well-fed birds.

One day someone brought a horse and put it in the field, and the two animals started to talk.

'I'm thinking of swimming across the river, to graze on some of that lovely ripening corn on the other side,' said the Horse.

'I can't swim. Take me on your back, please do!' said the Cat.

The Horse agreed, and soon they were crossing the river, with the Cat holding onto the Horse's mane.

On the opposite bank, the Horse started to graze, while the Cat leapt upon the pigeons, killing several and gorging himself in a very short time.

When he was completely full, the Cat started to howl and prance about; though the Horse tried to stop him. 'Be careful!' he said, 'the villagers will come out, hearing that terrible racket, and do us some harm.'

But the Cat only said, 'I always do this after I have eaten: it is my habit.'

The Horse was annoyed, because it took him much longer to eat his fill.

Presently the people of the village heard the cat's cries. They came with sticks and stones and attacked the two animals. The horse had to stop eating and, with the Cat on his back, he swam across the river once more.

'You've ruined everything!' the Horse told his companion. 'Now we can't go back, and I am still hungry.'

'Oh well,' said the Cat, 'I can't help it; it's a habit I have.'

Suddenly the Horse started to roll on the grass, trapping the Cat beneath him. 'Stop it!' gasped the Cat. 'You're killing me! I can feel my backbone crack! You don't know what you're doing . . .'

The Horse only said, 'Well, you see, it's my nature. After swimming I always roll.'

All in One Man

There was once a beautiful queen whom everyone wanted to marry, and suitors came from far and wide to seek her hand.

One day, three men – each with strange powers – met in a caravanserai in her capital city, each determined to win the lady.

They found that she had been abducted by genies. Talking together, the three teamed up to try to save her.

The first man was a Turk, who could see the unseen in a magical stone he owned. The second was a Persian, who knew how to construct a wonderful palanquin, which moved by its own power and as swiftly as light. The third was an Afghan, who had a demon-destroying bow and arrows.

The Turk looked in his stone and saw that the Queen was imprisoned in a far-distant castle. The Persian built a magical palanquin and they all leapt into it. When they arrived at the genies' castle, the Afghan killed them with his demon-destroying weapon: and they brought the lady safely home.

When she had recovered from the ordeal, the Queen called

the three heroes to her Court and asked each to name his reward.

The Turk said, 'I want to marry you; for I found you with my magical stone.'

'I claim you for my bride,' said the Persian, 'for it was my wonderful palanquin which took us to you.'

'I,' said the Afghan, 'deserve your hand, for it was I and my demon-destroying bow and arrows which made your rescue possible.'

The Queen laughed. 'I shall reward all of you for your gallantry,' she said, 'but, to win my hand, single-minded unity is needed. The three abilities you mention would have to be present in the same man!'

The Fish-Eating Monkey

An ancient dervish strode into a certain town one day, and began to preach that 'the reality which people generally take for how things really are is not true'. He insisted that people were deceived by appearances, and that even the things which supposedly spiritual people told them were imaginary, since the beliefs of people who could not tell truth from fiction could not be right.

Some people were impressed; but others said, 'Tell us in the form of a parable, for we have always been given stories to illustrate truths. Surely there must be something from your "other world" which can be used as a parable?'

So the dervish, after pondering for a moment, said, 'Yes, I will tell you, but people who think that apparent reality is truth will find real truth very odd . . .'

Nevertheless, he began to recite, and this is what he said:

'In ancient times there was a monkey, a fish-eating one, who was very miserable and hungry, because it was the season of deprivation – Winter – and the streams from which he was accustomed to getting his food were all frozen over.

'He wandered from one place to another in the broad acres of his world, wondering how to get something to eat. He was getting weaker and weaker, but thought himself lucky when he espied a rat, scurrying along.

'With his remaining strength, he managed to seize the rat, which fought hard but could not release itself.

'"Why are you molesting me?" it squeaked, "and since when did monkeys, and fish-eating ones at that, grab innocent rats, who have done them no harm?"

'"Ah," replied the monkey, "you see, circumstances alter cases. I may be a fish-eating monkey, but I am starving, and so I have to turn into a rat-eater for the time being, so as to get my strength back, until the rivers thaw and I can scoop fish out of them, and return to my normal ways . . ."

'Now all this was logical and understandable; just as when people desire something and cannot get it, they will try for something else, not knowing even as much as the monkey did. They simply reach for something to make up for their deprivation. Sometimes in fact, as we all know, they give strange accounts of their reasons for doing what they do.

'But, to return to our animals, the rat was not a fool. He thought as hard and fast as he could how to escape from his two problems. Two? Yes: he had already been wondering, before the monkey seized him, how he would feed himself. He was not strong enough to catch the monkey; even if he had been, he could not work out how to kill the monkey in order to eat him. So he devised a way to solve both the problem of food and the one of escape.

'The rat had an inspiration. He said, "Friend monkey! You don't really like rat's flesh, so why do you not choose fish instead?"

'"Imbecile!" shouted the ravenous and impatient primate, "I have already explained my position. If this is the best that you can do to induce me not to eat you, then we might as well get on with the feast."

"'It is not that at all," said the rat calmly; "it is just that you have not thought the matter through enough. I happen to know something that you obviously have not pondered: how to catch fish from a frozen stream . . ."

'The monkey began to be interested. "Indeed, I had no idea that one could do such things. How is it managed?"

"'When you have spent as long as I have among the abodes of men, those superior beings," said the rat, "you learn much of their arts. I have seen these men, and they perform miracles such as I have mentioned. I can tell you how to assuage your craving, so that you not only have food, but have guaranteed sustenance for all time. You will never have to be reduced to such a miserable predicament again, if you will only listen to me."

"'I am waiting," said the monkey. Even if he had not been hungry, he would still (like all monkeys) have been curious, inquisitive and avaricious. To show that he was also, like all monkeys, impatient, he now added, "Hurry up and tell me, or I'll squeeze you to death!"

'The rat said, "Although this is a high and esoteric art, it is simplicity itself when you know how. What men do is that they actually make holes in the ice."

"'But why should anyone do that? You can make a hole in something to eat it, but there is no point in eating ice," said the monkey, in puzzlement.

"'That just proves how little you understand," replied the rodent; "because the purpose of the hole is far more intricate than the immediate objective. The hole is made because under the ice, which does not extend the full depth of the water, the fish are still swimming. When the hole has been made, fishes swim past and can be caught."

"'That sounds possible," said the monkey, "but you would have to make a very big hole indeed to scoop fish out from it, and they will in any case not come up to the surface to be flipped out of the water, because this is the season when there are no midges for them to rise for . . ."

"'You are a fool!" said the rat; "observing men and penetrating their secrets, I have learnt the whole art of catching fish through holes in the ice in Winter, and I am trying to explain it to you, step by step, but all you do is to make objections before you have heard me out."

"'Oh, very well," said the monkey, "go ahead and finish your story."

"'Thank you. The fact is that the hole does not have to be as large as you think. The reason for this is that human anglers need a hole only large enough to lower what is called bait into the water. The fish see this and think that it is a morsel and snap at it . . . '

"'Oh, I see!" exclaimed the monkey. "Then all you have to do is to pluck the bait out of the water, with the fish's jaws clenched over it, and you have your fish on dry land and can eat it at your leisure because it cannot get back."

"'Precisely!" said the rat; "you are improving, Now, in your case, you are in a better position than a man, being a monkey and therefore having a tail. All you have to do is to make a hole large enough to put your tail in, lower it into the water and wait until the fish imagine that it is something to eat. When you feel the weight of the fish, you will know that you have caught something."

'So the monkey, still holding the rat in case he was being deceived, made a hole in the ice with one of his hands, and placed his tail in it.

'The water, of course, was very cold, and the monkey winced and complained that he was getting frozen.

"'That always happens," said the rat. "But, the interesting thing is that this sensation soon passes off, and you will feel the bliss which goes with no feeling at all."

'The rat knew, of course, that what would happen would be that the monkey's tail would become insensible and that the monkey would imagine that he was comfortable because of the contrast between the numbness and the former pain of the freezing.

'Sure enough, after a few minutes, the monkey released from the pain of freezing process, exclaimed, "Yes! this is indeed

267

comfort and bliss! What joy to be released from such suffering!" He even felt grateful to the rat, for he did not fully perceive that the pain was caused by the rat in the first place, in a manner of speaking.

'But soon the hole which he had made started to freeze over again, and the monkey felt as if a great weight had been attached to his tail, and he cried out in fear.

'"Now, now!" admonished the rat, "there is no need to make such a fuss. Anyway, what seems to be the matter?"

'"As an expert on higher, human affairs," said the monkey, "you will no doubt be able to tell me why I now feel as if I am being held tight."

'"Yes, of course," said the rat; "what is happening is that so many fish have taken hold of your tail that they must weigh a ton. Think of the crop which you will be able to bring up when they are all attached to you. You will be able to sell your surplus to the men who live in the village yonder. Relieved of the need to do their own fishing, they will honour you, will think of you as one of themselves instead of continuing to regard you as an undeveloped travesty of themselves; and they will have you do their fishing forever, welcoming you into their warm and illuminated abodes."

'The monkey was captivated by the thought. By now, of course, he was caught fast, as all the ice had frozen over again.

'"Can I bring up my catch now?"he asked, completely convinced that his experiences accorded with the words of his adviser, and trusting him implicitly. In token of this new relationship, he released his hold on his captive, now his teacher.

'"You may certainly do so,"answered the rat, settling himself nearby to watch that his stratagem had succeeded. Sure enough, he saw that the monkey was held fast by the ice. No matter how he struggled, he could not free himself.

'And what did the rat do next? He could not eat the monkey, as we have noted. So he went to the human village nearby, and did a deal with the people who lived there. In exchange for food they became the owners of the monkey, trading him from the rat. And the monkey stayed a captive of the men for the rest of his days, living on a subsistence diet and being trained by means of it to perform tricks whenever he was exhibited at fairs.'

The ancient dervish continued, 'And thus it is with you. You are like the monkey, and your instructors are like the rat. Things seem plausible to you, as they did to the monkey. But things were not what they seemed, and they are not what they seem to you. Therefore open your eyes now. What the monkey did not know is that there is always a normally unperceived solution to hunger other than being advised by a rat: especially when you think that you have captured the rat, and in reality it is he who has captured you.'

THE CORPSE IN THE GARDEN

Now the people were very impressed by what the old dervish had told them, but they were still puzzled about some things.

One of them, representing the others, said, 'Holy and Respected Dervish and Friend of Truth! We can now understand that the perception of the world is made up of our assumptions about it; that we lack information and experience, and that we follow the interpretations given about it and about things beyond by those who are only serving their own purposes.'

'In that case,' said the dervish, 'you will no doubt allow me to continue on my way, for I have things to do which should not wait.'

But the townspeople were not quite satisfied. One of them, himself a narrow cleric, brought forth a further question, which he was sure would be unanswerable.

'How, O Dervish,' he roared, 'can you justify the fact that our holy scriptures have lasted so long, and have been so universally admired; the fact that none dare challenge their validity with impunity (for we could kill you for suggesting this) and the fact that accepted beliefs and rituals have been handed down from one generation to another, generations of respected people, without serious challenge?'

'Those questions,' said the sage, 'are so easily answered that

269

to approach them without giving these poor people a chance to exercise their own brains would itself be a discourtesy and a wrong act. As I have said, I must continue on my journey, for there are things which cannot wait. But I shall return to you in the space of six months, during which time you can reflect on the matter. If, after that time, you still have anyone in this town who has not been able to understand the implications of your challenge, I shall be very glad to satisfy him.'

And the dervish picked up his staff, his begging bowl and his cap, slung his sheepskin mat across his shoulder, and went on his way.

The clergyman, of course, was delighted at the evasion of the dervish, and he lost no time in declaiming that his opponent had fled when faced by the irrefutable arguments of the truth and the properly appointed representative of theology and what he imagined to be divine ordinances.

Now some of the people who had been present had understood what the dervish meant. But others were confused, and still others were whipped up into unprecedented heights of fanaticism and excitement by the inflammatory words and frenetic gestures of the supposed man of faith.

When, after half a year had passed, the dervish was espied plodding along the dusty road towards the town, it was no longer quite the same place which it had been before. Those who had perceived the truth in the dervish's words had been transformed, and were working along lines which they had never imagined to be possible. Their ideas and their actions were operating on a higher, as well as a lower, level.

Those who were puzzled were badly in need of some direction, for instead of waiting patiently for the dervish's return they had allowed themselves to become tortured by doubts and assailed by impatience.

Those who were in the grip of the fanatic's putative teaching, actually only a form of madness imposed on otherwise normal people, ran into the streets to beat the dervish and thus convince themselves that right was triumphing over falsehood, pretensions and hypocrisy — all characteristics which they themselves had

270

in plenty, but whose presence in their minds they hardly allowed themselves to suspect.

The dervish walked steadily on. Brick-bats were thrown, catcalls echoed through the streets, small boys tugged at his robe, dogs barked and cowards boasted what they would do to him if they were given the chance.

When he entered the town square, the mob assembled and prevented him from speaking. The fanatic who was their leader howled with delight and jumped up and down, looking like the clown which he was but feeling like the saint he most assuredly was not.

The dervish sat down and waited for everyone to become a little calmer. This took some time, but when all the sensationalists were almost exhausted, he stood up and faced the alleged man of the spirit.

'Since you and your followers have obtained such intense, extensive and satisfying sensations from your opposition to what I have been saying,' he announced, 'you may care to hear even more, so that your not yet exhausted capacities for enjoying your sense of superiority may be even further animated, and your mission as upholders of the truth against falsehood allowed greater expression.'

The rabble-rouser could now see an opportunity for acquiring further glory, so he replied, in the manner which will not be unfamiliar to those clinicians who have seen his disease at its height. 'Accursed idolater! Dog and son of dogs! Enemy of truth and of the people! Satan and son of Satans, Damned emissary of the Places of Darkness! Speak, so that we may refute you and put to flight your obscene and impossible intrigues!' This is only a summary of some of his epithets, but the others may be imagined from this selection.

'Shall I then speak?' asked the dervish.

'Let him speak!' cried those who hated him, those who supported his insane opponent, and those who wanted to see blood spilt.

'Let him speak!' cried those who wanted to see justice done, and who believed that anyone should be allowed to express his opinions freely.

271

'Let him speak!' cried those who had only come for the sake of the entertainment.

So the dervish started to address the whole assembly of the people, each of whom was listening for his or her own reasons: those who knew what they were doing, those who knew a part of what they were doing, and those who did not know what they were doing. And all those in between.

'Once upon a time,' said the dervish, 'A man went into his garden and found a dead body there. It was the corpse of a man called Shakl, who had been a most successful and respected citizen of his town.

'Now the finder, whose name was Taqi (the Pious) recognised the corpse and was distressed to see that there was a crowbar beside him. It looked as if this apparently respectable man was in fact a burglar, who had died while exercising his trade, and that all his good works would now be lost.

'He said to himself, "In order to enable Shakl's good name and the continuing effect of his repute to be prolonged, I shall place his body near his house. People who find it will think that he went out for an early morning walk and collapsed near his home."

'So he started to drag the corpse towards Shakl's house. Hearing a noise there, however, he turned back and placed the body instead in the garden of the house on the other side of his. The garden gate was open. He knew that Shakl had sometimes visited this house, so he left the body there, thinking that people would assume that Shakl had died of natural causes in the course of a visit there.

'But the head of that household, Rassam, hearing a sound in his garden and fearing burglars, opened a window and threw a heavy club in the direction of the noise. When he went out, he found that the cudgel had hit Shakl on the head. He assumed, of course, that he had killed him.

'He immediately panicked, thinking, "We must conceal this murder, for people might think that we killed him on purpose, as we do not have a good reputation, and Shakl was a good man."

272

'So the whole family dragged the body to a nearby house where a family called the Muqallids were living. Then a thought struck them. They woke the Muqallids and said, "We have just seen this body in your courtyard, and it is evident that you have killed this important and good man, Shakl. Swear an oath of loyalty to us, and give us half of your money, or we'll bear witness against you!"

'The Muqallids agreed, and the villains took the body back to his own house, where they left it at the gate. When Shakl's parents went out of the house, which they shared with him, they were pleased to find that the corpse had returned: because in fact he had died the night before, in their presence, from an ordinary heart-attack. A burglar had stolen the body and tried to throw suspicion on Taqi the Pious, who was his enemy, and the burglar had dropped his crowbar by the window.

'So the only people who knew more or less what had happened (that Shakl had died normally, when his time had come) were his parents. All the others: Taqi, his neighbours and the Muqallids, continued for the rest of their lives to believe either what they imagined had happened or what the "evidence of their own senses" had told them.'

'Now Shakl,' continued the dervish, 'is the symbol of real teaching, for Shakl means the shape of a thing. His parents are those who brought the teaching into being. The teaching's life was over, it had fulfilled its purpose in that shape. It was due to be interred. The neighbours are the symbol of the people who continue to be impressed by something which has in fact no function to perform, but who insist, for some reason of their own, on doing something with it. Rassam acted as he did because he could not face truth, and because it often does not pay to do so. The Muqallids represent those who can be promised and threatened by things which have no reality, because of their own characteristics and because of the injustice of the world.

'Even the villains were confused, because, while they were watching Taqi's house to see what happened when the body was found, they could not understand why Shaql's parents, seeing the body, clapped their hands with joy.

'Everyone, of course, who is not aware of the true patterns which are acting in this world will always believe that things are as they seem obviously to be. But they are not.'

And, leaving the stunned people of the town to digest this lesson, the ancient dervish picked up his appurtenances and walked out of their lives.

The Chocolate Bar

Q: *If I am right and my Teacher is wrong, as Ghazzali says may happen, how can the rightness be useless and the wrong be useful?*

A: Because the apparent wrong is always ultimately right, while the imagined or short-term right is less right than the ultimate one.

You have to think of it in terms which make it easier for you to understand; and there is an anecdote of a certain Sufi who illustrated this mechanism as follows:

There was once a woman who went to this Sufi and asked him, 'Why should we do things against our inclinations; how do we know that you are not making us do things just for yourself?'

He answered: 'I will be able to answer if you go and get me a chocolate bar.'

She – and a lot of the people present – were annoyed. 'The Sufi is making fun of us', they thought.

'Get your own chocolate,' snarled the lady, and went away.

After a time, however, she thought she would see what happened if she complied, so she went to a shop and bought the chocolate. It so happened that, while she was out, a gas-main leading into her house exploded, and everyone there was killed.

She went to the Sufi and thanked him for this intervention,

as she now assumed it to be. He handed her the wrapper from the chocolate. When she got it back to the house where she was staying, she found a competition entry form on it. She tried the contest, and won enough money to buy a new house . . .

When she went back to the Sufi to thank him once again, he said, 'Things are mingled in this way, so that your inclinations may be untrustworthy; while what others seem to have as inclinations may in fact be something designed to serve you.'

Is this not an example of the 'undesirable wishes of the teacher' being useful, and the 'right thinking' of the pupil being useless?

The Vanishing Dirham

Many people do not understand Sufi thought simply because they make assumptions about Sufism, through thinking inefficiently. The cause is emotion or assumptions, and that is why Sufis try to teach how to set aside these two distorting factors.

Here is an ancient illustration of the muddled thinking in action:

There were once three travelling dervishes who arrived at a caravanserai late at night and sought lodging for themselves and their donkeys. The innkeeper had gone to bed, but the man on duty gave them stabling and a room for fifteen dirhams, silver coins, which the dervishes paid in advance.

In the morning, however, the proprietor realised that the dervishes had been accidentally overcharged: their rent should have been ten dirhams – so he sent a porter to give them back five dirhams.

Now the porter was not particularly honest and, besides, thought that five dirhams among three people was difficult to apportion. 'So that the dervishes do not fall out,' he told himself, 'I'll just give them three dirhams back, and take the other two coins for myself.'

This he did, with the result that the dervishes had actually spent only twelve dirhams.

That meant that the dervishes had been charged 12 dirhams, and the porter had stolen two: a total of 14 dirhams. But there had originally been 15 dirhams. Where had the one dirham got to?

Many people, when given this puzzle, believe that there is one dirham missing. But there really cannot be, can there?

In just the same sort of way, people imagine mysteries where there are none at all.

Diseases of Learning

Barriers to understanding in individuals and in groups.

'Traditionalism,' which often really means the servile copying of what are imagined to be valuable thoughts and actions, is the first conspicuous barrier to real understanding. We can abbreviate this with the word 'imitation', the first of the dozen-odd major disabling factors in real human development.

Over-simplification is the second: when a single formula is imagined to be enough to storm the gates of Heaven. Desire for emotional stimulus is the third, and the fourth is the compulsive collecting of information whether it is applicable or not at that stage of progress.

The fifth disabling tendency is to use a parable or tale as the representation of absolute truth, when it is always only a facet of a whole: thus imagining the part to be the whole, instead of a conductor to it.

The sixth problem is to seek to pursue artificially-formed hypotheses of virtue; the seventh and eighth cover the result of trying to teach oneself and trying to instruct others without the necessary perceptions for the job.

Ninth comes the failure to assess the needs of the learner; tenth being prematurely discouraged; eleventh the random mixing of teachings and techniques from various sources; and finally there is the mistaking of one thing for another.

All these forms of behaviour are easily to be found in both spiritual and other groups of human beings, because they are not essentially esoteric problems at all: but manifestations of the secondary personality, the self which people take to be their real one, but which is in fact a highly inefficient composition of instinct, emotion and half-learned or over-learned (conditioned) elements.

By illustrative exaggeration and transposition into more easily grasped equivalencies, these barriers can be examined fairly easily.

We may group them in the following categories of so-called jokes; those who scorn them are like those who want to learn to read without bothering with the alphabet:

1. Imitation and lack of perception.

The commonest mistake is the copying of rituals and observances which are obsolete or misunderstood. This gives some satisfactions sometimes, but no illumination. It is also one of the reasons why some devotional activities cause pain and bewilderment.

> The analogy is that of the man who was only barely literate and bought a can of soup. He was found wandering with a scalded foot because he tried to follow the directions. They said: 'Open the can and stand for 15 minutes in boiling water.'

Information without knowledge makes a prisoner instead of an escapee.

The tales which illustrate such conditions as this are often traditionally termed 'Land of Fools' jokes, because they are relatively grotesque in appearance. It should be remembered, however, that the behaviour of anyone who does not know enough about a specialised subject may appear bizarre to an experienced observer. So it is with psychological-spiritual matters.

The fact that such jokes as these can also stand on their own in their lower applications, as illustrations of idiotic behaviour, has of course caused them to be repeated only for amusement. This, in turn, has caused them to be regarded as essentially nothing but jokes, some of them feeble ones. But this deterioration of usage of important materials is itself a characteristic of human societies. From time to time the usefulness of procedures, techniques and knowledge itself has to be reclaimed.

2.   Drawbacks of relying on single formulae.

Over-simplification, in all belief-systems, will give great emotional stimulus and keep people busy. It will not solve many problems, nor will it lead to much educational advance.

To the informed observer, people can be doing things which seem perfectly reasonable to them; but which, without the context which is supplied by knowledge alone, prove to be useless.

> There is a story of two men who were sent to jail. They knew that plans to escape were made by people signalling through hammering upon water-pipes. So they perfected, through years of practice, a complete system of communication with each other by this method. Only then did they notice that they were both in the same cell . . .

The difference between education or development of knowledge and mere social stimulus is well illustrated here. Thinking that they were making progress, and were therefore developing their capacities, the men failed to assess the total situation to determine exactly what skills they needed in their particular variety of the prison environment.

This tale is also sometimes cited to emphasise the difference between spiritual knowledge and emotional activity. People are so engaged in the emotional that they often imagine that their experiences are spiritual.

Most people, as will be obvious to those who examine cults and various religious systems, are in fact happy enough 'living in one cell and practising signalling'.

We may point out their mistake, but we have no duty to disturb their amusements.

3. The would-be learner, instead of realising that there is an objective, becomes a bemused consumer of wonders and stimuli.

So-called 'teachings' and 'systems' are perceptibly, to the sociologist if not to the participant, social groupings affording satisfactions which could be obtained elsewhere and are social, not spiritual.

They do not give the fillip and the intervention to arouse him from his state of monotony which the learner needs, so he develops a taste for more of the same, for gaining a sense of pleasure, instead of progress.

This situation is illustrated in the tale of the man who was given three wishes by a genie.

He said: 'I would like to be able to do and be anything I happen to wish!'

'Certainly,' said the genie. 'And for the other two wishes?'

'More of the same!' said the man.

If we take this man as a citizen of the Land of Fools, we can laugh at the stupidity which wants everything and then more: but more which, of course, is only the same again.

As an exercise, you might care to take a look at the people who surround us in the world, and who are, through their life within various systems and teachings, in exactly the same case as the Land of Fools people.

279

4.   Compulsive information-gathering.

There are people who have been conditioned to ask questions; but only in some areas of life is it socially permissible to say: 'You are not ready for the answer to that yet. Indeed, to deal with this subject at this stage will only confuse everyone, including the questioner.'

People always want more information than they need. One way to help to remember this is to think of the doctor who gave out medicines 'to be taken two hours before the pain'.

5.   Imagining that all experiences are useful.

Some experiences may be useless, others are certainly harmful. In amusement-systems (whatever they call themselves) the emphasis is naturally on experience, because excitement and stimulus is what is really being demanded and offered.

In a true learning-system, however, as in all legitimate forms of education, what matters is the order of events and the preparedness of the learner, not the fact of the experience and what the individual happens to imagine it means, if anything.

The experience-cravers, of course, lack the perspective to see what effect the experience is having on them.

> The analogy might be taken from the story of the man from the Land of Fools who was reporting what happened to a friend:
> 'He was lucky. A bullet just missed his ear.'
> Someone asked:
> 'So he wasn't hurt?'
> 'Well, it went through his brain.'

It might surprise some of those pious and delightful souls who so much prize their supposedly mystical and religious experiences to know that this very pride, and the obsession with the significance of the experience which sometimes accompanies it, is equivalent to a bullet in the brain.

6.   Fragmentary use of parable material.

Parables, as well as having an immediate application, are

part of a whole in real teaching; but are more emphasised as individual items in less insightful systems.

To over-emphasise one story or parable, and to neglect to keep in mind that it is illustrating a part of a whole, and that it is the whole for which the enterprise is mounted, is to rejoin the consumer society: even if it is the respected parable-consuming society.

> One way to keep this fact in mind is to remember the story of the man who liked to read the dictionary.
> Someone asked him why he did not read full-length books as well.
> 'The dictionary,' he said, 'is so much more satisfying: it explains every word as one goes along, and this gives me satisfaction: I add to my knowledge every few lines!'

7.   Concentration upon far too few principles.

Almost everyone alive has been reared within a social system which powerfully emphasises certain virtues and vices, and also leaves many important attitudes unexamined.

It is usual, for instance, for people to teach that greed is a bad thing; while blithely ignoring the demonstrable fact that greed for supposedly good things (say greed for knowledge or for sanctity) is still greed. And yet, of course, it is the greed itself which damages the person, not what it is supposedly trying to do.

The result of ignoring the fact that certain attitudes are harmful is that these postures, such as greed, continue to take effect, to influence the individual, to prevent his learning or progressing.

The teacher is able to observe the working of such subjective attitudes, and to help to correct them. When he sees the manifestation of harmful but unobserved subjectivities, he is able to prescribe for them.

You can observe for yourself how strong is, for instance, the vanity of people who are believed to be humble.

The eluding of one's own censorship or discipline by the wayward characteristic is sometimes likened to the escape, from one part of the mind to another, of a malefactor.

Hence the following joke has an illustrative use:

'In the Land of Fools, a miscreant was tracked down to a theatre. The police immediately sealed all exits. Unfortunately the man escaped through one of the entrances.'

8. Difficulties of trying to learn by oneself.

People vary in their ability to put this kind of information into practice. Some can do so at once, others cannot do so at all. By far the largest number of people need a great deal of teaching, and this has to be done by someone who can see where the student actually is from time to time.

Highlighting the difficulty of the ordinary individual to prescribe for his own learning is the joke of the man who knew what he needed, but was unable to provide a solution which would really work. The predicament is, of course, emphasised by transposing the problem into a context where anyone can observe its absurdity:

A man from the Land of Fools bought a washing-line to send his mother for her birthday. He was unable to post it to her, however, as he could find nobody who stocked an envelope measuring one inch by thirty feet!

9. Self-appointed groups.

If self-teaching has its severe limitations, the establishment of groups often leads to even more bizarre results. The reason for this is that the leaders of these groups, although frequently full of good intentions, lack the necessary expertise. Skill in 'running a group' is not a substitute for the perception of the spiritual condition of the group and of all its members, constantly monitored.

The Sufi teacher, like any other specialist, can see the shortcomings of the supposed teacher, the individuals and the group in a way that they cannot. His position is like that of the man who knows what a screw is, observing how the Foolslanders try to fix one into a plank.

They manage to work out what the screw is, and how it holds something to a plank. They realise that it has to be turned, and they devise their method.

The result is that one man holds the screw, while a dozen others try to rotate the plank to get the screw into it. And, of course, all these people get in one another's way.

This 'joke' also emphasises that, in schools of the kind which the people of the Land of Fools are trying to imitate, not everyone is employed all of the time. The analogy would be that one man would get a screwdriver (missing from the Fools' calculations) and would drive the screw home. Then everyone would profit from the resulting table or whatever is being made . . .

10. Inability to assess the needs of the learner.

Another anecdote in this series about social groups which lack the equivalent of technical knowledge, is concerned with missed opportunities.

One of the saddest things about self-appointed esoteric groups is that there is a point at which the group and its members might reach a certain understanding of what they are doing – and that that point is almost always missed because there is no awareness of what to do: and when and where.

People continue to try to perform rituals and exercises, or to read literature, and so on, when they should be trying to do or to be something else. This is often because they are in fact pessimists: imagining, subconsciously, that they cannot reach any higher, and should therefore play about with minor and elementary stages of study. And these become games.

This situation is frequently seen, and it is dramatically obvious to those who have been accustomed to working with people who have been given the information that there is a flexible and ever-changing context to higher studies.

It is well illustrated by the tale of the employer who said to a workman who arrived back from a job very late: 'Do you realise,' he said, 'that it is 1800 hours?'

'It may well be,' said the other man, 'but my watch only goes up to 12.'

11.   Turning back.

There is no doubt that certain useful kinds of experience and understanding can be acquired by being in a study group. The value of the group will, however, disappear very soon after its most elementary potential is exhausted. This is why people who join groups gain the impression that there is something for them there. There is. But what they do not realise, in general, is that this potential is rapidly exhausted without continuing insight by the direction of the group.

The consequence is that many former members of groups either abandon them or try to form their own schools, seeking the teaching which, in the nature of things, they cannot find by such a method.

The world is full of people who have turned back from higher studies of the mind because they have not made enough progress.

They imagine that they have gained enough or else that they have gained nothing because there is nothing to gain.

Once more, the observer who has experience of such things can see both the difficulty and the limitations in understanding of these people, while they in general have no perception of their situation at all.

> They can be seen, from the objective viewpoint, to be in the position of the man who decided to walk to his home, 25 kilometres from his work. When he had gone half way, he was tired: so he walked the whole way back.

12.   Mixing various teachings.

At almost any stage, people try to mix the ideas and activities of various teachings, according to what appears to suit them. The consequence is never effective. You may produce something attractive by this method, but never anything which works.

Remember the story of the man who dug a hole and then

284

decided that the earth which he had brought up was untidy: so he burrowed into the ground again to make a hole to dispose of the earth . . .

13. Transposition of relevances.

One of the worst results of mixing various teachings is when the relevance of a teaching activity is transferred: producing entertainment but removing the effect. When Jalaluddin Rumi's 'whirling' exercises, designed, according to his own words, to stir up the feelings of certain thick-headed people of Asia Minor, became 'holy movements', their real effect was lost.

A modern story which pinpoints this tendency is the one of the man who bought a clock which gained, instead of one which kept correct time.

> 'Why have a clock which shows an hour extra every half-hour?' someone asked him.
> 'Don't you understand? It's doing 50% more in the same time as yours!'

14. The fourteenth observation in this series really subsumes the whole list. It is the need to abandon the assumption that humour is out of place in serious matters. Such an assumption is just as foolish as to decide that one should roar with laughter all the time.

But, of course, people who believe either of these things are not in need of entertainment, for they have it in their fantasies; or education, as they are almost insusceptible to it. They do, however, need normalising – by whoever has the capacity to help them in that direction.

SECTION IX

Guide to Major Principles in the Use of Humour in Human Development

Outward show and appearances of all kinds are the mainstay of human institutions when they reach the stage where the inner component, that which actually makes them work, is absent.

This outward show is so effective that it can be mistaken by people for the essence of the thing itself. It is no accident that conservatism in ritual, dogma and belief is so powerful and so energetically maintained: and so hysterically defended.

WHY NOT?

There was once a Sufi who was approached by a peerlessly-devout scholar, noted for the punctilious performance of his external duties. This man said to the Sufi:

'I note that you are not to be seen at public prayers.'

'That is so,' said the Sufi.

The man continued:

'You wear ordinary clothes, and not the parti-coloured robes affected by many Sufis.'

'True.'

'And,' went on the other man, 'you do not congregate with people who discuss spirituality; we seldom see you with a rosary in your hand. You never refer to great teachers, and are apparently not attracted to holy personalities.'

'True, true, true,' agreed the Sufi.

'Then may I ask why?'

The Sufi said:

'Because concerning myself overmuch with such things would interfere with my spiritual activities.'

So the Sufis, above all, are not people of externals. They are concerned with the effect of the inward development upon the outward: not so much the other way about. And note the use of the word 'overmuch'. This stresses the Sufi concern with measure. Measure means the necessary amount of attention placed upon anything. You should note, too, that the more devout or sincere people imagine themselves to be about something, the fiercer becomes their selective attention towards detail and intensity of belief and action. The principles of measure go by the board.

These principles obtain in all fields of human effort. If you want to develop something, or in something, you must be able to adopt and progress the right balance and measure towards that thing. To become obsessed about it will end only in conditioned blindness or in obsession for its own sake.

One's objectives, both in the ordinary world and in one's learning process, will yield results to the extent to which they are correctly focused upon a relevant aim: what we call 'a destination'.

Here is how one individual's attempt to concentrate upon a certain purpose ran straight up against another's assumptions and purposes: it is a parable of the difference between the teacher's attempt to communicate what he has and the learner's attempt to get what he thinks he could have:

SOMEWHERE BETTER

A man once advertised in a paper: 'House and contents for sale. Owner emigrating.'

He had a large number of replies.

A friend asked him:

'Did you get a good price?'

'A good price?' he said, 'I didn't even get a sale. Everyone wanted to know whether I knew of a good place for them to emigrate to!'

The irrelevancy here is that the purpose of the seller does not necessarily coincide with the needs of the would-be emigrants. If, for example, our advertiser is emigrating to the United States because he has landed a job as a nuclear physicist there, what is the use of numerous plumbers, bus-conductors, professors of philosophy or cabinet ministers asking him about emigration?

The tale, I think, neatly illustrates the absurd activity of the greed (the basic human desire to gain something) and the conditioning (widespread belief based on repetition that things are better in other countries) which together form the commanding self. This element, far from being that which helps people to gain anything, is the factor which actively stands in the way of progress and especially of human development and the finding of the real self.

So, in the first story, we have the behaviour of the people of externals, which all people are until they learn something about externals and alternatives. In the second we have the display of the greed and habit mentality which reinforces the external behaviour.

Now these two tales have shown us that it is possible to perceive the working of these things in ourselves. The major purpose of Sufi study activity is to 'freeze' this behaviour-pattern, first in examples and then in personal life, so as to perceive it and to avoid it. Concurrently, of course, we have to encourage the development of the True Self which lies behind this secondary one.

Here, in frozen action, is an example of the way in which people think, though they seldom catch themselves out at it, unless they have been told that it is possible:

HAVING AND GIVING

There was once a Sufi who asked a would-be disciple:

'If you had a house, would you give it up for the Sufi Work?'

'Yes,' answered the applicant.

'And would you abandon your family, if you had one, and follow only the Path of Truth?'

'Certainly.'

'And would you give one of your shirts, if you had two, for the Cause?'

'Certainly not!'

'But why not?' asked the Sufi.

'Because I have got two shirts!'

This is the secondary self looking after itself.

People can be judged only on performance, which is why the Sufi specialises in performance, and not in words. Note, too, that when we talk of performance we do not mean externals in the sense of a charade, where people are merely pretending. Performance has to involve test: as in the case of the shirt of the would-be disciple.

It is because what is truly spiritual and of the realm of real higher consciousness is difficult that most of the manifestations of religion and supposed spirituality are in fact just a part of social life. When the vanity and the emotional life have not been observed and understood, these will then attach themselves to the social life now termed 'spiritual' and we have the formula for the myriad of cults – some of them regarded as major religions or versions of them – which fill the earth.

Nowhere is this self-deception more widespread than in India. Not long ago a huge sign was erected outside one of the menageries which cater for Western self-imagined 'seekers', reading:

'TRY MEDITATION'

Some wag, who was perhaps more aware of his real state than some of the others, had scrawled below this legend the words:

'IF YOU CAN'T BE A SUFI'

He, at any rate, had realised the problems of impatience and superficiality.

Unlike other systems, Sufism is not a matter of merely getting people to believe something; not a matter of acquiescent disciples and supposedly miracle-working Masters. Indeed, it is more than likely that many people who will come to understand Sufism are those who find it most hard to accept. Look at this story and you may be able to see why:

> 'Don't try to convince a student if you see him looking unconvinced during one of your lessons,' counselled a Sufi to one of his deputies.

'But why not?' asked the man.

'Because he may be the only student who is actually listening to you.'

Do you see the point?

Those who show no sign at all may or may not be listening, and this will be seen sooner or later.

Those, however, who may be trying to get to grips with the Sufi teaching, and hence listening, are almost certainly focusing their 'commanding self', the secondary self which is what almost everyone uses to assess anything, upon your words, your actions, your reality. Quite naturally, this raw and self-seeking element is likely to agree or to disagree. Disputing with it will get nobody anywhere. The student has somehow to come to the working assumption that there may be a different way of learning than acceptance and rejection. This, too, is why Sufis number so many former scholars in their ranks, and also why scholars cannot usually stomach Sufis: at least until they are dead, and cannot answer back.

Acceptance and rejection, again, you should understand, are much more often than is recognised just ways of amusing oneself. People, in other words, take pleasure in believing something or in disbelieving it, and the reasons why they supposedly accept or reject come later. These are what psychologists nowadays call 'rationalisations'.

The ideologue, whether in religion, politics or the advertising and selling of commodities, specialises in the engineering of belief. That is to say, he causes people to want things and to convince themselves that they want them for good reasons. Centuries ago the Sufis, publicly and privately, asserted that this kind of belief was not faith or religion, and that there was a real version of which this was the counterfeit. The position today is that this is fairly well established in theory in the East and less well known in the West (where people tend to respect belief as if it meant something by itself) but in both areas it is little understood and even less practised.

The importance of the right kind of belief or faith cannot be over-stressed if it is realised that the wrong kind leads to a wasted life and the right kind alone leads to enlightenment.

Now look at this story:

THE REASON

A revivalist preacher was crying out:

'Those who want to go to Heaven, stand up!'

All rose, except for one rather tattered looking dervish in a corner.

'And why,' thundered the agitator, 'do you not want to go?'

The other man looked up mildly. 'Because I still have such a lot to do here!'

What the dervish had to do, of course, was to liberate the real self from the toils of the secondary self; which is the reason for the Sufi saying: 'Die before your death.'

Specific and important tasks have to be performed 'in the world'.

Sufis, and many of their students, can see beyond the outward face of things: they aim for perception of reality beyond appearances. Unless you know what the reality is, you will always tend to pursue the appearance, which includes all kinds of beliefs and pleasures which are unproductive though pleasing. The ordinary student, the scholar, the ideologue, is constantly misled by appearances and driven astray by assumptions.

The effect of these elements on the ordinary human being is to make him or her look very different to the Sufi than he looks to himself or to his fellows. There is a tale which expresses this rather well, for it shows how futile such a person appears to be, in all his concerns, to those who really do know what he might be doing with himself:

AGE

A young man, it is related, once saw a reverend-looking man walking along the road, dressed in a swami's robe. He looked about a hundred years old, although he walked with a certain vigour.

The youth said to him:

'What is the secret of your attaining this venerable age in this excellent physical condition: your hair, though white, is abundant, your face, though wrinkled, is calm. Your gait, though you walk on two sticks, is good for an aged one, and you are hardly panting at all as you walk.'

The ancient said:

'I follow the orders of such-and-such a spiritual Master.'

'And how old are you, may I ask?'

'I am nearly twenty-five years old!'

The Story of the Fool

There was once a youth, a citizen of the Land of Fools, whose whole life seemed to operate on a basis of misunderstanding and misinterpretation. Sometimes he thought that things were other than they seemed, sometimes others thought that he did things for reasons other than he really did. The resulting pattern took up a great deal of time. But everyone in the Land of Fools thought that the way in which they saw things amounted to 'history', or 'how things are' – or even 'ordinary life with coincidences and extraordinary happenings'.

Their lives, of course, were so different from ours that we can see what happens to them as entertaining stories.

One day (just to give you a flavour of these remarkable people) this youth of whom we are speaking saw that the family dog had unearthed his mother's purse from behind a cushion and was running out of the house with it. He called out, 'Mother! The dog has found a purse!' His mother, afraid that someone might find out how much money she had, quickly threw some cakes onto the branches of a tree growing beside the house. 'Quick, son,' she cried, 'get those cakes which have just grown on the tree!' and she ran after the dog while the boy was thus occupied.

The woman got her purse back, and hid it again. Her son, after eating all the cakes, wandered into the street and looked around for the dog. Presently he met two thieves. They asked what he was doing.

'I was looking for a dog which stole my mother's purse. She has a lot of money, you know,' he said. The thieves looked at one another, thinking that they would find out where he lived and rob his house.

'When did the dog take the purse?' asked one of the men, by way of carrying on the conversation. 'It must have been just before the cakes started to grow on trees,' answered the idiot. Now, of course, this made the thieves think that nothing their new friend said was true, and they gave up the idea of robbing his mother.

But they were annoyed. 'Your brain is made of wood,' said one of them. 'Does that mean I'm dead?' asked the lad. 'Yes, of course – at least as near as makes no difference,' snarled the second thief. And they went on their way.

'If I am dead, I should be buried,' thought the fool. He started to dig a grave for himself, but at that point a travelling merchant came along and asked him what he was doing, for he wanted someone to help him carry his wares, and he could see that the fool was strong.

'I am dead. A man told me, when I told him that the dog stole the purse after the cakes grew on trees,' answered the youth.

'You may be mentally dead, but physically you are not, and you should be doing something useful,' replied the merchant, who reckoned that he could get the fool to work for him for nothing. 'Pick up this box and follow me, and if you carry it properly, and to my satisfaction, I shall give you a copper piece.'

The fool was delighted. Picking up the box which contained

a jar of honey, he followed the merchant, thinking about what he would do with his reward. First he would buy a hen, he would sell the eggs and buy a cow, he would sell the milk and buy a farm, he would become rich. At that point he tripped and fell, spilling the liquid honey all over the dusty road.

Now the merchant was really furious. He was also afraid, for the King whose castle they were approaching had asked him to bring the honey. The merchant took the fool into the castle, and the fate of the honey was explained to the monarch.

Instead, however, of punishing the fool, the King only said, 'Your fantasies are very much like my own life. I keep trying to get more and more, and things always go wrong. As you have amused me, take these gold pieces and go on your way.'

So the fool set off for the town, imagining what he would do with all that money. He would buy shoes, a robe, a fine shirt and a hat. He would go to the next country, where he was not known, and ask for the daughter of their King in marriage. They would be wed, and in due time he would inherit the kingdom . . .

And, believe it or not, he managed to buy the clothes, and eventually present himself before the palace of the King of the neighbouring country.

But this was another country of the Land of Fools, and things which seemed set to go right often went wrong, and the other way about. So it was that the King hereabouts was waiting for a suitor, another King, to arrive to claim his daughter. When the fool presented himself at the palace gate, saying that he was going to marry the Princess, everyone believed that this was the expected suitor. After all, they had never met either the fool or the other King.

The wedding was held immediately, and everyone went into the banqueting hall to celebrate. Now the fool, as we remember from his gobbling the cakes, had a good appetite, and he not only started to eat but concealed in his robe a large jar with a narrow mouth, into which he placed as many choice delicacies as he could, thinking that they would come in handy later.

But after slipping three of four sweetmeats into the jar, the fool forgot to unclench his fist, and so he could not get it out again. This slowed down his eating, and his host, assuming that he was finished, declared the feast at an end, and sent the happy couple to the bridal apartments.

The fool was still hungry; and, with the jar hidden in the folds of his cloak, he tried and tried to get his hand out, but to no avail. Finally he confessed his problem to his bride. The Princess, no brighter than anyone else in those parts, said, 'There is a white rock outside the door of this room. Go and break the pot on it, and return to me.'

Our hero opened the door and swung his arm at what he took to be the rock. Unfortunately it was the head of a guard who had been posted outside; and the man collapsed with a loud cry.

'They will find out that I have murdered him, and kill me!' said the fool to himself.

Without a moment's hesitation, he ran out of the palace and along the highway beyond, still wearing his fine clothes.

Now the moon was full, and as the fool looked behind him he saw his shadow, which looked very much like someone following him. Taking off his hat, he threw it at the shadow, and moved on at a faster pace. Looking back, he thought that his pursuer was still close behind: so he took off his robe and flung it down, thinking that the other would be delayed by picking it up. Time and again he flung away some article of clothing, calling out, 'Take this finery and call off the hunt!', until he was stark naked; but still the shadow followed him.

In desperation, the idiot climbed a tree, and shouted wildly at his persecutor until he was hoarse.

Now it so happened that a band of thieves was coming along that road some way behind, and came upon the clothes. They gathered up each of the rich garments and stopped at the bottom of the tree to share out the loot. The fool listened while they handed out his clothes: 'This is for you, this is for me,' and so on.

He became so interested in the share-out, and so overcome with desire as he looked at the clothes, that he involuntarily called out, 'What about me?'

298

The thieves, peering in alarm into the branches, saw what they imagined to be a naked demon, with a harsh voice. They panicked and fled, leaving the clothes lying in confusion.

When it was dawn, and there was no sign of anyone, the idiot went down from the tree and put on his clothes again. He said to himself, 'People may think that I am not very clever, but here I am all ready to resume my life as a man of distinction, richly apparelled and free from care!'

He did not know, however, that there was no inhabited place for many miles, and so he had to walk all that day, until the night became cold and he could only find a hollow tree in which to sleep.

The decaying trunk was full of honey, since a nest of wild bees had deserted it, and the fool was soon covered in the sticky stuff. Half asleep and unable to understand what was happening, he fled from the tree and stumbled into a barn, lying down on a pile of wool which was stored there.

The wool stuck to the honey, and soon our friend looked exactly like a sheep.

In the morning, woken by the sun shining down, he looked down at his body and limbs and decided that, for his sins, he had been transformed into a sheep. He wandered hither and thither until he came to a flock and, quite logically, joined it.

Another band of thieves, looking for something to steal, crept upon the sheepfold and carried away what they thought to be the largest animal they could find. This, of course, was none other than our hero.

He did not enjoy being stolen.

'I may be only a sheep,' he yelled, 'but that does not give you the right to steal me from my master!'

At this the thieves, imagining that their prey was bewitched, let him go and ran headlong in all directions, swearing to live exemplary lives in future.

The fool, meanwhile, had fallen into a pool of water, and the honey and wool were washed off him. 'Fancy that!' he marvelled, 'I have resumed my human shape!'

He dried himself, and found that the robbers had, in their

299

panic, dropped a bag of gold. 'This is my recompense for having been stolen,' thought the fool, and limped down the road until he came to an inn.

Now the innkeeper was a crafty and dishonest fellow. The fool called for food, and placed the bag of gold on the table, to show that he could pay for it.

'Good Sir,' said the landlord, 'pray stay with me, without any charge at all. I can see that you are a man of distinction and breeding, and it will be an honour to have you in our humble abode.'

Happy that at last he had met someone who appreciated his worth, the fool agreed.

That evening, while supping with the innkeeper, the fool listened to one tall story after another, which his host was telling deliberately to deceive him.

Finally, the rogue said, 'You may not believe this, but the fact is that I have a cat which carries a lamp in its mouth!'

'Nonsense!' said the fool, 'everyone knows that cats cannot be trained like dogs.'

'Would you wager on it?' asked the landlord. 'Of course I would!' answered the fool; 'in fact, if you can train a cat to do things like that, I'll not only give you my money, but my clothes and my freedom.'

But, horror of horrors, it turned out that the innkeeper indeed did have such a marvellous cat. Shortly afterwards, when he called it, it came across the courtyard and into the room, carrying a lamp in its mouth.

The innkeeper took the fool's gold, and his clothes – and made him his slave.

When some months had passed, and the guard who had been hit on the head had recovered, the Princess was almost desperate for news of her husband. She felt sure that some evil had befallen him, and she constantly besought her father to have him found, if he were still alive.

Since, however, this was the Land of Fools, nobody knew how to mount such a search, and most people thought that it was quite natural for someone to appear and marry a Princess and then disappear in the middle of the night.

But the fool, working day and night for the innkeeper, thought and thought about his life, and about what he had done and had not done – until he came to the conclusion that his fate was connected with his folly.

One evening, when he was serving a wayfarer, a sage, as it happened, who was staying at the inn, he managed to confide his dreadful story to him, and sought his help.

The wise man said, 'I can help you, but you will have to wait, for there are preparations to be made.'

And he went on his way. The fool, of course, thought that the wise man was merely making excuses: until, several months later, he returned. This time he carried a wooden box, and was accompanied by a foppishly dressed youth.

That evening, while relaxing beside the fire, the fop said to the innkeeper, 'This is a dull place, indeed! If I had not promised to accompany this sage as his disciple, I would be indulging in my favourite pastime, which is gambling . . .'

The innkeeper pricked up his ears. 'If you are a betting man, perhaps you would like to wager that I have not got a cat which carries a lamp in its mouth?'

The youth immediately wagered a thousand gold pieces against the inn itself. While they were talking, the sage slipped out of the building, and into the courtyard.

He sat down with his wooden box and waited. Presently the landlord called his cat, which appeared from the stables with a lamp in its mouth. As soon as he saw it, the sage opened his box and a mouse ran out. The cat looked at the mouse, hesitated, and then walked purposefully on its way. Now the wise man let loose another mouse. Again the cat paused, half moved towards the mouse – and, recovering itself, continued towards the parlour of the inn. Finally, when the cat had nearly reached the door, the wise man let his third, and last, mouse out of its captivity. It ran past the cat; but this time the temptation was too much. Dropping the lamp, the cat tore headlong after its prey, disappearing into the nearby fields.

Meanwhile the sage quietly returned to the fireside. After a suitable lapse of time, and amid much disputation, the landlord was adjudged to have lost his bet. The inn was given to the fop, and the idiot, now very much wiser, returned to his bride.

And everyone lived happily ever after.

Choosing a New Teacher

Q: *The Great Sheikh (Ibn el Arabi) has, I think rather harshly, said that a disciple who takes another Master while his own is alive cannot be a disciple, and betrays his trust.*

A: Like other Sufis, Ibn el Arabi is not being harsh or gentle: the Sufi's task is to be descriptive and to exercise or provoke the teaching function. If you put the matter in other terms, you may not be able to understand the answer, but I hope that you will. 'Harshness' or 'gentleness' is how people see things subjectively.

By definition, your teacher can teach you, and does so. What is the purpose of another teacher? You can't eat two meals at a time, so to speak. A 'disciple' who goes from one teacher to another is not a disciple: and someone who 'teaches' him under such circumstances is not a teacher. This is the Sufi reality on the subject.

If you are thinking of some other sort of learning or teaching – a little here and a little there – you are not talking about the Sufi way. You may, however, have made the customary confusion between what you like and what you do not, seeking pleasure and avoiding discomfort. This is not consistent with Sufism.

Fire and Straw

Q: *You have quoted Rumi as saying that the 'dervish dance' and music were instituted by him only for the phlegmatic people of Asia Minor, even though they are today imitated even in the West. But this principle — that Sufi practices are carefully prescribed according to the needs of a community — seems to be a dramatic underlining of the absurdity of the people who still imitate, throughout the centuries, what were intended only for one locality. Is this an indication that virtually all systems known to us are mere relics, and therefore ludicrous?*

A: I can only tell you the facts, which are as you have put them. If you want to note anything further, look at the words of Saadi:

An Indian, he reports, was giving lessons in making fireworks, and a wise man said to him, 'This is hardly a suitable occupation for you, whose house is made of straw . . .'

When you use the word 'ludicrous', you should decide what seems ludicrous to you and to others looking at it.

I only have to remind you that an old jar may look good or it may look bad, but due to its age and handling it may have leaked all its contents away . . .

And Wear them Out . . . ?

Q: *Can we not set aside many of the questions which form the subject of discussions between Sufis and their pupils?*

A: Mulla Nasrudin was seen one day trudging towards the town with his shoes slung from a string around his neck.

The man who saw this said, as he passed:

'Hey, Mulla - why don't you put your shoes on?'

'What — ,' said Nasrudin, 'and wear them out?'

303

A little later a nail went right into one of his feet.

'Thank goodness I've saved my shoes,' said the Mulla to himself . . .

If you do as you say you want to, you may set aside certain protective elements, like the shoes in the Nasrudin tale.

The question, surely, is the *nous*: the knowledge of what is the best thing to do: 'What port is reached by the captainless ship?'

Mystical States

Q: *What do people feel like, and what do they seem like, in mystical states, and what preparation, if any, is needed for such experiences?*

A: People who develop states without preparation will experience all kinds of contaminated states, which is what generally happens with self-appointed experimenters. Sufis* call the mystical state, where it is perceived as anything strange at all, the action of the higher impulses on the lower, unaltered and therefore unsuitable, consciousness. 'States', therefore, are regarded as prisons and vicissitudes: 'realised people' – as Hujwiri says – are those who have escaped from having 'states', mystical experiences.

The true states, however, cannot be described, because they are an annihilation of speech.

The stage of self-realisation is called *Tamkin* (stabilization). In order to reach it, however, the individual has to proceed through stages (*Maqam*). There are a number of these, and one must not depart from one until it has had its appropriately maturing effect upon the inner consciousness.

So *Hal* (state) denotes insufficient preparation, as the lower

*Ali b. Uthman al Jullabi al Hujwiri: *Kashf al Mahjub* (11th Century).

self is mixed with the incoming impulse. *Tamkin*, however, is repose. There are thus three stages, the first two of which are usually mistaken for the end result by those who do not understand, whereas they signal unpreparedness: *Maqam, Hal, Tamkin.*

People who imagine that something important has happened when they have experienced *Hal* through their Commanding Self show that self to be in the state of self-congratulation: hence the participant is 'commanded by the prideful self to imagine that he is one of the elect'.

In a Sufi School

Q: *I have heard that the major woman Sufi of ancient times, Rabia, was asked why she used a rosary, the Tasbih, which was regarded by some devout people as superfluous. Her answer was, 'I will not abandon something which has taken me close to God.' How can an inanimate thing like a rosary take anyone 'near to God'?*

A: This question illustrates rather well the perils of reading or repeating things without context. The quotation is what a sociologist would call a 'test question'. Students of Sufis are asked to comment on such supposed quotations and to find the flaw in them, in the spirit of 'What is wrong with this quotation?'

Sufi schools are full of these tests. One familiar one, often used against Sufis by outward commentators, is 'the disciple must conceal his teacher's shortcomings'. Another one is to recommend the writings of Ibn el Arabi to an individual or a group. The idea is not to understand Ibn el Arabi, but to show the students that they cannot make real progress with this writer without guidance and insight: that is to say something else is needed first. Some of these techniques are well known in the East, of course, and cannot be used again until they are forgotten, so they become 'teachings' or 'facts'. In the case of Ibn el Arabi, the fact is that his own list of his writings, compiled in the year 1234, contains 289 works. His Sufi commentary on the Koran alone fills eight volumes.

There is another story about Rabia and the prayer-beads. Asked what she had to say about them, it is reported that she replied: 'A little every day means a great deal in one year.' Those who approved of rosaries imagined that she thereby supported them, while the others quoted the saying as against beads, since 'it was obvious that the little evil of every day would amount to much in a year'.

In the East, of course, there are many people who are familiar with these devices; and one does not need even to be a Sufi to see the misguided literalists who, increasingly in East and West, adopt such formulae without insight.

Where the People of Learning go Wrong

Q: *What exactly is the Sufi criticism of the learned profession? Surely the acquisition of knowledge is in itself good and to be encouraged?*

A: The professionally learned are constantly criticised by the Sufis for two obvious but far-reaching faults. The first is the claim to have a virtual monopoly of learning, so that only their limited way of approaching things is recognised as the 'learned way'. The second is the consequence of this: the wastefulness of dealing in innumerable facts and arguments at the expense of self-development. The hypertrophy of the drive towards wisdom is the obsessional collection mania which sometimes takes it over.

Al Ghazzali, himself a former academic and the Islamic world's greatest explainer of Sufi principles, deals with this at length in his Book of Knowledge in the *Revival of the Sciences of Religion* (*Ihya al Ulum al Din*).

He states that the man who avoids experiential religion and instead discusses it is like a man who is ill and has many ailments who encounters an able doctor; but, with little time to ask for a cure, talks and asks all the time about medicines and treatments, and about the profession of medicine. He does not deal with his own sickness. He has wasted his time.

This is still the major affliction of scholarship. Ibrahim ibn Adam tells of a stone which he saw on the ground at Mecca. On it was written: 'Turn me over and read a warning'. He turned it over. On the other side was inscribed:

> 'If you are not acting on what knowledge you already have, why are you seeking to know more?'

The Sufis are not purveyors of information, but initiators of experience.

And there is an old saying in the mysterious West, that someone may be a fool, but he cannot become a really big one without a scholarly education.

> You can't make a fool of biggest pattern
> Until he's learnt both Greek and Latin.

Working through the World

Q: *The Sufi way, traditionally, except for deteriorated forms, works within the world, and opposes withdrawal from the world. But surely it is better to get completely out of worldly matters, so as to concentrate upon the spiritual?*

A: There are three main answers to that one. First, this is the Sufi way, and both Sufis and non-Sufi commentators upon them have always attested to the sublime results of this procedure. Secondly, if you make a study of people who are supposed to have severed worldly connections, you find that they have usually done so only in name, but are still obsessed, for the most part, by what are in fact worldly things. They give them different names, or abandon greed for money and encourage greed for spirituality, and so on.

Thirdly, the things of the world are there, when such things are understood by the Sufi, as means to escape: 'When you were born into this pit, a ladder was placed before you.'

> There is a tale of Mulla Nasrudin in which he was looking at a small reed-bed near his house. He thought that he would extend the bed and cultivate reeds, then he would be able to sell the reeds and with the money he could lay out a beautiful garden. Suddenly realising that a reed-bed would look ridiculous in a garden, he tore up all the stems, as a first step towards this garden which, of course, depended upon their being extended . . .

Today and Yesterday: Jami

Q: *Are there any analogies between the use of Sufi behaviour and arguments today and the times when famous Sufis used to deal with bigots and limited understanding in the East, in the past? Perhaps there are, in humour, for instance? It seems a pity that we do not know more about the day-to-day activities of those Sufis.*

A: There are indeed analogies. One Sufi of the past who would find himself very much at home today among our contemporary limited thinkers was Nuruddin Abdur-Rahman Jami (1397-1474), a major Persian-language poet and Afghan Sufi, a disciple of the Naqshbandi teacher Saaduddin Kashghari of Herat, whose daughter he married. Jami, through this relationship, met the formidable Sufi divine Abdullah Ahrar ('Lord of the Free').

Jami, in addition to writing his Sufi classics, also lived the part of the Sufi corrector of idiocy. The religious scholar Haidari of Baghdad once challenged him to a discussion. Jami asked: 'On religious law or mystical perception?' Haidari chose the first. Jami then said: 'Before we start, we must put your moustache right: according to the religious law it is too long.' Scissors were sent for, and the hairs trimmed, first on one side and then on the other, until there was nothing left. The religious scholar then withdrew, as he would have to grow another moustache to conform with the religious law before debating it.

Once when Jami saw a man with a huge turban on his head being paraded through the streets of Herat on a horse, he asked what was happening. People told him: 'The man is a former infidel who has been converted to Islam by the chief divine of the city, whose turban he is wearing.'

'It is most appropriate,' said Jami, 'that the turban which is now on a former infidel's head should have come from the head of a Moslem infidel.'

A poet once complained to Jami that all his best thoughts had been stolen by another. Jami asked to see the poet's works, and then said: 'Yes, I can see that your poems have no meaning: the ideas must have been stolen from them . . .'

When he was on his deathbed, people brought in a large number of Koran-readers to recite the holy words loudly over him.

Jami raised his head. 'What is the point of all that?' he asked, 'Can't you see that I am dying?'

The Taste of No Taste . . .

Q: *Many of the procedures which are familiar in mystical and extra-sensory activity do not seem to have any rationale. Further, their effect is not instantly perceptible – they even seem to have no effect at all. What can you say about this?*

A: There is a fruit in Nigeria which has no taste at all. So what is the point of eating it?

Simply this. If you eat something else after tasting the 'miracle fruit', called *durumi*, the second thing's flavour is altered.

Eat the miracle fruit and then chew a lemon. The experience is like tasting a sweet orange.

If you were in a place where there were no oranges, only lemons, and you could also find miracle-fruits there – you could arrive at the taste of sweet oranges if you needed it.

But if you were a person who insisted that everything should have a taste, you would, if logical within this insistence, not be able to get the orange flavour.

So it is with all kinds of metaphysical and higher-consciousness systems. Since the participants demand 'taste' and insist that taste is significant, they will not take part in the equivalent of eating the tasteless fruit.

Emotional stimulus is, of course, the equivalent of 'taste' here. Nothing is wrong with it, but just to assign importance to it because one has imagined that importance is not only ridiculous, it is ineffective.

Protecting People against false Teachers

Someone keeps saying that we should do something to prevent so many people resorting to the myriad false Eastern gurus who fool them and they end up fed up and pitiful sights when they find out how absurd their behaviour has been.

I am reminded of the man who had a pain in his eyes, as recalled by Saadi. The man went to a farrier and asked him to do something about it, as he understood that he had a skill in dealing with horses' eyes.

The farrier put a horse-ointment into his eyes, and the man became completely blind. He took the matter to court, but the judge said:

'You can have no damages. If you had not been an ass you would not have gone to a farrier.'

Pleasing all the People

Q: *You meet and work with people, and they no doubt learn from these occasions. Then, I take it, materials from these encounters are put into your books, and you publish them. But what about those of us who live at a great distance, and cannot ask to come to see you?*

A: According to our tradition, much the same question was asked of the Master Bahaudin Naqshband of Bokhara. He told this story of the Land of Fools:

> Two men from the Land of Fools were visiting a fair in another country. They saw an ox being roasted and asked someone what was happening. 'Well,' he said, 'we roast an ox on the first day of the fair and distribute the hot meat to whoever is there on that day. Then, on the second day, we give out the remaining cold meat.'
> 'That's not very versatile,' said the chief Foolslander, 'supposing someone wants cold meat on the first day?'

How to Find the Right Way

Q: *It has been said that the Ways are as many as there are stars in the sky. Jami said this, and also quoted someone as saying that in spite of this, he could not find even one. What is the answer to this question of seeking?*

A: The answer is very simple. Your quotation is from the classical book *Nafahat al Uns (Fragrances of Companionship)*. Jami explains in the same book that: 'He cannot be found by searching: but the Seeker finds him . . .'

This means that it is not the seeking which finds, but the seeking which provides the training which enables the seeker to adopt thereafter the posture which eventually finds. This is akin to saying, for instance, that the co-ordination capacity which you learnt as a baby in holding a feeding-bottle is later a part of the skill which you activate in writing a letter, also needing co-ordination. Naturally there seems to be no connection between learning the first and the expectations of the second. People who are looking for 'Paths' are generally looking for something which feels to them like a path. How wrong they can be! This is why, incidentally, Sufi teachers have people do and think things which seem to have nothing to do with what the students are aiming for.

That this is not better known is due mainly to the fact that those who know it do not have to talk about it, while those who do not are usually in the process of learning it, or else completely alien to this field.

Conduct

Q: *Can the Sufi always behave in the same way to everyone? Surely behaviour is something which comes from training and emotion?*

A: There are two kinds of behaviour: that which rules you and that which you yourself rule. The former is that of animals and lesser people, the latter is that of Sufis.

It is a matter of the difference between what you cannot help, versus that which helps you.

Al Ghazzali, quoting a Sufi, summarises (in *Revival of the Sciences of Religion*) the three ways in which you should be able to behave:

> 'Courteously towards the people of the world;
> With wisdom towards those of the other;
> In accordance with your will to the Knowers'.

Testing the Disciple

Q: *Is the purpose of testing a disciple done in order to show the teacher what aspects of the person need attention, or to display this to an audience, or to manifest his hidden characteristics to the disciple himself?*

A: It may be done for any or all of these reasons. It should never be assumed that it is only done for a single reason, for otherwise part of its useful effect may be lost. For instance, if a teacher causes someone to display certain behaviour and observers imagine that this is being done only for the good of that individual, they may fail to apply the lesson to themselves. Similarly, if they think that the action is performed only to show something to them or to others, they can fail to grasp that it is also dedicated to the self-knowledge of the person so exposed.

The great Sufi, al Ghazzali, in the section on brotherhood in his *Revival of the Sciences of Religion*, recommends the advice of Abu-Said al Thauri. He suggested that, before entering into fellowship with someone, you should make him angry and then arrange for him to be in touch with someone who will question him about you. Then, continues Thauri, if this man nevertheless says good things about you, you may admit him to companionship. So, you see, the Sufi attitude is that harmonisation between people cannot take place properly unless it is at a sufficient depth. How many people known to you would pass this test?

Criticism by Sufis

Q: *We are accustomed to regarding men of spirituality as gentle and self-effacing. Yet I have heard that Sufis often criticise others, who claim to be Sufis, very severely. They are also said to upbraid people who are not Sufis for pretensions, for attitudes and for actions, in such a way as to make them appear quite unreasonable. What is the traditional justification for this? Is it known in any of the great classical teachers of the Sufis?*

A: If a theologian or priest, adhering to a doctrine in which some things are good and others are bad, comes across anyone who upholds the supposed evil and avoids the stated good, he will be quite likely to denounce that person, whether he has been told to be gentle or whether he has not. So much for the 'men of spirituality' of whom you speak.

Now, if someone can be permitted to speak or act with such vigour when his principles are based not on knowledge but on a conviction of right and wrong; supposing there is someone

314

with knowledge about objective good or bad: is such a person not to be allowed to pronounce on the matter?

This latter argument is the one which has been used to explain the vigorous behaviour of Sufis, in the past and present. Jami is one who was most severe in this regard. Read Rumi and you will not find him lacking in forthright expressions. If you read, for instance, the seventy-third Discourse of the great Abdul-Qadir of Gilan, in his *Futuh al-Ghaib* (*Revelations of the Unseen*) you will find him plainly stating that, since the Sufi has a direct perception of the facts of someone's falsity, he is impelled to denounce him or her. Gilani goes so far as to say that those who oppose the Sufi for behaving like this themselves do so because they are guilty and fear his opposition to their real deceitful selves, and thus seek to neutralise his efforts.

So, he continues, acceptance of this behaviour of the Sufi on the part of the observer will be to the advantage of the latter himself.

What the Master Does

Q: *How does one view the role of the Sufi guide in relation to the learner? Is he the source of knowledge, which he imparts; does he conduct the Seeker to places and experiences which cannot otherwise be reached?*

A: Sheikh Ibrahim Gazur-Ilahi has put it well when he says – in his *Irshadat* – that the process is like a journey. The teacher, he observes, follows the path and knows it well. Then, in the case of each and every disciple, he retraces the way with him. This is allegorised as starting a circle with a point, which then describes a complete revolution and ends with the point, which is itself a part of the circle.

The sheikh, the teacher, is also likened to the activity of a seed; which becomes a plant and which gives rise to another seed, which has to complete the cycle, and so on. This is the meaning of the Path, the Journey, and so on.

It is because of the ignorance of the learner and the accurate perception of the Teacher (his main capacity relevant to the student) that the relationship must be one of complete obedience to needs.

As the Master Gharib-Nawaz (Moinuddin Hasan Chishti of Ajmer) emphasises:

> 'It must be remembered that whatever the Guide instructs the disciple to do and to carry out, this is for the disciple's own good'.

You and Me

Q: *Why should people in study groups be specially selected, and not, as laid down in such classics as the Dhia al-Qulub, the Radiance of the Hearts, collected at random?*

A: People have to harmonise, otherwise, through everyone going through the same experiences at the same time, people merely learn to imitate one another, and you get a processed, not an organic, group.

The way in which people see themselves and others makes all the difference. There is a 'Land of Fools' tale which illustrates this: it underlines the result of two people, each thinking about himself.

> Two citizens of the Land of Fools are walking together when one of them picks up a piece of mirror from the wayside.
>
> He looks into it and shudders, then turns away.
>
> The other Foolslander takes it from him and looks into it. 'What's the matter? This is me inside!'
>
> 'Thank goodness,' says his companion, 'I thought it was me!'

316

This is, in reality, one of those matters which are best described as being so because they are so. If Sufi authority for this question is accepted, why the question? If it is not, this is not a question about Sufism.

There is a saying which indicates how such things must accord with possibilities: 'You are praying for rain, but the wind is in the North.'

Just as Useful

Q: *What is the result of people seizing, so to speak, Sufi exercises which should only be carried out under special circumstances, and using them mechanically, hoping to produce results?*

A: They may take them – and a lot of them have done so. They may use them, and they do: I constantly meet people who have been carrying out Sufi exercises under people who have no Sufic status, and people who just try exercises from books. The most probable result is that nothing happens. But there is a risk that they will be made sick: as in the misuse of many things.

There is a Nasrudin tale about this:

> Nasrudin and his wife were washing clothes one day by the river bank. A blackbird swooped down and swept up their soap in its beak.
>
> 'He's stolen our soap!' shouted the Mulla's wife.
>
> 'It's too bad that he can't use it,' said the Mulla, 'for his clothes need it even more than ours.'

317

Webbed Feet

Q: *I have read how often and how successfully the ancient Sufis scored off scholars: with their limited ideas and narrow vision. Trying to emulate the Sufis, I find that the scholars often get the better of me. Should one argue with pedants?*

A: If you are as limited as they can be, you should not. Perhaps you have not heard of this adventure of Mulla Nasrudin:

One day a Sufi was being harangued by a scholar, while Nasrudin watched.

The Sufi suddenly said:

'Of course, everyone knows that all scholars have webbed feet . . .'

This so infuriated the man of letters that he tore off his shoes and shouted:

'That just shows how foolish you are! I haven't got webbed feet at all!'

And everyone laughed, because the scholar had allowed himself to be manoeuvred into a position where he had to answer an absurd challenge.

Some time later, Nasrudin was listening to another scholar's words when he remembered what the Sufi had said.

He shouted:

'All scholars have webbed feet!'

But the scholar simply stepped down from the platform and knocked the Mulla down.

Authenticity

Q: *I cannot accept your statements, as I have not experienced the states mentioned or received authoritative assurances that they exist. Can you convince me or provide proof?*

A: Fortunately I do not have to do either.

If you demand experience without the preparation which alone makes it possible, you are preventing yourself from experiencing. Almost anything I might do or say would only, in such a case as yours, strengthen your existing prejudices.

Al Ghazzali, who was as great a Sufi authority as any, has said in *The Alchemy of Happiness:*

> 'There can be no greater foolishness than to deny the reality of something only because one has not experienced it.'

It is not I, but the classical Sufi masters who affirm and authoritatively confirm the reality of Sufi states. They constitute the authentication and a verification.

No Sufi activity of which I am aware aims at conviction. Sufism provides information and methods, not controversy and debate. Sufism is studied by means of itself.

Speech and Silence

Q: *Has it not been said that 'Silence is better than speech'? If this is so, why do Sufis use words so much?*

A: Silence of itself cannot be better than speech. It all depends on what the silence is for and like and what the speech contains or can do. Superficialists and hypocrites flourish in an atmosphere where slogans like this are used instead of knowledge: as when, for instance, people insist that it is 'better to smile than frown' – when a good man frowning is better than a bad one smiling. This is an important question, because mere appearances and slogans pass in most cultures for reality and conceal ignorance while opposing truth.

In his chapter on 'Speech and Silence' (*Revelation of the Veiled*), Hujwiri a thousand years ago reported an anecdote about this: 'Abu Bakr Shibli,' he relates, 'was in Karkh one day when he heard an impostor say: "Silence is better than speech".'

Now, because Shibli was accustomed to telling the truth and was in no way intimidated by externals and hence not a hypocrite, he was able to reply:

> 'Thy silence is better than thy words, and my words are better than my silence: because thy speech is nonsense, and thy silence is a fraud. And my words are better than thy silence, because my silence is patience and my speech is knowledge.'

If someone said that today, he would probably be regarded as a fraud, because the frauds have persuaded people that sententious catch-phrases are better than speaking direct truth.

Fire-Worshipper

Q: *Why do you show so much patience with people whom you are also not slow to point out as being obtuse?*

A: Because I cannot forget something which appears in Saadi's *Bostan* (*The Orchard*):

He relates how Abraham once welcomed and sat down to eat with an old man one day. Finding out that the ancient was a fire-worshipper, the Patriarch was enraged, and drove him away.

Then a divine message came to him, saying: 'I have fed him for a century, yet you detest him in a moment!'

SECTION X

The Giving of Knowledge

Q: *Why do Sufis in general not give public lectures; and why do they not share what they have of knowledge equally with everyone in the world?*

A: The great Imam al Ghazzali said, in his *Niche for Lights* (*Mishkat al-Anwar*), a Sufi classic, quoting a poet:

> Whoever gives knowledge to a fool loses it
> And who keeps it from the deserving does wrong.

Almost all Sufis who are publicly known are constantly surrounded by people who want their attention. If this attention is given to those who are not ready for it, or who merely want social activity, it inevitably means that those who can actually make use of it will be excluded, because the majority always floods out the minority.

If charity money were given to everyone, even to all the needy, there would not be enough for all.

Take another subject, the counterpart of spiritual knowledge: technical skills. Let us suppose that you are trying to introduce these into an Eastern country where everyone wants this knowledge. If you try to teach everyone, all hundred million of them, perhaps, what progress will you make? You will not manage to teach even one. Similarly, some sort of discrimination must be made in inner knowledge.

Religious and Wise

Q: *What is the difference between the devout and the wise?*

A: It is easier to be devout than to become wise, and generally the former produces greater worldly rewards than the latter.

It is also observable that those who call themselves religious people are far more concerned about themselves, in general, than the wise. This is widely denied as soon as it is said, but it is not difficult to establish it if the people whom you are observing are off their guard.

Saadi, in *The Bostan*, tells of an instance which illustrates this:

> There was a holy man who left a monastery of supposedly spiritual people, and went into a study seminary.
>
> Saadi asked him what the difference was between the wise and the religious.
>
> He answered:
>
> 'The religious man is trying to save his own blanket from the fire, while the wise one is trying to save other people from drowning.'

The Three Chests and the Balance

A famous Eastern story, *The Three Chests*, provides one very good framework for studying the Sufi psychological system.

The figures in the story represent traits of the human mind, their actions show balance and imbalance. Since, until very recently, psychology was unknown in the West, the tale has been seen as anything but what it is: as entertainment, as a satire or mockery, as an illustration of the wiles of women or of the injustices found in Eastern cultures. Let us look at how the Sufis see it.

First the synopsis: A merchant of Baghdad fell ill, and lost his money through unwise investments and the failings of friends and associates. His beautiful wife went to see their last hope, another merchant who owed her husband money, to plead for its repayment.

This man at first denied the debt, for which there was no

326

documentation, then said that he would pay even double the amount if the woman would yield to him. She went to the *Qadi*, the judge, asking him to compel the debtor to pay. The Judge, however, would do so only if she would sleep with him. She now applied to the Governor of the city, with the same kind of result.

The woman and her husband were wondering what to do when their ancient night-watchman gave them a plan. The woman, pretending to relent, invited the debtor, the judge and the governor to visit her, timing their appointments at half-hour intervals, and each unknown to the other. When each arrived she welcomed him; but within a few minutes the watchman appeared, saying that the husband was about to come to the women's apartments. Each was put into one of three large chests which were then locked.

The following day the woman went to the King and told her story. Accustomed to unsubstantiated allegations, the King doubted that people of such repute could have behaved in such a way. The chests were then brought and the three naked men were brought out in front of the entire Court.

The ruler ordered the villainous merchant to be fined almost his entire wealth, which was given to the ailing merchant. The exploiter was also forced to return to his original trade of a market greengrocer. The judge was demoted and sent back to where he came from: the stall of a public letter-writer. The Governor was returned to his first post as a minor administrator, a clerk. And everyone lived happily ever after. That included the three malefactors, who were grateful not to be executed.

Each part of the human mind returned, that is to say, to its own proper function.

Who are the figures in the story? The unhappy merchant is the real self of the human being; the wife is the potentiality which everyone has for self-realisation. The unscrupulous merchant is the emotional, material self, which has over-reached itself. The judge is the intellectual faculty which is not operating as it should. The governor is the balancing factor, the sense of what should be co-ordinated and put right. The night-watchman is the teaching which is extant and available to everyone: while the King is the teacher. The courtiers represent the moment of realisation of truth by the whole mind of the individual. The audience, to whom the story is told, may be entertained, helped or heedless, according to circumstances.

When is a Prayer not a Prayer?

The Sufi attitude towards religious requirements and rules is not, as people imagine, to abandon them or to decry them, but to define them in a particular way.

One of the Suhrawardi Order's founders in India, the Master Jalaluddin of Tabriz, used a characteristic scheme to illustrate this difference.

He visited the eminent religious Judge, Qadi Kamaluddin, author of numerous books on prayer, while he was praying.

Informed that the man of law was at prayer, the Sufi asked whether the judge knew how to pray.

This remark naturally caused the greatest indignation, and the Judge immediately sent a message asking what the Sufi meant by challenging the knowledge of one who was such an established authority.

The Master Jalaluddin was only too glad to have the dispute on record, and the occasion is still remembered. He informed the Judge that 'whereas the religious authorities prayed in the direction of Mecca, the Sufis would only pray when they actually saw the Throne of God.'

(Quoted from Amir Hasan Sijzi's *Fuwa'id al-Fu'ad*)

328

Wisdom . . .

Pashtun sayings, proverbs and similes:

A pure gold dagger cannot stab.
If you can't give me a halfpenny, at least call off your
   dogs!
Cats don't catch mice to please God.
Even the Judge was drunk when the wine was free.
He reckons his importance by the elephant-load.
There is no currant without a stalk.
A frog hopped onto a wall and cried, 'I can see Kashmir!'
The wood is burnt, but the ashes are a nuisance.
While the butchers were arguing, the cow dropped dead.
A sandal is not a shoe, a cap is not a turban.
When the shopkeeper has no work, he weighs his mud.
He is sinking in too little water.
Heed the troubadour, burn the dinner.
The yellow dog is brother to the wolf.
A lame crab walks straight.
It's your donkey, but you still have to pull it out of the
   ditch.
Storing milk in a sieve, you complain of bad luck?
You can beat anyone – if you have a golden slipper.
He saved his ears, but lost his head.
An intelligent enemy rather than a foolish friend.
When an ant says 'ocean', he's talking about a puddle.
Five of them would run from the bang of one empty
   gun.
He learnt the language of pigeons, and forgot his own.
When the hen gets fat, she stops laying.
The blind man asks God for two eyes.
Annoy the tailor, but you may go shirtless.
Not cheap without reason, nor dear without value.
If you are a rose, leave it to the nightingale to praise you.
His stomach is full, so he thinks he speaks Persian.

Try to get action by soft words: but don't complain to me.

It may smell like a melon, but is it going to make you sick?

If you want to keep camels, have a big enough door.

Don't show me the palm-tree, show me the dates.

Learning makes some Mullas and some into devils.

Go out from your village: don't let your village go out from you.

If the master gnaws bones, what will he give the dog?

In the shop of the sightless jeweller, ruby and pebble are one.

A mother and daughter fought, and a fool thought they meant it.

The crow is clever – but look at what it eats!

Hot milk burned him – so he's afraid of yoghurt.

A duel of hawks – and a pigeon wanted to join in.

Grumbling and carping are the muscles of the weak.

The night may be dark, but the apples have been counted.

Yes, the nephew is a thief: but the uncle is a magistrate!

Your aspirations are in heaven, but your brains are in your feet.

The mud of one country is the medicine of another.

A stick for the nobody, a hint for the nobleman.

No deceit, no merchant.

Same donkey, different saddle.

The rose is beautiful, yet its feet are in the mud.

The Half-Blind King

Once upon the time there was a king who desired his portrait painted.

He was blind in one eye.

The King invited the three greatest royal portraitists in the world to paint his picture, saying: 'If you do a bad portrait, I shall punish you; but if you do a good one, I shall reward you beyond your dreams.'

The first painter produced a picture which showed the King's eye to be blind. The King had him executed for disrespect.

The second painter showed the King's eyes as perfect. The King had him thrashed for falsification.

The third painter, however, pictured the King in profile, showing only his good eye.

This man was made the official portraitist, and heaped with gold and honours.

Sufi Introduction

An introduction can be carried out by inviting interested people to read certain books, etc., and then to formulate their own questions and observations.

The next stage is to hold a meeting at which the materials are considered, after which the questions and observations are looked at.

Following this, it is decided which questions and observations are answered or have been sufficiently looked at: the knowledge resident in this group has been shared so far as is possible at this juncture.

This concludes this phase of the attention to introductory written materials and responses.

An appropriate group of individuals may then carry on to either:

Further study and consideration – or – taking part in exercises.

EXERCISES:

The group is demonstrated the exercises and then performs them, without expectations, acceptance or rejection.

When the exercises have been carried out by everyone in such a way that they all know how to do them, the session is ended. Members of the group may choose whether they wish to carry out these exercises by themselves for a period of two weeks, daily. Each day after the first three days (when no notes are taken) each individual checks in the evening whether he feels that there has been any effect of the exercise, and what it seems to be.

This feedback is reported at the next meeting of the members of the group.

According to the reactions, further studies, or none, are prescribed for the group.

If further studies are prescribed, people are asked to register the pitfalls of auto- or self-indoctrination, to help prevent the enterprise developing, as most human groups will, into a conditioning system.

The programme continues from there.

Sufi Attitudes towards Religious and other Cults:

1. Sufis are opposed to fanaticism and closed minds, believing that these lead to oppression.
2. Many cults using the name 'Sufi' have arisen over the centuries. They have caused harm to their followers, and have, at times, given the word *Sufi* an undesirable flavour.
3. For the above two reasons, initial Sufi activity has, for centuries, aimed at explaining the nature of real Sufi aims and also at clarifying the undesirable effect of what today are called conditioning systems.
4. It has been observed by scholars and others that the Sufis are almost alone in having assessed and described the two undesirable factors referred to above. In so doing, they may have paved the way for contemporary knowledge on mind-manipulation. While others, for example, were still thinking in terms of 'the Devil is behind cults', the Sufis have pointed out the causes of cults as being purely psychological.
5. Among the characteristics of a 'false or misguided path', the Sufis have noted the following features which help to identify it:

    i) The claim that the organisation is the sole repository of truth, or is the only 'path';
    ii) The mistaking of emotional for spiritual states;
    iii) Separation of the followers of the group from the populace at large;
    iv) Failure to do one's human duty to everyone, regardless of such people's confessional position;
    v) The emphasis upon hope and fear, and upon reward and punishment;
    vi) Material richness of the organisation, and especially of its leaders;
    vii) The uniqueness of a leader, asserting superhuman or other qualities or responsibility;

viii) Secretiveness;

ix) Inability to laugh at things which appear funny to people outside the 'path';

x) Employment of stereotyped techniques and/or rituals and exercises, not adapted according to the principle of 'time, place and people';

xi) 'Idolatry': which includes investing people, animals or things with a special meaning;

xii) 'Teachers' who are themselves ignorant.

6. Sufis do not actually oppose such cults, since Sufis are tolerant: but they find it essential to describe them, in order to show the differences between cults and Sufism, and to help to prevent people interested in Sufism from forming or joining such organisations or groups.

SUFIS AND CONTEMPORARY PSYCHOLOGY:

The great development in the knowledge of psychology during the twentieth century has made it possible for Sufis to communicate in these terms to a world audience.

In earlier days, due to the general backwardness of most cultures, Sufis were obliged to communicate in established terminology, which reduced communication. Today, many of the contentions of the Sufi teachers of the past, still preserved in numerous classics, can be seen as pioneering the understanding of spiritual as distinct from sociological groups. Numerous modern observers have noted this contribution, though it is not yet fully disseminated among either the general public or even the specialists, though the process is accelerating.

There are now many references in books, monographs, etc., to the above facts.

One of the most conspicuous contributions of the Sufis has been the assertion that someone's conviction about the truth of a doctrine may be engineered, accidentally or deliberately;

and to label that as 'religious faith' or anything similar is no more than a display of ignorance of how the human brain works. Reluctance to accept the reality of indoctrination as taking place in all human systems marks the lower-level thinker.

INDICATIONS OF AN AUTHENTIC SUFI SCHOOL

First, elimination: the school, its teachers and students should be observed for signs of the features (item 5, above) which identify a spurious school. Second, it should be noted that the following are among the marks of an authentic Sufi school:

i) It does not restrict attention to any specific literature or teachings, but expects its students to have a good knowledge of a wide range of literature, while at the same time specialising in appropriately measured studies;

ii) It will be able to explain and interpret past formulations of the Sufi Way, as contained in the whole range of Sufi literature;

iii) It will be able to explain the process of supersession of materials;

iv) It will not be culture- or language-based. That is to say, it will not need to bring in, except at times for illustration or analogy, words or practices belonging to cultures and/or languages other than those of the people among whom the Sufis are working;

v) It will not use outlandish clothes (robes) or words, etc., extraneous to the local culture;

vi) It will not accept slogans or 'sayings' from past teachers unless they have an illustrative function;

vii) It does not use intonations, movement, music, etc., as a quasi-religious ceremony or as a spectacle, but has knowledge of such things as parts of a comprehensive system of applying stimuli;

viii) It will neither claim to have a mission to teach everyone, nor will it enrol everyone. It will first make sure that the interested person has enough information and experience to come to a decision about Sufis and Sufism in an appropriate manner;

ix) It will make clear the nature of the 'instrumental function' of ideas, techniques, etc., rather than regarding them as immutable, sacrosanct, 'traditional' and so on;

x) It will deal with everyone according to capacity and character, being neither benevolent nor the reverse: for kindness and cruelty, while effective and understood in ordinary relationships, operate as part of a conditioning system within a teaching or group situation.

SUFIS AND LITERATURE

There are two kinds of literature. The first kind is Sufic: that is to say, it is designed for teaching purposes. It is by Sufis, and essentially directed towards the people of the time in which it is issued. Subsequent generations have to understand the plan which underlies it, which the school has a duty to make clear.

The second kind is literature from the outside: materials *about* Sufis and Sufism. There is a vast body of this. It is often written by scholars, who do not understand Sufism, as they assess it from the academic and mechanical or emotional standpoints. This is useful only in illustrating the nature and pattern of the academic mind. It does not teach anything else. The very abundance of this literature has caused many people to imagine that they can learn from it. The Sufis, down the centuries, have often commented upon this material as 'trying to send a kiss by messenger', or 'teaching the taste of jam through the written word'. Such, however, is the prestige of the written word that even otherwise sensible people often fail to understand that an external assessment can hardly be useful, except of another external phenomenon.

The Tale of Two Frogs

Q: *Western civilisation is based on experiment and success, trial-and-error. Bit by bit, knowledge is built up, and such things as science emerge. If you have no knowledge, you can still achieve things, by making sure that you struggle: and that you don't give up! Yet Sufis say that you should have knowledge first, otherwise effort is not likely to be useful.*

A: Quite right; you need knowledge first.

Q: *Then how do you explain the following Sufi story, which places a premium on not giving up?*

THE FROGS

There were once two frogs, which jumped into a pail of milk. The first was a logical one, and, realising that he could not get out he calmly gave up and drowned. The second, though he did not know how to get out, went on struggling for hours. In due course, the milk turned to butter in sufficient quantities for the surviving frog to jump out.

A: As is usual, you have been told the story in a defective version. It does not end there. The end of the story is: 'The turmoil engendered by the surviving frog's struggles had alerted a crane, which, as soon as the frog jumped out of the pail, pounced on it, impaled it on his beak and made a dinner out of it'.

Q: *Then?*

A: There was, in fact, a third frog in the tale. He knew how butter is made. When the crane had gone away, he jumped in, made butter by flailing around, called in friends to give the dead frog a decent burial, and they ate the butter.

Q: *But what about the poor owner of the milk — he lost it . . .*

A: You can't have everything at once: he turns up in another story.

The 'Net' at the Meetings

You can soon see the difference between a Sufi lecture and a preaching one.

The preacher, didactic, etc., always has a theme which he affirms or tries to persuade the people about, or relates to some part of his or her beliefs.

This is, in fact, largely indoctrination in action or in reinforcement.

There is usually, too, a moral 'meaning', and the use of logic, intellect or emotion, sometimes all of these.

With the Sufis, the address or other initiative by the teacher is based on his perception of the needs of the individuals and collectivity in the audience. In other words, he casts a 'net' to find out how people are thinking, and then stimulates them in such a way as to help develop their consciousness.

The two methods are entirely distinct. The former is one which is shared by religious people with political, national, tribal and other projections. The latter is only operative on the interior spiritual plane.

As examples, using similar materials: the religionist may point to art or nature as wonders and encouraging and aesthetically and emotionally satisfying; the Sufi will use them to stimulate understanding and development rather than indulgence.

Shearing

Q: *People write to you, you say, asking to join study groups, or to have a meeting with you, or to be given help, or to get interpretations of things you have written, and so on. And, you say, again and again, you can't – or don't – help them with these things.*

Don't you think that this lack of help may make you unpopular, and certainly make you misunderstood, if there are good reasons for not being more helpful?

A: As to being unpopular, almost anything you do or do not do will make you unpopular with *some* people.

If I did some of the things I am asked to do, this would lead to results which would make me *more* than unpopular with the people who think they're the right thing to do!

Yes, there are reasons for not being apparently more helpful.

In fact, there is a single reason, which can be summed up in a very short anecdote, supposed to be true:

DO IT NOW

A London company bought a controlling interest in a sheep farm in Australia. Noting that the price of wool had suddenly shot up, the Chairman of the Directors cabled to the head of the sheep station: START SHEARING.

A reply arrived: CAN'T SHEAR BECAUSE LAMBING.

To which the Chairman answered: STOP LAMBING START SHEARING.

Efficiency

Q: *There surely are more efficient ways of doing things than those which limited the ancient Sufi teachers?*

A: Some things can certainly be improved, but very few. There is a true story I very much like, since it shows limitations and strengths where they might not be expected. Although in another area of interest, there is a parallel with Sufi matters:

HUMINT

ELINT is the word used in the intelligence community for 'Electronic intelligence' – information acquired by electronic means.

In the 1970s, the Pentagon in the USA wanted to know the calibre of a gun on the new Russian main battle tank. They decided to use *ELINT*.

Employing satellites, computers and all the rest, they spent eighteen million dollars before confessing failure.

Now it was known that there were examples of this tank in East Germany, and the British Army undertook to try to get the necessary information.

A small unit of *HUMINT* (human intelligence) was got together, composed of ordinary soldiers. They broke into the tank shed and measured the gun, all at a cost of four hundred dollars – one-45,000th of the cost of the failed *ELINT* attempt!

Working within limitations is not always as difficult, and often more effective, than thinking and trying to act sophisticatedly.

Uncomplimentary

Q: *How can one stop people saying and writing unfounded and uncomplimentary things about Sufis?*

A: My poor friend, I wonder where you have been all your life, that you don't know that people go about saying and writing uncomplimentary things about everyone?

What you are asking is how to change the human race: and you can't do this in the terms you seem to expect.

Haven't you noticed that almost everything in the news media, in advertising, in dozens of areas of human life, in all kinds of communities, advanced and otherwise, depend on gossip and often malice?

Who are you, either in competence or authority, to try to stop all this?

No doubt you would also like those who are most deserving to get appropriate rewards, and those who deserve it to be our rulers and mentors?

Why don't you think again?

The American

There are real dervishes in America, but not among those who claim that they are such. According to one of the real American dervishes, this is because they have to work outside of and beyond the transactional mentality which comes from business-mindedness – and which some people in the United States wrongly imagine to be the only way to do things.

He tells this story to illuminate the pitfalls of thinking only in terms of gain:

> All the human souls were being paraded out before an angel, before being born on Earth, to be allocated their propensities and opportunities.
>
> The first was to be a Sufi, who was asked what he wanted. The potential Sufi said, 'I wish to be without desire.'
>
> The second was designated as a Dervish, and said, 'I desire to be a Sufi.'
>
> The American businessman was next. He said, 'All I want is information. Who has been given out the money?'

Confrontation

'Showing people to themselves', an ancient Sufi speciality, is well illustrated by one incident which I observed in London. It needs, however, a certain amount of attention to observe what is happening.

A Sufi teacher had attached himself to a group of journalists who were about to attend a press conference held by a certain highly unpopular businessman. He had figured in newspaper publicity which implied that he had been guilty of improper share dealings.

In conversation with the pressmen, the Sufi had noted that they were all preparing to attack this man, each one in accordance with the policy of his employers. The representative of the mass-circulation daily newspaper, for instance, was looking for material on a wasteful life-style and possible marital infidelities; the right-wing correspondent sought damaging material, to write a piece about how isolated an incident this example of the 'unacceptable face of capitalism' was, and so forth.

The interviewee was late, and the journalists began to discuss him informally.

This gave the Sufi his chance. Taking the floor, but not identifying himself, he started to attack the tycoon. He spoke, with increasing vehemence, about his background, his personality, his associations, his general awfulness. I was the only other person present who knew the identity of this strange figure.

As he spoke, getting more and more reckless and intemperate in his statement, the mood of the pressmen changed. Within a fairly short time, they were objecting, right and left, to the distortions, until one was vying with another to say something *in favour of* their intended victim.

When the businessman appeared, they were kind to him in their questions. When their reports appeared in the Press, they made every allowance possible, mostly stressing that judgement should be reserved.

342

I asked two psychiatrists for their interpretations of this reversal of behaviour. The first one said that 'such behaviour patterns are common where people have been seeking a victim and then find that blood has been shed. The Sufi acted as a surrogate interrogator. The heat had been taken out of the situation'.

The second expert on the mind believed, and still believes, that 'unconsciously the journalists saw the error of their ways when someone acted out their own likely behaviour before their eyes'.

The Sufi's version? 'People crave excitement, not truth. But they cannot just say, "I crave excitement" – indeed, they do not know that this is their condition. So they have to attach the desire to a likely source of excitement. In this case, the source was the businessman, the pretext was his alleged villainies. The act which I put on gave them their excitement. They dealt kindly with the man afterwards because they were in a better frame of mind, and had "worn out" their bitterness.'

I asked the Sufi where, in all of this, the interests of truth, of journalism, of commerce, and so on, were served, if at all . . .

He said, 'If any of these ends is in fact served, it is served only after the primary desires – excitement and so on – are assuaged. You cannot assume that the businessman or the Press are going to give priority to the essential, while none has any conception that he is not dealing with the essential. Indeed, this has been rationalised to such an extent that the people believe, and constantly repeat, that people will investigate something only if they are inflamed about it, or if they are doing their duty. We have not yet arrived at the point where *function* – to discover and publish the facts – is understood as far exceeding in quality such conceptions as duty or excitement.'

For More Information about Sufism,
and to be on our mailing list, write:
The Society for Sufi Studies
P.O. Box 43
Los Altos, CA 94023
or go to the web at http://www.sufis.org